WORKS ISSUED BY
THE HAKLUYT SOCIETY

———

YERMAK'S CAMPAIGN IN SIBERIA

SECOND SERIES
NO. 146

ISSUED FOR 1974

The conquest of Siberia by Yermak, by V. I. Surikov, 1895

Painting at the State Russian Museum, Leningrad

YERMAK'S CAMPAIGN
IN SIBERIA

A selection of documents
translated from the Russian by
Tatiana Minorsky and David Wileman,
and edited,
with an introduction and notes,
by
TERENCE ARMSTRONG

THE HAKLUYT SOCIETY
LONDON
1975

ISBN 0 904180 03 4

Printed in Great Britain
by Robert MacLehose and Company Limited
Printers to the University of Glasgow

Published by the Hakluyt Society
c/o The British Library
London WCIB 3DG

CONTENTS

v

ILLUSTRATIONS AND MAPS

vii

PREFACE

The Russian conquest of Siberia was an event of which the conse-
quences have only slowly become apparent. Already great, they may
come to dominate much of our world; with today's technology, a
resource base of this size and richness confers immense power on the
owner. The conquest was a gradual process of absorption. But if one had
to assign a time and place for its start, then one would certainly choose
the campaign of Yermak in the 1580's. This enterprise was by no means
wholly successful, and probably fewer than a thousand Russians partici-
pated in it. But it was the first entry in force into Siberia, and Russian
historians have long regarded it as crucial.

Among English-speakers, the events are not so well known. The object of this book is to provide the reader of English with translations of the
most important documents relating to the campaign. There are several
narrative accounts, collectively known as the Siberian chronicles. They
tell a reasonably coherent story, but can be usefully supplemented by
some background information about the region, the times, and the
documents themselves. The introduction covers the more general points.
Matters of finer detail are commented on in footnotes; but a footnote is
not repeated, if the same matter arises in another chronicle, so the series
should be read consecutively.

A new Russian edition of the Siberian chronicles is reported to be in
preparation. Two groups of scholars are involved, one at the Institute of
History of the Academy of Sciences in Moscow, the other at the
Academy's Siberian Division at Novosibirsk. While the new edition will
surely contain interesting new material, the scope and detail of that
edition are likely to be such as to carry it far beyond the relatively
modest aims of the present one, so that to delay publication until the
appearance of the Russian edition does not seem justified.

The territory in which the events took place has been, ever since, part
of Russia. So the place-names used here, if they are to be found on
modern maps, should be those in current Soviet official use, which, in
the best British and American usage, are transliterated according to the
system approved by the Permanent Committee on Geographical
Names for British Official Use and the U.S. Board on Geographic
Names. The same transliteration system has been used, for conven-
ience, in rendering personal names and bibliographical references.
Certain proper names in the accounts are non-Russian in origin, but the
Russian or russianised forms are used here, because they are most
commonly found in the literature, which is predominantly Russian.

Thus Kuchum, Mametkul, Khodzha are preferred to Kucum, Memetkul, Hoca. The foregoing refers to editorial use of proper names. The translations retain in transliteration whatever oddities and inconsistencies of spelling are found in the original documents. Variant forms are brought together in the index.

Many people have helped in the preparation of this edition. First I must record special thanks to Mrs Tatiana Minorsky and Mr David Wileman, the translators. Mrs Minorsky translated the Remezov chronicle and the royal charters and letters, and Mr Wileman translated the Stroganov and the Yesipov chronicles. Both performed their exacting task with great skill and meticulous care, and both also contributed many points of critical commentary. But as editor, I must accept responsibility for any error in the translations, for I made a number of adjustments in the cause of consistency.

I would like to record my appreciation of the late Mr A. M. Richwood, who took the initiative, together with Mr G. R. Crone, in proposing the edition to the Hakluyt Society, and who carried out a considerable amount of background research while serving on the library staff of the Royal Geographical Society. Mr W. Harrison of Durham University kindly contributed the section of the introduction on 'Yermak as folk-hero'. Very special thanks are due to Dr Nikolay Andreyev, Professor Elizabeth Hill and Dr Will Ryan for the care and trouble they have taken in checking my typescript. Help and advice on various matters was freely given by Professors Lucien Lewitter of Cambridge, M. I. Belov of Leningrad, Menahem Milson of Jerusalem and Marc Szeftel of the University of Washington; by Mr Paul Putz of Luxembourg; by Mr Peter Avery, Mr Nicholas Penny, and Dr Susan Skilliter of Cambridge; and by Mademoiselle de Bonnières, the most helpful librarian of the Institut des Langues et Civilisations Orientales in Paris.

The Library of the Academy of Sciences of the USSR (Librarian, Dr D. V. Ter-Avanesyan) kindly allowed me to reproduce in its entirety the Mirovich version of the Remezov chronicle, which is held in the collection of that library. I am likewise indebted to the Director of the State Russian Museum in Leningrad for permission to reproduce Surikov's painting. The Bibliothèque Nationale in Paris provided much appreciated help in locating rare publications.

The maps were drawn by Miss Anne Swithinbank.

Scott Polar Research Institute, Cambridge   TERENCE ARMSTRONG
March 1975

INTRODUCTION

Muscovy's eastern frontier in the 16th century

Ivan III, who ruled in Moscow from 1462 to 1505, earned his title of 'the Great' largely by his absorption of the territory belonging to Novgorod, hitherto the dominant Slav state in the Russian plain. In so doing, Ivan advanced his frontier to the northern Urals, for the Pechora basin, a region renowned for its fur resources, had long been a colony of Novgorod, and Novgorod, which was above all interested in trade, attached special importance to the fur trade. Ivan sent expeditions to this newly-acquired territory: one under Prince Fedor Kurbskiy in 1483 and another under Prince Semen Kurbskiy in 1499. These consolidated the Russian presence, chastened the native inhabitants, and carried their operations beyond the Urals into the lower Ob' valley. From 1484 Ivan added to his titles 'Lord of Yugra' – a somewhat vague place-name connoting the land on both sides of the northern Urals.[1]

But this eastward advance took place only north of about the 60th parallel, in a region, therefore, far to the north-east of Moscow. The more direct route to the east was blocked by the Tatar khanate of Kazan'. This was all that survived, in much diminished form, of the Golden Horde, the Mongol state which emerged in south Russia after the great conquests of half the world under Chingis (or Gengis) Khan. The Mongol, or Tatar, domination (Tatar is here used to signify the Turkic-speaking peoples who served in the Mongol forces) held Muscovy and other Slav principalities in subjection for well over two centuries, but for the latter part of this period its power was crumbling. The independent khanate of Kazan' was formed in the middle of the 15th century, and soon afterwards the land of Sibir', on the Irtysh river, also subject to the Golden Horde, broke away to become another independent khanate.[2] The process of dissolution made it likely that when a resolute blow was struck, resistance would not be great. That time came in 1552, when Ivan IV defeated the Tatar army and took Kazan'. Four years later, he took also the khanate of Astrakhan, and the

---

[1] Yugra comes from *yögra*, a word the Zyrians used for the Ostyaks, so it came to mean the lands the Ostyaks lived in (see below, pp. 22–3). In early times this was on both sides of the mountains, but later Yugra connoted only the eastern side. See L. S. Berg, *Istoriya russkikh geograficheskikh otkrytiy* (Moscow, 1962), pp. 59–60.

[2] The name Sibir' is used in these translations, in preference to the anglicisation Siberia, because Sibir' then connoted a very small part of what we now understand by Siberia; and the adjective Siberian refers to Sibir'.

I

whole length of the Volga was in his hands. The more direct route to the east now lay open.

The Siberian khanate was untouched directly by this conquest, but it was now, of course, dangerously exposed to Moscow's power. The only protection was the Urals, and not only are they a rather unimpressive physical barrier in these latitudes, but the Russians had already given ample evidence of their ability to cross them. The rulers of the khanate at this time were Yediger and Bekbulat, sons of Kasim, and in 1555 Yediger thought it wise to send ambassadors to Moscow, who acknowledged him a vassal of Ivan IV, and agreed to pay an annual tribute of furs. In this way Moscow secured some influence in their territory. Yediger's reason for making the arrangement seems to have been a desire to find an ally against his neighbours. But the arrangement was not long-lasting, for in 1563 both Yediger and Bekbulat were deposed and killed by Kuchum, son of Murtaza, the ruler of the Uzbeks. This move was one more act, and not the last, in the long-standing rivalry between the descendants of Taibuga and those of Sheiban, grandson of Chingis Khan. Yediger and Bekbulat were Taibugids, Kuchum was a Sheibanid.

The arrival on the scene of Kuchum, who was to be one of the chief actors in the drama of Yermak's campaign, and the one cast by all Russian historians in the role of villain, did not at once change things. He started by continuing the payment of tribute, but the last time he did so was in 1571. His emissaries to Moscow on that occasion came just after the city had been besieged and partly burnt by the Tatar army of Devlet-Girey, khan of the Crimea, and they reported back, no doubt, on the disarray they had seen. Kuchum clearly intended to put an end to Russian encroachment. In 1572 the Cheremis (now called Mari), a Uralian people living on the Volga above Kazan', revolted against the Russians and pillaged settlements on the Kama and Chusovaya rivers. Kuchum, their neighbour across the mountains, may have had something to do with this. But the more open break came in the following year, when Ivan IV's ambassador, Tret'yak Chebukov, or Chubukov, who had arrived in 1572 to receive the tribute, and had been welcomed by Kuchum, was killed on Kuchum's orders when on his way back to Moscow. At the same time Kuchum's nephew Mametkul led a raid across the Urals into Russian territory. The vassal period was over, and Moscow reacted in 1574 by empowering the merchant family of Stroganov to establish strongholds on the *eastern* slopes of the Urals.

Before considering the role of this important and energetic family, let us take account of the nature of the frontier and of Moscow's attitude towards it. There was no exact line of demarcation on any map, much less on the ground. Persons owing allegiance to Moscow lived in lands which adjoined those of persons claimed by the khan of Sibir'; but much more than this could not be said. The situation was further complicated by the fact that there could be many degrees of vassaldom. The people of Vyatka, for instance, though not necessarily whole-hearted in their allegiance, were at this time more reliable than the Cheremis, who were in turn less friendly than the Permians who lived to the north of them. Even the khanate of Sibir' itself might have been thought of as within the frontier after Yediger's agreement of 1555 to pay tribute; and indeed Ivan IV dubbed himself at that time 'Lord of all the Siberian land' (i vseya sibirskya zemli povelitel') – and instructed his ambassadors about how to answer questions foreigners might ask about this.

The eastern frontier was therefore an indefinite concept; and Moscow's attitude towards it was also somewhat indefinite. While there were no carefully-considered expansionist plans, there was no disinclination to move eastwards if opportunity offered. The economic motivation for such a move had long existed: it was the search for fur – a commodity which continued to be very valuable. It is not necessary to elaborate here on the great importance of the fur industry in the Russia of the 16th century, for it has been admirably described by R. H. Fisher in *The Russian fur trade, 1550–1700* (Berkeley, 1943).[1]

The Stroganovs

Records of the Stroganov family go back to the 14th century (Vvedenskiy, 1962, pp. 15–16. This work is also a main source for the account which follows). Originally probably from the White Sea – the idea that they are descended from a *murza*[2] of the Golden Horde is now discounted – they moved eastwards and settled at Sol'vychegodsk, on the Vychegda near modern Kotlas, towards the end of the 15th century. Anika Fedorovich Stroganov (1497–1570) built up a great trading concern, based in Sol'vychegodsk, and dealing in agricultural products, furs, and salt. As regards salt, he was a pioneer in this region (Sol'vychegodsk means the salt works on the Vychegda), and he extended his operations over a wide area. Iron, both mining and working, was another major interest; copper followed. In 1558 Anika acquired from the tsar rights in the region of Perm' ('the Permian patrimony'), and soon Stroganov agents were seeking iron and copper on the Kama and its tributaries which come down from the western slopes of the Urals. In the other direction, the family was trading at Kola, close to the frontier with Norway; and there were even links with central Asia. So the firm's interests embraced a tremendous stretch of territory. Not all of it was owned by the Stroganovs, of course; but a remarkably large

[1] The main sources, for this section in particular, but also for much background information elsewhere, are the researches of Soviet scholars: S. V. Bakhrushin, *Nauchnyye trudy* (Moscow, 1955), Tom III, Chast' I, pp. 15–71; A. P. Okladnikov, ed., *Istoriya Sibiri* (Moscow, 1968), Tom II, pp. 25–41; A. A. Vvedenskiy, *Dom Stroganovykh v XVI–XVII vekakh* (Moscow, 1962), pp. 15–110; and A. A. Preobrazhenskiy, *Ural i Zapadnaya Sibir' v kontse XVI–nachale XVIII veka* (Moscow, 1972), pp. 15–26. Full references are given in the list on pp. 296–303.
[2] Minor nobility in Turco-Tatar tribes. There is no glossary; the index may be used.

3

amount was. Anika had three sons, Yakov, Grigoriy and Semen. Yakov and Grigoriy took special interest in the eastern domains, while Semen, the youngest, was concerned more with the affairs at the headquarters, Sol'vychegodsk.

A commercial empire of this size was bound to attract the close attention of the central government. Moscow was very interested in many products of the Stroganov industries, and indeed it is chiefly through the surviving orders and instructions from the tsar that we learn of their activities. Not only did the tsar buy Stroganov goods, he also borrowed Stroganov money. A rather special relationship grew up. In a certain sense the Stroganovs became agents of the tsar, especially in the Urals region.

Anika died in 1570. He was a deeply religious man, caused many churches to be built in his domains, and a short time before his death became a monk (an action not unusual at that time). The patrimony was to be divided equally between the three sons. But there was a family row, for in 1573 we find Yakov and Grigoriy complaining to the tsar that Semen had got more than his share. This was adjusted, but bad feeling naturally remained.

Yakov and Grigoriy continued to spend most of their time in the Permian lands. But in 1577 and 1578 they died, and their mantles fell upon Yakov's son Maksim Yakovlevich and Grigoriy's son Nikita Grigor'yevich, young men of twenty-one and sixteen years of age respectively. It was these two who were most closely concerned, a year or two later, in the events described in these chronicles. It should be remembered, however, that Sol'vychegodsk remained, for the rest of the century, the main centre of the Stroganov commercial empire. Semen Anikiyevich lived there until his death, at the hands of some of his retainers, in 1586.

Let us now revert to the role of the Stroganovs in the eastward expansion of Muscovy. The fact that Ivan IV had approved in 1558 (text of charter on pp. 281-4) of the Stroganovs exploring and exploiting the Permian lands may be interpreted as a first move, at government level, in feeling the way eastwards. In 1572 another royal charter (see pp. 288-9) authorised the Stroganovs to send troops against the Cheremis. Then, in 1574, came the decree already referred to (see pp. 289-92) which authorised the building of strongpoints across the Urals, on the Tobol, Irtysh and Ob'. Ivan was clearly using his merchant friends to further aims in which his government was just as much interested as they were.

A central point in our narrative is now reached, when the cossack Yermak Timofeyevich first appears on the scene. The background to this is still controversial. His name is first mentioned in the royal charter of 16 November 1582 (see pp. 293-4), which roundly dresses down the Stroganovs for sending him and his men to the wrong place. The point still hotly debated is this: did the Stroganovs summon Yermak and his band to come and fight their war for them across the Urals; or did he come of his own accord? In other words, was the initial Russian penetration into Siberia a Stroganov idea, planted in their minds perhaps by Moscow, or was it an idea of the simple man of the people, Yermak? The historians of Siberia take opposite sides on this issue. In the 19th century, most thought Yermak was summoned by the Stroganovs: N. M. Karamzin, N. G. Ustryalov, S. M. Solov'yev, L. N. Maykov, Ye. Ye. Zamyslovskiy, and A. A. Dmitriyev;[1] but P. I. Nebol'sin and S. A. Adrianov[2] held the view that the Stroganovs played no part in Yermak's campaign. The first group was joined in the 20th century by S. F. Platonov, V. I. Ogorodnikov, B. Nolde, S. V. Bakhrushin, V. I. Sergeyev, A. A. Vvedenskiy, and G. Vernadsky;[3] while new adherents to the second were A. M. Stavrovich and A. I. Andreyev.[4] Thus the two major contributors of the last twenty years, Vvedenskiy and Andreyev, are divided on this issue. A compromise position, that the Stroganovs provided none of the initiative, but were obliged, through fear of Yermak, to furnish him with supplies, was held by G. F. Müller, J. E. Fischer, P. A. Slovtsov and D. I. Ilovayskiy,[5] writing in the 18th and 19th centuries, but its only recent adherent is V. G. Mirzoyev.[6] The point here is that the so-called Stroganov chronicle (one of the three major chronicles

[1] The exact locations are as follows: N. M. Karamzin, *Istoriya gosudarstva Rossiyskogo* (St Petersburg, 1821), Tom IX, pp. 380–8; N. G. Ustryalov, *Imenityye lyudi Stroganovy* (St Petersburg, 1842), pp. 17–19; S. M. Solov'yev, *Istoriya Rossii s drevneyshikh vremen*. 2nd edition (St Petersburg, 1897), Tom VI, column 337–8; L. N. Maykov, 'Khronologicheskiye spravki po povodu 300-letney godovshchiny prisoyedineniya Sibiri k russkoy derzhave', *Zhurnal Ministerstva narodnago prosveshcheniya*, Tom CCXVII, Otdel 4 (1881), p. 26; Ye. Ye. Zamyslovskiy, 'Zanyatiye russkimi Sibiri', *Zhurnal Ministerstva narodnago prosveshcheniya*, Tom CCXXIII, Otdel 2 (1882), p. 232; and A. A. Dmitriyev, *Permskaya starina* (Perm', 1892), Vypusk 4, pp. 61–3, and 'Rol' Stroganovykh v pokorenii Sibiri', *Zhurnal Ministerstva narodnago prosveshcheniya*, Tom CCXCI, Otdel 2 (1894), p. 45.
[2] P. I. Nebol'sin, *Pokoreniye Sibiri* (St Petersburg, 1849), p. 63; and S. A. Adrianov, 'K voprosu o pokorenii Sibiri', *Zhurnal Ministerstva narodnago prosveshcheniya*, Tom CCLXXXVI, Otdel 4 (1893), p. 548.
[3] S. F. Platonov, *Proshloye russkogo severa* (Berlin 1924), pp. 100–1; V. I. Ogorodnikov, *Ocherki istorii Sibiri do nachala XIX st.* (Vladivostok, 1924), Chast' 2, Vypusk 1, pp. 25–7; B. Nolde, *La Formation de l'empire russe* (Paris, 1952), p. 160; S. V. Bakhrushin, 1955, pp. 20–32; V. I. Sergeyev, ' K voprosu o pokhode v Sibir' druzhiny Yermaka', *Voprosy istorii*, Tom I (1959), p. 129; A. A. Vvedenskiy, 1962, p. 97: and G. Vernadsky, *The tsardom of Moscow 1547–1682*, Part I (New Haven, 1969), pp. 178–9.
[4] A. M. Stavrovich, 'Sergey Kubasov i Stroganovskaya letopis'', in *Sbornik statey po russkoy istorii, posvyashchennykh S. F. Platonovu* (Petrograd, 1922) pp. 279–93, and an unpublished work by her called *Sibirskiye letopisi. Etyud po istorii voprosa i analizu sibirskikh letopisey* (1920), in which she probably expresses the same views more fully (see Bakhrushin, 1955, p. 31); and A. I. Andreyev, *Ocherki po istochnikovedeniyu Sibiri*. 2nd edition (Moscow, Leningrad, 1960), Vypusk 1, p. 215.
[5] G. F. Müller, *Opisaniye Sibirskago tsarstva* (St Petersburg, 1750), p. 99; J. E. Fischer, *Sibirskaya istoriya s samogo otkrytiya Sibiri do zavoyevaniya sey zemli rossiyskim oruzhiyem* (St Petersburg, 1774), pp. 114–15; P. A. Slovtsov, *Pis'ma o Sibiri* (St Petersburg, 1826), pp. 49–52; and D. I. Ilovayskiy, 'Yermak i pokoreniye Sibiri', *Russkiy vestnik*, No. 9 (1889), p. 31.
[6] V. G. Mirzoyev, *Prisoyedineniye i osvoyeniye Sibiri v istoricheskoy literature XVII veka* (Moscow, 1960), pp. 128, 163.

translated in this book) shows the Stroganovs as the motivating force; while the Yesipov chronicle – the other early one of the three – does not mention them at all. So the issue is closely connected with the view one takes of the Stroganov chronicle. If one believes it to be written by a Stroganov hireling who was willing to twist facts in order to glorify the family name, then one may doubt the whole Stroganov story. But, as Dvoretskaya and Vvedenskiy[1] show, Yesipov's silence is not conclusive, and the Stroganov writer need not have been doing anything more than interpreting facts from the Stroganov point of view. The important thing, says Vvedenskiy, is to judge the whole matter from the standpoint of Moscow's eastern policy; and in this context, Stroganov initiative was certainly to be expected: had Ivan not authorised them in 1574 to build strongpoints across the Urals? I find this view convincing. Besides, the New Chronicle (see pp. 278–80 below), probably written in 1630 and possibly the oldest account we have, states clearly that Maksim Stroganov summoned Yermak. Platonov (1924, p. 103) goes further than this, and postulates a two-pronged campaign against the Siberian khanate by the Stroganovs. For in 1581, he says, the Stroganovs were organising a sea-borne expedition to the Ob' by way of the Arctic Ocean, under the command of the Netherlander Oliver Brunel. But this seems somewhat far-fetched, for although Brunel did make journeys to the Ob' for the Stroganovs about this time, they were scarcely campaigns, serving rather the ends of trade and intelligence-gathering.

The event immediately preceding Yermak's advance over the Urals was the attack on the Stroganovs' Kama lands by Begbeliy Agtakov, a Vogul princeling. Although the Stroganov chronicle has this occurring on 1 September 1581, Vvedenskiy concludes this is a mistake for the year before (and not the only one of this kind in the chronicles, as we shall shortly see). Yermak's campaign was not just a reaction to this attack, however; for it had been planned (if we accept the Stroganov line) since some time before that.

The campaign

The progress of the campaign itself is best told by the chronicles. Although their tales are in some ways fanciful and in many ways confused, the story comes across quite clearly and requires no summarising here. The movements of Yermak and his men can be followed on Map 1, facing p. 18. A few points, however, require clarification or emphasis. The first of these concerns chronology.

The dates of various stages of the campaign, as given in the three major chronicles, are not always consistent either between one chronicle and another, or within a single chronicle. Impossibilities and unlikeli-

[1] N. A. Dvoretskaya, 'Ofitsial'naya i fol'klornaya otsenka pokhoda Yermaka v XVII v.', *Trudy Otdela drevnerusskoy literatury*, Tom XIV (1958), p. 334; A. A. Vvedenskiy, 1962, pp. 81–4.

hoods of several different kinds occur. For instance, the captured Tatar prince Mametkul is reported by the Remezov chronicle as being sent to Moscow in 1582, where he was brought before Tsar Fedor Ivanovich; but Fedor Ivanovich came to the throne only in 1584. In the Yesipov chronicle, Yermak's first advance into the Siberian khanate is given as 1581, and the capture of its capital, Isker, as 1580. There is generally good agreement as to day and month, but often there is doubt about the year. It would be tedious to discuss the reliability of every date given in the chronicles, for argument would be long and intricate. There are certain possibilities of cross-checking with outside sources, notably royal charters. On the basis of this kind of critical evaluation, Bakhrushin suggests[1] that the likeliest dates for the key events are as follows: Yermak's advance across the Urals started on 1 September (old style) 1581, that winter was passed in the mountains, and the party moved on down the rivers on the Siberian side in May–June 1582, the fight at Babasany was on 21 July, the capture of Karacha's stronghold on 1 August, the capture of Kuchum's capital, Isker, in October 1582; a message informing Moscow was sent off in December, and on 10 May 1583 the decree authorising reinforcements was issued; these, under Bol'khovskiy, spent the winter of 1583–84 in Perm', and reached Yermak only in November 1584. That winter there was famine in Sibir', and Yermak was killed on 1 August 1585. Mansurov, the next emissary from Moscow, arrived on the Ob' in the summer of 1586. These dates are fairly widely accepted now, but Sergeyev (1959, p. 126) has suggested that the initial advance could have been as early as 1578. Vvedenskiy (1962, p. 100) finds this suggestion 'interesting', but wants more documentary evidence before he accepts it. Preobrazhenskiy (1972, pp. 40–3), the most recent commentator, prefers the later date (1581) for the start of the campaign, and adduces more evidence in its support. Many points in the chronology are still unclear, and future research may clarify them. But the margin for doubt is generally only one year, and never more than three.

Something should be said about the adversary, Kuchum. From the chronicles he emerges as a double-dyed villain. It is clear that he was a redoubtable adversary. Kuchum son of Murtaza, the Sheibanid, took the khanate of Sibir' by force in 1563 from the Taibugids Yediger and Bekbulat. Thereafter he showed great energy, tenacity, and determination to resist any Russian advance, a contingency he no doubt foresaw. When it came, he organised a vigorous defence with the small numbers at his disposal, but lost. The Russians, after all, had firearms and their opponents did not. What impresses the non-partisan reader of the chronicles, however, is Kuchum's continuing resistance after he has lost

[1] In G. F. Müller, *Istoriya Sibiri* (Moscow, Leningrad, 1937), Tom I, pp. 482–6, 492. This a modern edition, in two volumes out of a projected three, of Müller's *Opisaniye Sibirskago tsarstva* (St Petersburg, 1750), and has annotation by Bakhrushin, Andreyev and others.

his capital and many of his men. The old fox was prowling in the steppes and forests, always a threat, and finally, to Yermak, a fatal one. His victory at that time could not be followed up, however, for his Taibugid rival, Seydyak, deposed him. But he still had followers, and still played the part of the nomad marauder, attacking Tatars and Russians alike. Determined attempts were made to crush him, in 1591, 1595, and 1598. In the last, much of his army was killed or captured, as were many of his family, but he escaped. A surviving letter to him at this time from the khan of Bukhara urges him to stop fighting his own kind and to rally all Mohammedans against the Russians.[1] Finally he is said to have been killed soon afterwards by the Nogais, to whom he had turned for help. The fullest account of his wanderings after Yermak's death is given by Nebol'sin (1849, pp. 115–30), and Sinyayev, a more recent investigator, has looked into the final Russian campaign against him in 1598.[2] He is a figure worthy of respect, for although he was perhaps little more than a roving brigand who had usurped a throne, nevertheless he strove desperately for seventeen years to defend his country against what became hopeless odds. He was taken seriously in Moscow, and exchanged letters with the tsar (part of this correspondence survives[3]). But no historian, not even Soviet champions of the downtrodden, speaks well of him. Even the 16th-century Turkish historian Seyfi Çelebi regards him as a backwoodsman of little account, who lived among peoples (Ostyaks and Voguls, presumably) who were 'strange, of astonishing external appearance, no one understando their language, without religion or rite, almost like animals'.[4] The nearest thing to an appreciative reference to him is perhaps the 'Song of Khan Kuchum', one surviving verse of which was discovered by Radlov among the Siberian Tatars in the 19th century.[5]

Yermak's campaign, as such, ended in ignominy. The leader was killed, and the hard-pressed survivors of his small force, probably only about 150 men under the cossack Matvey Meshcheryak and the professional soldier Ivan Glukhov, slipped away from Sibir', leaving it to be reoccupied by the Tatars. But reinforcements under Ivan Mansurov, sent from Moscow, arrived on the scene soon afterwards. The Russians re-entered Sibir', and joined by further reinforcements under the *voyevodas*[6] V. B. Sukin and I. Myasnoy, established with very little

---

[1] Printed in H. Ziyayev, *Ortä Asiya vä Sibir'* (Tashkent, 1962), pp. 41–2, and kindly translated for me by Mr W. Feldman.

[2] V. S. Sinyayev, 'Okonchatel'nyy razgrom Kuchuma na Obi v 1598 godu', *Voprosy geografii Sibiri*, Sbornik II (1951), pp. 141–56.

[3] *Sobraniye gosudarstvennykh gramot i dogovorov* (St Petersburg, 1819), pp. 52, 63–5.

[4] J. Matuz, *L'Ouvrage de Seyfi Çelebi, historien ottoman du XVIe siècle* (Paris, 1968), p. 88.

[5] W. Radlov, *Die Sprachen der Türkischen Stämme Süd-Sibiriens und der Dsungarischen Steppe. I Abtheilung. Proben der Volkslitteratur. Übersetzung. 4 Theil* (St Petersburg, 1872), p. 141.

[6] Military leaders. The word came later to mean the military governor of a town or region. The plural of transliterated words is anglicised with an s.

THE CAMPAIGN

resistance a series of Russian strongpoints: Obskiy Gorodok (1586 – but it lasted only a few years), Tyumen', on the site of Chingiy (1586), Tobol'sk, close to Sibir' (1587), Berezov (1593), Tara (1594). By a shabby trick Danilo Chulkov, another Russian leader, broke the power of Seydyak and his adherents. This time the Russians had come to stay. Yermak's campaign had, after all, shown the Russians the way. It had been primarily a private affair, run, as I think, by the Stroganovs; or, if you will not accept that, then by Yermak himself. One thing certain is that it was not run directly by Moscow. Government support, which came only when there were clear indications of likely success, was too late in the first instance to stave off defeat. But the second and third waves made victory certain. So was the foundation laid of Russian power in Asia – of a great colonial empire, which was to grow up almost unnoticed by the countries of western Europe.

The cossacks, Yermak, and his band

Yermak is referred to in the chronicles as a Volga cossack, or an *ataman*, which means a cossack leader. Who were the cossacks in general, and the Volga cossacks in particular? And who was Yermak? The chronicles themselves say nothing about the first question, assuming the reader will know, and almost nothing about the second.

There is much obscurity about the origins of the cossacks. Lantzeff[1] thinks they were a social element of uncertain origin, existing in several different forms from early times: thus it was a militant border population, according to Solov'yev; bands of Turkish warriors, according to Karamzin and Pogodin; itinerant workers on the land, according to Klyuchevskiy; and border settlers holding back nomads, according to Ukrainian historians. The position is examined in detail in three recent books,[2] and Vernadsky devotes much space to them in his histories.[3] The word itself (Russian *kazak*) is plainly derived from the same word in Turco-Tatar languages, where it means a free man, hence a vagabond (Vasmer[4] specifically dissociates *kazak* from *kasog*, the early Russian term for a Circassian, from which some have derived cossack). Cossacks were by no means only Russian. On the contrary, in the fifteenth century they were often Tatars in Russian service.

By the time of Yermak, there were two main kinds of cossack. One kind was a sort of frontier force composed of men who were not nobles

[1] G. V. Lantzeff and R. A. Pierce, *Eastward to Empire* (Montreal and London, 1973), p. 73.
[2] G. Stökl, *Die Entstehung des Kosakentums* (Munich, 1953), P. Longworth, *The cossacks* (London, 1969), and A. A. Gordeyev, *Istoriya kazakov* (Paris, 1968–71).
[3] G. Vernadsky, *Russia at the dawn of the modern age* (New Haven, 1959), pp. 8, 112–13, 249–68; *The tsardom of Moscow, 1547–1682, Part I* (New Haven, 1969), pp. 8–11, 178–81.
[4] M. Vasmer, *Russisches etymologisches Wörterbuch* (Heidelburg, 1953–58), sub nomine.

9

but were not serfs either, and who were paid for their service by grants of land and remission of taxes. They were known as service cossacks (*sluzhilyye kazaki*), and were under direct government control. The other kind were independent settlers, especially in the south-east corner of Muscovy on the Don and Terek rivers, and lived in villages called *stanitsas* and were ruled by their own elected leaders, or *atamans*. The allegiance of these cossacks was to themselves, and only to the government when it suited them, which it seldom did. From this second group, loosely known as Don cossacks, some moved across to the lower reaches of the Volga, where a number became river pirates, plundering passing travellers. Hakluyt relates[1] how Jeffrey Ducket of the Muscovy Company of London had a very unpleasant experience near Astrakhan in 1573, when 'certain Russe Cassaks, which are outlawes or banished men' seized his ship and got away with much of his freight. The situation became so bad that Ivan was obliged to take action and sent a force under Ivan Murashkin in 1577 to disperse these cossack bandits. It was after this punitive campaign that one of the Volga cossack groups, led by the *ataman* Yermak, left the region and went upstream to the Kama and the Permian lands of the Stroganovs.

Yermak son of Timofey first appears in the chronicles as a fully-fledged *ataman*. No hint is given about his origin. But some relevant information is found in a later source, known as the Cherepanov chronicle. This is a crude compilation made in 1760 by the Tobol'sk coachman I. L. Cherepanov, and it contained an item called 'some Siberian history' (*Nekotoraya sibirskaya istoriya*). It was for some time disregarded as worthless. Nebol'sin (1849, pp. 65–6) was sceptical, and it was turned down in 1876 by L. N. Maykov for publication in the standard series then being prepared by the Imperial Archaeographical Commission.[2] But in 1894 the historian A. A. Dmitriyev showed that Cherepanov's 'some Siberian history' was probably derived from a genuine 17th century document, 'the story of the Siberian land' (*Skazaniye sibirskoy zemli*), part of which Dmitriyev discovered in a village near Solikamsk in 1893–94 (Vvedenskiy, 1962, pp. 86–8). Andreyev too (1942, p. 322) concluded that the Cherepanov chronicle was a valuable source after he had studied an unknown copy of the manuscript.

The part of the 'story of the Siberian land' that interests us here is a section called 'On Yermak, and where he was born'. This is the section Cherepanov is supposed to have seen, but which has not been found in other surviving copies. The section seen by Dmitriyev is written in an 18th-century hand, but internal evidence leads to the conclusion that this is a copy, or paraphrase, of a mid-17th-century document. It may

---

[1] R. Hakluyt, *The principall navigations, voiages, traffiques and discoveries of the English nation* (London, 1598), Vol. I, p. 421.
[2] A. I. Andreyev, 'Cherepanovskaya letopis'', *Istoricheskiye zapiski*, Tom XIII (1942), p. 311.

have been written therefore about the same time as two of our major sources, the Yesipov and the Stroganov chronicles. The information it gives about Yermak is as follows, and it purports to be derived from Yermak himself. His grandfather was called Afonasiy Grigor'yevich Alenin, and was from Suzdal', north-east of Moscow, where he was a *posadskoy chelovek*, or inhabitant of the town outside the walls of the central fortified area. Famine drove him to Vladimir, and he became a coachman, was hired by some robbers, captured in the forest near Murom, and imprisoned; he escaped, and died at Yur'yevets Povol'skoy on the Volga. He had two sons, Rodion and Timofey, whose poverty caused them to seek their fortune in the Stroganov lands on the Chusovaya river, a tributary of the Kama. Rodion had two sons, and Timofey three – Gavrilo, Frol and Vasiliy. Vasiliy was strong and self-confident and worked in the Stroganovs' river fleet on the Kama and Volga. There he gathered a band together, left his employment and became a river pirate. As leader of the gang, he was called *ataman* and acquired the nickname Yermak. So runs Cherepanov's story, which will be found in print in Karamzin (1819–29, Tom 9, note 664) (only odd pieces of this chronicle have ever been published).

Vvedenskiy, who quotes this information (1962, pp. 88–9), finds it plausible that Yermak Timofeyevich's real name should have been Vasiliy Timofeyevich Alenin. None of the other chronicles mentions his family name, and Vvedenskiy provides contemporary examples of Stroganov employees who had nicknames. A. Voronikhin is another historian of this century who supports this view, and he quotes[1] a source of 1792 which uses the name Yermak Vasiliy Timofeyevich. If this piece of genealogy is true, Yermak turns out to be a Volga cossack only in the sense that he spent some time cossacking (the Russians use the verb) on the Volga; he was brought up in the Stroganov lands and worked for a Stroganov enterprise. Vvedenskiy (1962, p. 90) finds it typical of the Stroganovs that they should turn to an old employee when they needed a man to do a particular job. Preobrazhenskiy (1972, p. 44), however, raises the awkward point that if Yermak was really brought up on the Chusovaya, then it is rather strange that he should lose his way on that river, as the Remezov chronicle (chapter 5) states that he did, when leading his band over the Urals. But many mysteries remain in this fragmentary story.

If one rejects the Cherepanov account, then all one is left with is the qualifying adjective Volga (or in some cases Don), signifying a region he was associated with. N. M. Mel'nikov, an émigré cossack writer,[2] lists sixteen reasons why Yermak should definitely be regarded as a Don cossack; but they are not very convincing, and their author is highly partisan.

[1] A. Voronikhin, 'K biografii Yermaka', *Voprosy istorii*, No. 10 (1946), p. 99.
[2] N. M. Mel'nikov, *Yermak Timofeyevich, knyaz' sibirskiy, yego spodvizhniki i prodolzhateli* (Paris, 1961), pp. 59–63.

There is no specific evidence to support the often-repeated view that Yermak had a price on his head when he left the Volga. But it is true in a general sense, in that he undoubtedly was a pirate, and the punitive expedition of 1577 had orders to hang any they caught (see the Remezov chronicle, chapter 5).

One rather unobtrusive ghost may be laid at this point. The suggestion has been advanced[1] that Yermak was a cossack leader from Mogilev, sent to the Urals by Ivan IV in 1581. Mel'nikov takes the same line (1961, p. 11). But it is clear that this is a case of mistaken identity. A letter to King Stephen Batory of Poland does indeed mention 'the cossack *ataman* Yermak Timofeyevich' as one of fifteen *voyevodas*; but the timing of events in 1581 makes it impossible that this could be the same man (Vvedenskiy, 1962, p. 62). A rather odd coincidence, perhaps, but history is full of them. Indeed, G. Ye. Katanayev[2] records yet a third Yermak Timofeyevich, and a Don cossack at that, active in 1581–84.

Despite the general lack of knowledge about Yermak's antecedents, a monument was erected to him at the end of the last century at Novocherkassk (Katanayev, 1893, p. 14) – the capital of the Don cossack country, a region which has long claimed him, but which he may never have visited. Some historians – Ilovayskiy, for instance – cast doubt on the enterprise at the time. For the statement sometimes made (see Mel'nikov, 1961, p. 11), that he was born at the cossack village of Kachalinskaya on the Don, there is no early documentary evidence.

There are several other statues and portraits of Yermak. There is a statue at Tobol'sk, one in the State Russian Museum at Leningrad by M. M. Antokol'skiy, another by S. G. Korol'kov; and there are paintings and engravings by A. Skarl'man, P. P. Beketov, Korol'kov, V. I. Surikov (the frontispiece of this book), by the illustrator of the Remezov chronicle, and no doubt others. Many of those mentioned are reproduced in Mel'nikov's book. All of them, of course, are imaginary. No one recorded his likeness; and the only guide of any authenticity that the artists might have had is the words of the Remezov chronicle, written over a century after Yermak's death, that he was 'flat-faced, black of beard and with curly hair, of medium stature and thickset and broad-shouldered' (chapter 106).

In short, little is known for certain of Yermak. But many legends grew up, and they are not to be disregarded as a historical source. Something is said of these in the section below, 'Yermak as folk-hero'. Yermak has been the subject of poems: K. P. Ryleyev (1795–1826), who was executed for his part in the Decembrists' uprising, wrote 'The death of Yermak' in 1821; and I. I. Dmitriyev (1760–1837) wrote a dramatic

[1] N. Shlyakov, 'Yermak Timofeyevich letom 1581', *Zhurnal Ministerstva narodnago prosveshcheniya*, Tom CCCXXXVI, Otdel 2 (1901), pp. 33–45.
[2] G. Ye. Katanayev, 'Yeshche ob Yermake i yego sibirskom pokhode', *Zapiski Zapadno-Sibirskago otdela Imperatorskago Russkago geograficheskago obshchestva*, Kniga 15, Vypusk 2 (1893), p. 13.

poem 'Yermak'. His name has been used in various ways. There have been two icebreakers called *Yermak*, one the first major vessel of this kind ever built (completed in Newcastle in 1898 to the order of Admiral S. O. Makarov), the other the first of a powerful new class, which entered service in 1974. The town of Yermak lies on the upper Irtysh, and gives the name also to a giant thermal power station nearby. Derivatives of the name (Yermaka, Yermaki, Yermakovka, Yermakovo, Yermakovskoye) are attached to at least eight other places or geographical features in the Soviet Union. Thus the impact of Yermak on Russian cultural history has been significant.

The size of Yermak's army is another point on which it is hard to determine the truth. The Yesipov and Stroganov chronicles (chapters 7 and 8 respectively) mention that the band which came from the Volga numbered 540 men. The Stroganov chronicle (chapter 11) adds to these a further 300 men recruited on the Chusovaya, making an army of 840 which advanced into Siberia. The New chronicle has 600 men coming from the Volga, and 50 joining them – total 650. But the Remezov chronicle, in its chapter 6, which is one of the chapters interpolated from the Short Kungur Siberian chronicle, makes this an army of 5000 men. Bakhrushin (1955, p. 41) and Vvedenskiy (1962, p. 98) dismiss this as fantastic, and most contemporary scholars, including Vernadsky (1969, p. 179), agree with them. Only Sergeyev (1959, p. 123) and Mel'nikov (1961, p. 18) think a larger figure is right – and Sergeyev compromises at a suggested 1600 men. Their argument is that fewer men could not have done the job. But this depends on how numerous one thinks the opposition was. I have more faith in the broadly consistent figures which appear in the older chronicles (even if probably derived from the same source), than in the often fanciful Short Kungur Siberian chronicle.

Yermak as folk-hero[1]

Although folk-songs and legends about Yermak originated amongst the cossacks, on the Volga, Don, Ural and Terek rivers, in the Urals and Siberia, the distribution of songs collected since the 18th century (over 150) shows that his fame as a folk-hero spread throughout central and northern European Russia.

Most of the 'historical songs' (*istoricheskiye pesni*) begin with lines setting the scene, sometimes the Saratov steppes, sometimes the Caspian Sea, but, in the opinion of Ye. A. Aleksandrova[2], on the evidence of the songs the historically authentic location for Yermak's early exploits was the river Kamyshinka, a tributary of the Volga which rises near the

---

[1] This section was contributed by W. Harrison, University of Durham.
[2] Ye. A. Aleksandrova, 'K voprosu o metodike analiza istoricheskikh pesen', *Uchenyye zapiski Gosudarstvennogo pedagogicheskogo instituta, Daugavpils, seriya gumanitarnykh nauk*, Vypusk 2 (1959), p. 82.

Ilovlya, a tributary of the Don. Yermak and his men are brigands who have pillaged boats, both Russian and foreign, on the Volga and the Caspian for many years. In one song they attack a Turkish caravan and abduct a *murza*'s daughter, an incident which Likhachev links[1] with the incident when the Siberian chieftain Yelygay offered Yermak his daughter (Remezov chronicle, chapter 100). In another song Yermak is a captive of the Turks, and elsewhere he fights the *murza* Itslamber. It has been suggested[2] that songs of this group reflect a period when Yermak served Ivan IV and may have met Islam-Girey of the Crimea or the Nogai prince, Ismail, between 1555 and 1562. In another song Yermak's men kill the Muscovite ambassador to Persia named as Semen Konstantinovich Karamyshev.[3] Karamyshev was actually slain by the Don cossacks in 1630, but the Remezov chronicle (chapters 3–5) does tell of raids by Yermak and other cossack leaders on foreign envoys and merchant vessels. In folklore there is some merging of Yermak in these acts of piracy with the 17th–century figure of Stenka Razin, who apparently succeeded him as hero of the folk-drama 'The Boat' (*Lodka*).[4]

But the songs indicate that Yermak's deeds became troublesome to Moscow and so the cossack *krug*, or 'circle', convenes to debate where they should spend the winter, threatened as they now are by troops sent to curb their brigandage:

'Now the summer passes, the warm summer,
And winter approaches, brothers, cold winter,
How and where, brothers, shall we winter?
To go to the Yaik the way is long,
On the Volga to ply is to be branded as thieves,
If we go to Kazan, there the awesome tsar stands,
The awesome tsar, our sovereign Ivan.
He has there a mighty multitude of men
And you, Yermak, there will be hanged
And we cossacks there shall be seized
And imprisoned in sturdy gaols.'[5]

A version of the Stroganov chronicle not translated here[6] contains a passage very similar to this song.

One solution to their predicament is to win the tsar's favour by some

---

[1] D. S. Likhachev, *Russkiye letopisi i ikh kul'turnoistoricheskoye znacheniye* (Moscow, Leningrad, 1947), p. 416.
[2] A. M. Listopadov, *Donskiye istoricheskiye pesni* (Rostov-na-Donu, 1946), p. 4.
[3] V. F. Miller, 'Istoricheskiye pesni russkago naroda XVI–XVII vv.', *Sbornik Otdeleniya russkago yazyka i slovesnosti Imperatorskoy Akademii nauk*, Tom XCIII (1915), pp. 477–81.
[4] V. N. Vsevolodskiy-Gerngross, *Russkaya ustnaya narodnaya drama* (Moscow, 1959), pp. 38 ff.
[5] V. K. Sokolova, 'Russkiye istoricheskiye pesni XVI veka, epokhi Ivana Groznogo', *Trudy Instituta etnografii im. N.N.Miklukho-Maklaya*, Tom XIII (1951), p. 90.
[6] *Sibirskiye letopisi* (St Petersburg, 1907), p. 56.

14

deed of service. In the songs of the Don cossacks,[1] this service is usually the capture of Kazan' - which had taken place twenty-five years earlier. Yermak appears at Ivan's court and offers to take Kazan' in order to redeem himself and his men. As a reward Ivan grants the cossacks the lands of the Don. So persistent is this theme in cossack folklore that the question of some connection between Yermak and Kazan' must arise - but are we concerned with the same Yermak? As implied earlier, Yermak was not so very rare a name in the 16th century. It is generally thought, however, that the scene at Ivan's court is an echo of the arrival in Moscow of Yermak's envoys after his Siberian successes.

In some songs the cossack *krug* decides to seek its fortune in Siberia: this solution is put forward in the songs of the Ural cossacks (Sokolova, 1960, p. 76):

'Shall we go, shall we not go to the river Irtysh,
From the river Irtysh we'll take the town of Tobol
And then go to the tsar and give ourselves up,
To him we will take our rebellious heads
And in the right hand take a block and axe.'[2]

Almost all versions of this song, without describing the Siberian cam-paign, pass straight to a scene at Ivan's court where Yermak cuts off the head of a boyar who demands that our hero be hanged; and then Yermak is commissioned to take Kazan' and Astrakhan. The absence of a warm welcome may be significant, implying that Yermak's actions were not entirely approved of in Moscow.

It seems that references in this song to places beyond the Urals could be later inventions, and that in the original version Yermak urged that they make for the Kama. It is true that the *Kama* is not mentioned and the river named is the *Kuma*, but as Aleksandrova points out, Yermak's description of the river with its dark forests abounding in marten, fox and sable is more appropriate for the Kama (Aleksandrova, 1959, p. 101; Miller, 1915, pp. 495-6). This point is all the more convincing if our Yermak *was* Vasiliy Timofeyevich Alenin: he was proposing to take his men to his native region which he accurately describes.

In the Urals and western Siberia oral accounts of Yermak's deeds were preserved and legends were created, not only by Russians but also by Tatars and other peoples (see for instance Radlov, 1872, pp. 141, 179-81). It may be that the Orthodox Church contributed to the for-mation of legends, for Archbishop Kipriyan in striving to enhance the prestige of his new archbishopric of Tobol'sk sought to present Yermak as champion of the faith, a saint almost, which would require miracles to be associated with him. In the 1890's Nemirovich-Danchenko found that the religious element persisted in Ural legends in which Yermak was

[1] V. K. Sokolova, 'Russkiye istoricheskiye pesni XVI–XVIII veka', *Trudy Instituta etnografii im. N.N. Miklukho-Maklaya*, Tom LXI (1960), p. 76.
[2] V. F. Miller (1915), p. 511.

remembered as conquering evil with the aid of the Cross (Sokolova, 1951, p. 35). At any rate we have the legend of Yermak's suit of armour with its miraculous powers, the healing power associated with his grave, the appearance of his ghost to Seydyak and the fiery pillar observed in the sky over his tomb (Remezov chronicle, chapter 113). The influence of folk legend is evident in the song 'Yermak took Sibir' in the 18th-century *Sbornik Kirshi Danilova*.[1] Scholars have pointed out that parts of this piece do not read like a song and that it seems to be a combination of folk-song with an oral prose account of Yermak's expedition. This makes it the most important of the songs as a historical source. There is no mention in it of an invitation from the Stroganovs, but in the deliberations of the cossack *krug* Yermak says:

Let us go to Usol'ye to the Stroganovs,
To that Grigoriy Grigor'yevich
To the lords Voronov:
We'll collect there powder and shot and stocks of grain.

(It seems that in Grigoriy Grigor'yevich the song confuses two people, Grigoriy and Nikita Grigor'yevich; in some songs a Voronov is mentioned as a *prikazchik*, 'steward', of the Stroganovs.) The cossacks accept Yermak's advice, and after taking provisions and ammunition from the Stroganovs, they set off up the Chusovaya.

The route they follow is the Chusovaya-Serebryannaya-Zharavlya-Barancha-Tagil-Tura-Yepancha-Tobol-Irtysh. According to Gorelov[2] the song commits two errors: there is no river Yepancha (though there is a person and a place); and Yermak would have left his boats between the Serebryannaya and the Zharavlya (a tributary of the Tagil), not between the Zharavlya and the Barancha, as the song has it. The song also invents a manoeuvre by which at the confluence of the Tobol and Irtysh the cossacks split into three groups, Yermak taking the upper stream, whilst the others take the central and lower streams and reach the Irtysh just below Tobol'sk: the Tobol does not flow into the Irtysh by three streams.

The song continues in the realm of fiction with the capture of Kuchum by Yermak's band and a visit by Yermak to Ivan's court. It ends with his death in a clash with a superior force of Kott Tatars on the Yenisey. Leaping from one boat to another Yermak slips, breaks his head, and is killed. (According to some cossack legends, Yermak drowned because of the weight of his armour given him by the tsar.) Yermak never did battle with the Kott, who lived much further east than he ever reached: this is a reflection of the exploits of another *ataman*, Yermak Ostaf'yev in the 1620's (Gorelov, 1961, p. 371).

But this 'song' does contain some interesting historical details. We are

[1] A. P. Yevgen'yeva and B. N. Putilov, *Drevniye rossiyskiye stikhotvoreniya, sobrannyye Kirsheyu Danilovym* (Moscow, Leningrad, 1958), pp. 86–90.
[2] A. A. Gorelov, 'Trilogiya o Yermake iz Sbornika Kirshi Danilova: polemicheskiye zametki', *Russkiy fol'klor. Materialy i issledovaniya*, No. 6 (1961), p. 365.

told that Yermak spent the first winter in a cave in a cliff overhanging the Chusovaya river where, according to Ural legends, Yermak hid treasure. Writers who mention the cave include Witsen in *Noord en Oost Tartarye*, G. F. Müller who traversed those parts in the 1730's, and Mel'nikov-Pecherskiy, who was there in 1830. It is worth noting that in Ural legends Yermak still pursued from his cave a career of robbery and piracy.[1] We are told in the song that Yermak reached the Tagil and made a halt at Bear Rock where he stayed till Trinity Sunday building larger boats. The chronicles do not mention this halt, but excavations have shown that Kirsha Danilov was correct (Gorelov, 1961, p. 365).

Interesting too is the story of the straw warriors. Having reached the mysterious river Yepancha, the cossacks halted until St Peter's day. There they made figures of straw and put clothing on them:

'Yermak had a *druzhína* of three hundred men,
But with them [i.e. the straw figures] they
became more than a thousand.'

When the cossacks attacked, the Tatars showered arrows on them and, deceived by the straw figures, believed that the cossacks could not be harmed. The origin of this story may have been the use of straw bales as protection, but its authenticity is supported by Tatar folklore. Müller heard it (see Remezov chronicle, chapter 38, note). According to A. Dmitriyev the Tatars of Tobol'sk recounted this legend in the 1890's (Gorelov, 1961, p. 366); and it is still current in the Urals today.[2]

The song in the *Sbornik Kirshi Danilova*, then, contains information of historical interest. The same is true of the folk-songs as a whole, though in trying to interpret them as a historical source we can speak only of probabilities. But the story which the folklore seems to tell us about Yermak is as follows. He was active on the lower Volga for many years before his Siberian expedition. In that time he may have performed services for Moscow, but eventually he became a nuisance to the government and was forced to move from the Kamyshinka to the Urals, where he expected he would be more welcome. According to the songs the initiative for the expedition into Siberia is naturally Yermak's, not the government's, nor the Stroganovs', though he obtained supplies from the latter. He is an enterprising, daring, popular hero. As such he passed into the *byliny*, the epics set in Kievan times, where he stands alongside the other great warriors, the *bogatyri*, Il'ya Muromets, Dobrynya Nikitich, Alyosha Popovich, champions of Russia against foreign foes. But he is different from the others: he is impetuous, foolhardy. When told by the other *bogatyri* to climb a tree to spy out the Tatar host, instead of carrying out the reconnaissance mission he sets

[1] V. P. Kruglyashova, 'Predaniya reki Chusovoy', *Uchenyye zapiski Ural'skogo gosudarstvennogo universiteta im. A. M. Gor'kogo*, Vypusk 18 (1961), pp. 35, 44.
[2] Ye. Dergacheva-Skop, *Iz istorii literatury Urala i Sibiri XVII veka* (Sverdlovsk, 1965), p. 107; Kruglyashova, 1961, pp. 37–8.

off to do battle single-handed and, in some versions, come to grief. Perhaps there is a historical message there for us.

Routes into Siberia

The routes used by the men of Novgorod, who were the earliest known Russian travellers from Europe into Asia, were water routes and crossed the Urals at their northern end. The reasons for the relatively high latitude were that it allowed the travellers to outflank first the Bulgars and then the Tatars and others who barred the more direct routes to the east, and that the fur-bearing animals they were looking for lived in the northern forests. Use started probably not later than the 12th century.

The travellers headed for the Pechora river (see Map 1), which they could do either by way of the Severnaya Dvina system (Vychegda – Vym' – portage – Ukhta – Izhma) or the Mezen' system (Peza – portage – Tsil'ma). Once on the Pechora, they ascended it and took one of two main routes across the Urals. The most northerly – just north of the Arctic Circle – followed the route Usa – Yelets – portage – Sob' – Ob', while the other, 500 km further south, took the Shchugor and portaged into the Severnaya Sos'va, a tributary of the Ob'. None of the portages on these routes was more than a few kilometres long, and the mountain passes were less than 1000 m high. The routes were essentially for summer use; for, although a frozen river can provide a good highway, the passes in these cases were difficult in winter, and would be used only in emergency. The Shchugor route was the one taken by Prince Semen Kurbskiy in 1499. Both were frequently used by hunters and traders in the 16th and 17th centuries.

The next route to be used by the Russians was the next obvious one to the south, 250 km south of the Shchugor. This started from the Volga system and went by way of the Kama – Vishera – portage – Loz'va – Tavda – Tobol – Irtysh – Ob'. The town controlling access to this route was Cherdyn', and the Russian acquisition of the lands of Perm' in 1472 made it accessible. A punitive expedition against the Voguls on the Tavda in 1483 made use of it, and likewise the Voguls used it a bit later when attacking the lands of Perm'. This route in fact became, after Yermak's time, the official road joining the new domains to Moscow, and along it went government money and stores, and, in the reverse direction, the harvest of furs; but it lost this traffic after only eight years, when the town of Verkhotur'ye on the Tura, one of the next convenient pair of rivers to the south, was built in 1598. The Verkhotur'ye route remained the official one until 1763.

The Verkhotur'ye route was close to the one which Yermak and his companions used. Theirs crossed the mountains a little further south again, and followed the line Kama – Chusovaya – Serebryanka – portage – Zharavlya – Tagil – Tura – Tobol – Irtysh. The Urals passes in this region are quite low – never exceeding 500 m. This was the obvious route

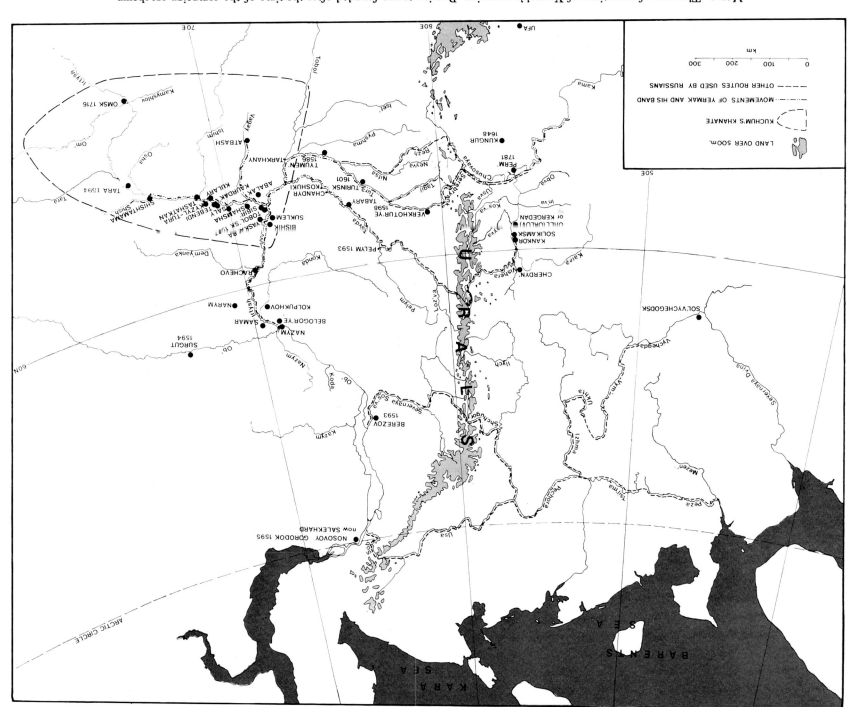

MAP 1. The area of operations of Yermak's campaign. Russian towns founded after the time of the campaign are shown with date of foundation. Main source: map at the end of G. F. Müller, *Istoriya Sibiri* (Moscow, 1937), Tom I. Müller himself travelled in the Tobol-Irtysh region in the 1740's and identified many places mentioned in the chronicles.

for Yermak to choose, because the Tatar grip on the area was so greatly weakened by the fall of Kazan' in 1552. It had been used before that for trade between Perm' and the Voguls. It seems to have been the route used by the Tatars travelling between the khanates of Kazan' and Sibir', and was used by the unfortunate ambassador Chebukov in 1572. After Yermak it remained in use, but with an altered course on the Siberian side. The connection with the Tagil and Tura dropped out; they were replaced by the Rezh, Neyva and Nitsa, a shorter route to the Tobol. A detailed study of these routes, and the basis for the preceding paragraphs, is found in the work of Bakhrushin (1955, pp. 72–111).

Thus Yermak's route was not pioneered by him, but was one of a number which were in more or less regular use. Of considerable interest, but little emphasised in the chronicles, is the mode of travel. It was by water, not land, except for the short portages. The best evidence, although it must be at least 100 years later than the events, is provided by the illustrations in the Remezov chronicle, where ships appear in many of the drawings. The Russians had already acquired great experience of inland navigation, so there was no need to apply new techniques in order to make this journey possible. The ships used are likely to have been flat-bottomed river vessels called *doshchaniks*, which could carry a load of anything between 35 and 150 metric tons (the latter for the biggest ones, which were probably rare). If the illustration to chapter 121 of the Remezov chronicle is any guide, those used were big enough to require use of a dinghy to reach the shore. The motive power came mostly from the river current, but oars could be used, or they could be towed from the shore, and the ships mounted a sail which could be used for down-wind travel. Zagoskin, the leading Russian historian of inland water transport,[1] mentions a big one – 18 *sazhens*, or 38 m long, which carried an enormous sail. No iron was required for their construction, beyond the axe-heads of the skilled Russian builders. Such ships had been in use for some time by the late 16th century, and they were to continue for some time longer. Verkhotur'ye soon became the major shipyard for the Siberian traffic, turning out up to a hundred *doshchaniks* a year in the early 17th century.[2]

While the chronicles do not use the term *doshchanik*, they use the term *strug*. This word was unfortunately often used in a loose sense in the 17th century (Zagoskin, 1909, p. 425), and may mean no more than 'ship'. But properly speaking, a Volga *strug* was primarily a rowing boat, three to eight *sazhens* (6–17 m) long in the 16th–17th centuries, and flat-bottomed. A seven-*sazhen* *strug* was capable of carrying 600 metric tons. Olearius[3] describes what must be a Volga *strug* he saw in 1636 (he calls it

[1] N. P. Zagoskin, *Russkiye vodnyye puti i sudovoye delo v do-petrovskoy Rossii* (Kazan', 1909), p. 454.
[2] M. I. Belov, *Istoriya otkrytiya i osvoyeniya severnogo morskogo puti* (Moscow, 1956), Tom 1, pp. 196–7.
[3] A. Olearius, *Vermehrte Newe Beschreibung der Muscowitischen und Persischen Reyse* (Schleswig, 1656), pp. 341–2.

a *struse*, but he often got names a bit wrong). It had 200 persons on board, was flat-bottomed, and could sail. Such ships, he tells us, could carry up to 500 *last* (or 1000 metric tons). He has a picture of this one in his book, and it is a boat not unlike those in the Remezov chronicle illustrations. Yermak might have been using ships of this sort, but certainly not so big as that one. The letter of 7 January 1584 from the tsar to the Stroganovs (see p. 295) mentions *strugs* capable of carrying 20 men and their stores.

Non-Russian peoples

As the Russians advanced into Siberia, they encountered many peoples (see Map 2). The local population was sparse and disparate and so lacking in cohesion. Those mentioned in the chronicles fall into two main groups. First, there were persons the Russians called Tatars, who were the Russians' main opponents. The word Tatar covered many peoples living in and around the Urals, especially on the southern side. These peoples' ancestors had achieved prominence when Chingis Khan organised them into fighting groups for his tremendous conquests in the 13th century. By the 16th century they had fragmented into a number of geographically distinct groups, of which some were descended from the Golden Horde, the state which emerged from the Mongol conquests. All these peoples were Sunnite Moslems and spoke Turkic languages of the north-western group.[1] Their centre of gravity was to the south of the Russian line of advance. Second, there were more primitive hunter-gatherers who lived in the northern forest, mainly to the north and east of the Tatars, and therefore to the north of the main Russian line of advance. These were members of the Uralian language family (containing Finnic, Ugrian and Samoyedic languages), and were shamanists. Some members of this group were in European Russia and therefore already subject to Moscow, but others offered various degrees of resistance.

Tatars

The *Kazan'* or *Volga Tatars* were defeated by the Russians in 1552 when Kazan' fell, and are seldom mentioned in the Siberian chronicles. But their cousins the *Siberian Tatars*, who lived to the north-east of Kazan', play a central part. They were the people of the Siberian khanate under Kuchum, and claimed descent from the White Horde, originally led by Chingis's grandson Batu. They were cattle nomads who settled to crop-growing with the advent of the Russians. They are believed to have numbered only 5000 at first contact with the Russians, according to a modern estimate based on a critical evaluation of fur-tribute returns preserved in Russian archives;[2] but the number of subjects of the

[1] W. K. Matthews, *Languages of the USSR* (Cambridge, 1951), p. 64.
[2] B. O. Dolgikh, 'Rodovoy i plemennoy sostav narodov Sibiri v XVII v.', *Trudy Instituta etnografii im. N.N.Miklukho-Maklaya*, Tom LV (1960), pp. 48, 52, 59.

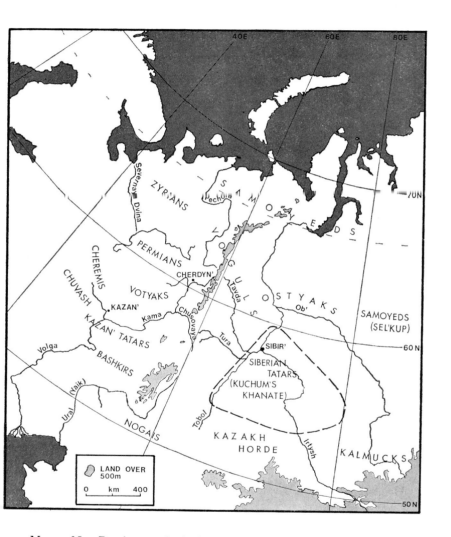

MAP 2. Non-Russian peoples in the Urals region in the late 16th century.

Siberian khan in the 16th century was reported to Moscow at that time to be 30,000 (Vvedenskiy, 1962, p. 75). The latter figure would no doubt include non-Tatar subjects of the khan, so the two may be compatible. Today there are 100,000 Tatars in western Siberia, and no doubt many of them are descended from the subjects of Kuchum.

The *Kazakh Horde* was a political rather than an ethnic grouping, but its subjects were chiefly Kazakhs. Its area was immediately to the south of Sibir'. It had become a khanate by the beginning of the 16th century, and, like Kazan', incorporated remnants of the Golden Horde. Its numbers would probably have been some tens of thousands at most. The Kazakhs have increased greatly since then, and numbered 4·23 million in 1970.

The *Bashkirs* were subject to Kazan', and lived to the south-east of it, in the Urals foothills. They live in the same region today, and numbered 1·24 million in 1970.

The *Noguls* (also spelt Nagai in the chronicles) were nomadic tribes descended from Nogai, a famous prince and general of the Golden Horde in the 13th century. Their warlike activities took them through much of southern Russia, but by the 16th century they were living mostly in the area north of the Caspian.[1] They were described by Anthony Jenkinson, who visited their lands in 1558.[2] They survive today as the *Nogaytsy*, a national group of 52,000 living in the northern Caucasus.

The *Chuvash* lived on the middle Volga and were descended from the Turkic Bulgars who settled on the Kama in the 8th century. The Chuvash were subject to Kazan', and thus were taken into Moscow's territory in 1552. They numbered 1·7 million in 1970.

Uralian peoples

Chud' was a general term used in the Russian chronicles to designate the tribes, primarily Finnic, found by the Russians in the north of European Russia, and, by extension, in Siberia.

The *Ostyaks* lived in the middle and lower Ob' basin, and spoke a language of the Ugrian group. They are thought to have numbered about 11,000 at first contact (Dolgikh, 1960, pp. 60, 76, 85), but the word was then as loosely used as the word Tatar. Indeed, to many Russians in the 16th century the natives of Siberia would have been known as Tatars and Ostyaks. The Ostyak proper are today called Khanty. They live in the same general region and numbered 21,000 in 1970.

The *Voguls* spoke a language related to that of the Ostyaks, whom they closely resembled in life style, but they lived further west, in the foothills

---

[1] H. H. Howorth, *History of the Mongols from the 9th to the 19th century* (London, 1880), Part 2, Division 2, pp. 1011–39.
[2] R. Hakluyt, *The principall navigations, voiages and discoveries of the English nation* (London, 1589), pp. 348–53.

of the Urals on the Siberian side. Both Ostyaks and Voguls had learnt reindeer breeding from their northern neighbours, the Samoyeds. Dolgikh (1960, pp. 23, 32, 39) estimates that they numbered about 5000 when the Russians came. Today they are called Mansi and number 7700. Bakhrushin has made a detailed study of the political and social organisation of the Ostyaks and Voguls at this time (1955, pp. 86–152). An older term for both peoples was Yugrians (Yugrichi)–see Berg (1962, pp. 59–60).

The Samoyeds mostly lived further north than the Ostyaks and Voguls, in the northern forest and the tundra, and were hunters, fishers, and reindeer-breeders – true Arctic nomads. They are now known to comprise several distinct groups, with related languages in the group called Samoyedic, one of the three sub-divisions of Uralian. Those around the lower Ob' are thought to have numbered 5700 at the time of the chronicles (Dolgikh, 1960, pp. 60, 76, 85) but another 9000 of them were living further east and north, in areas not yet reached by the Russians. Most of these peoples are ancestors of today's Nentsy, who numbered 29,000 in 1970. One sub-group of the Samoyeds lived higher on the Ob', east and not north of the Ostyaks: these were the people who came to be known as Ostyak Samoyeds, today called Sel'kupy; their numbers then and in 1970 were 645 and 4300. This is the people referred to as the Skewbald (or Piebald) Horde.

The Cheremis lived on the Volga above Kazan', and were subject to Kazan' until 1552. Their language was one of the Finnic group. They were agriculturalists and skilled also in forest crafts. They live in the same region today but are called Mari, their self-appellation. They numbered nearly 600,000 in 1970.

The Votyaks were neighbours of the Cheremis to the east, and shared many aspects of their culture. The languages are also related, Votyak being another of the Finnic group. They too continue to live in the same region today, and, known as Udmurt, numbered over 700,000 in 1970.

The Zyrians were neighbours of both these peoples, to the north, living in the forests of the Pechora basin. Their language is the closest to Votyak in the Finnic group (the two form the Permian sub-group). Today they are known as Komi, and numbered 322,000 in 1970. Closely related to the Zyrians, and living close by, were the Permians, today called Komi-Permyaki and numbering 153,000.[1]

Others

The Mongols occasionally referred to in the chronicles were probably the Khalkha Mongols of what is now Outer Mongolia. Their homeland was well beyond the reach of 16th-century Muscovy; but of course the Russians knew plenty about them from the period of Mongol domination. The Kalmucks, also known as Western Mongols or Dzungars, whose

---

[1] The main sources for this section are: Dolgikh, 1960; M. G. Levin and L. P. Potapov, ed., The peoples of Siberia (Chicago, 1964); W. K. Matthews, 1951; and Itogi vsesoyuznoy perepisi naseleniya 1970 goda (Moscow, 1973), Tom IV.

language is close to Mongolian in the Altaic family, were encountered more frequently. They were cattle nomads and had established themselves on the northern shores of the Caspian and lower Volga. Today there are 137,000 in the Soviet Union.

The chronicles

There seems to have been one contemporary account of Yermak's campaign, written by a participant. This, referred to in later accounts as the *Relation* (*Napisaniye*), has not survived. What have survived are certain chronicles, or historical tales, which seem to derive in varying measure from a common source, no doubt the *Relation*. The most important of these, selected for inclusion in this volume, are, in descending order of length, the Remezov, the Stroganov, the Yesipov, and the New chronicles (as a chronicle, the New is the longest, but only two paragraphs of it refer to Yermak). In order of antiquity, however – in so far as one can be at all clear about dates of origin – the list is reversed, the New being perhaps the oldest.

The texts of all these – the Remezov in one version, the Stroganov in three, the Yesipov in seven, the New in one – were published by the Imperial Archaeographical Commission in St Petersburg in 1907–10. The texts of the first three were established by P. V. Pavlov, L. N. Maykov and V. V. Maykov, and published in a volume called *Sibirskiye letopisi* in 1907; and that of the New was established by S. F. Platonov and P. G. Vasenko and published in the *Polnoye sobraniye russkikh letopisey*, Tom 14, 1914. Where more than one version of a chronicle exists, the editors decided which one was to be considered as basic, and these are the texts used for the translations in this book.

The basic version of the Stroganov chronicle is that known as the Spasskiy, so named because the manuscript, which at the time the edition was made was in the library of Count S. G. Stroganov, had previously been in the possession of the historian Grigoriy Ivanovich Spasskiy, who had discovered and then published it in 1821, and presented it to Count Stroganov in 1843. The text is written in a 17th-century hand. The other two versions published in the 1907 volume – out of eight then and sixteen now known – are later and shorter. The name Stroganov was first attached to this chronicle by N. M. Karamzin.

The Stroganov chronicle was for long generally considered the oldest of the three longer ones. There is no direct indication of either date or authorship, and there has been much argument. Karamzin himself, Spasskiy, Solov'yev, Pavlov, and Maykov all thought the date of writing was in the first quarter of the 17th century. Until the late 19th century only P. I. Nebol'sin (1849, p. 8) thought it later, pointing out that it could not in any case be earlier than 1621, since it mentioned the Siberian archiepiscopacy, which was created only in that year. Andreyev (1960, pp. 207–9), a leading authority in Soviet times on Siberian source material, came out in favour of a view expressed by A. M. Stavrovich that it must have been written between 1668 and 1673. Her full exposition of the case is in a work which has never been published,[1] but a paper published in 1922 outlines it,[2] and the reasoning is subtle. The royal charter as quoted in chapter 12 of the chronicle includes Semen Stroganov, as well as his nephews Maksim and Nikita, among those who sent off Yermak to conquer Siberia; but the official version (see pp. 293–4) does not mention him. Stavrovich suggests the name was inserted at the request of his descendant, G. D. Stroganov, who became in 1668 the sole representative of the male line, and could plausibly have wished to claim direct descent from the empire-builders. In 1673 another royal charter was issued in which Semen's name was mentioned in this connection – the information being taken, presumably, from the chronicle. These, then, should be the termini. Both handwriting and paper, in Andreyev's view, support this date. But S. V. Bakhrushin, another leading historian of Siberia of this century, does not think this clinches the matter, although he admires Stavrovich's skill. He regards the question as still open (1955, pp. 31–2). And Vvedenskiy takes a somewhat similar line, taking issue with Andreyev on a number of points (1962, pp. 65–72, 106). For myself, I too admire Stavrovich's ingenuity, but do not regard this single fact as conclusive.

The pendulum is now swinging again, and the current tendency in Soviet scholarship[3] is to suggest, on textual evidence, that the Stroganov chronicle was a source for the Yesipov – not easy to do, given that both chronicles also used the same, lost, source; but if this were accepted, it would date the Stroganov chronicle before 1636. V. I. Sergeyev (1970, pp. 52–3) suggests 1621 as the likely date, arguing that the Stroganovs would have wished to emphasise their role at a time when the creation of the archiepiscopacy was cementing union with the Russian state. This argument seems to me by no means conclusive either. But the evidence seems to be pointing now towards a date in the second quarter, rather than the third quarter, of the 17th century.

The authorship is more doubtful still. Only one suggestion has been made, by Stavrovich (1922): that Sergey Kubasov, a secretary at Tobol'sk, wrote it. But Bakhrushin (1955, p. 32) regards this as very unlikely, and Andreyev (1960, p. 216) does not disagree with him.

There is no doubt, however, as to the reason for writing this chronicle. It is plainly to emphasise the role played by the Stroganov family in this expansionist activity. The author, whoever he was, must have been a Stroganov man. To achieve this end, he incorporated in the main story a series of facts, and indeed documents, which he must have found in the

---

[1] *Sibirskiye letopisi. Etyud po istorii voprosa i analizu sibirskikh letopisey* (1920).

[2] 'Sergey Kubasov i Stroganovskaya letopis'', in *Sbornik statey po russkoy istorii, posvyashchennykh S. F. Platonovu* (Petrograd, 1922), pp. 279–93.

[3] V. I. Sergeyev, 'U istokov sibirskogo letopisaniya', *Voprosy istorii*, No. 12 (1970), pp. 45–60. Ye. K. Romodanovskaya, *Russkaya literatura v Sibiri pervoy poloviny XVII v.* (Novosibirsk, 1973), pp. 72–3.

Stroganov archives. Particularly significant among these are the royal charters, like the one just mentioned. (For purposes of comparison, and to complement the story, seven relevant charters and letters, whose texts have come to light from various sources, are included in this book on pp. 281–94.)

The basic version of the Yesipov chronicle is that called the Sychevskiy, after Ivashka Andreyev Sychev, the scribe who wrote on the copy that he completed the transcription on 15 March 1649. Fifty other versions of this chronicle are known, many of them much abbreviated. By contrast with the Stroganov chronicle, the Yesipov chronicle offers no problem of dating or authorship. Its final chapter, the *Sinodik* or book of names for the commemoration of the dead, has an addendum in which the year the chronicle was composed is given as 1636, and even the day (of completion, presumably) as 1 September. There follows a letter code of a type then common, in which the chronicler concealed his name – Savva Yesipov. Yesipov was in the service of the Archbishop of Tobol'sk, and his object, it is equally plain, was to emphasise the religious aspect of Yermak's campaign, and in particular the role of the Orthodox Church. The literary quality of this chronicle is perhaps the greatest of the three, and has been the subject of recent study by Ye. K. Romodanovskaya (1973, pp. 69–124). If we accept the view of Stavrovich and Andreyev, then of course the Yesipov chronicle is older than the Stroganov. Andreyev (1960, p. 213), following Adrianov (1893, pp. 546–50), avers that the writer of the Stroganov chronicle used Yesipov as one of his sources. Bakhrushin (1955, p. 26) does not agree, and now we see attempts to show that Yesipov used the Stroganov chronicle as a source. But the *Sinodik* is ascribed in the chronicle to Kipriyan, the first Archbishop of Tobol'sk, who, the chronicle says, composed it in his second year, that is, 1622. This, then, may in any case be older than the Stroganov chronicle, and perhaps the earliest surviving record of the events. It has sometimes been thought to be the original source, but Bakhrushin (1955, pp. 22–6) has shown that there must have been an earlier document – the *Relation* – from which *Sinodik*, Yesipov and Stroganov all derive. That document was probably quite short, and its date, Bakhrushin thinks, cannot have been later than 1600.

The Yesipov chronicle in turn served as the principal source for the third major account, the undated and apparently unsigned Remezov chronicle. This is found in two versions, of which one, the Mirovich, is printed in the 1907 volume. A note on the manuscript tells that P. F. Mirovich gave it to the historian G. F. Müller in Tobol'sk (it is likelier, in fact, that Mirovich merely helped him to find it), and Müller handed it over to the Academy of Sciences in 1744. Müller called it the Tobol'sk chronicle. The handwriting is 17th–18th century. A striking feature of the manuscript is the illustrations, of which there are 154, one to illustrate each paragraph of the story. The lay-out is that of a modern strip-cartoon. The next section deals with this aspect.

Although apparently anonymous, the chronicle was in fact written by the Tobol'sk boyar's son (a noble rank, not unlike esquire) Semen Ul'yanovich Remezov. Müller was told this when he found it in Tobol'sk in 1734 (Müller, 1750, p. 39); and there is also evidence in the text itself, for again there is a letter code in the last paragraph, and it reads, when solved, 'written by Semen Remezov', followed by the names of his four sons Leontey, Semen, Ivan and Petr in the genitive case (*Sibirskiye letopisi*, 1907, p. xxxv). It is thought, therefore, that his sons played some part in compilation. The handwriting of most of the chronicle is generally thought not to be that of Semen Ul'yanovich Remezov (which is known from another source). L. A. Gol'denberg, a recent biographer of Remezov, thinks that the eldest son Leontey may have written it; but does not rule out the father altogether.[1]

Knowing who the author is helps greatly in determining the date. Semen Remezov (1642 after 1720) belonged to a family which had lived in Tobol'sk since 1628. He made a number of geographical and ethnographic studies for the government, including three atlases, or outlines for atlases, of Siberia.[2] The principal one of these, the *Chertezhnaya kniga Sibiri*, was completed in 1701. In the five or six years before this, he was collecting material, and there is much geographical information in the chronicle. Analysis of the handwriting and paper indicate the late 17th century. Andreyev (1960, pp. 254–5) goes further, and points out that the reference to the Turks at the end of chapter 136 is unlikely to have been written before the Russian victory over the Turks, and the capture of Azov, in 1696; a telling point. It is now generally accepted that the date is around 1700.

But the Mirovich manuscript itself has insertions. They are readily identifiable, because they are literally stuck in, and they comprise chapters 5–8, 49–52, 73–80, 99–102, and 140–7. The first four of these five insertions come from an otherwise unknown account of these events called the Short Kungur Siberian chronicle. Neither author nor date of this account is known, but some guesses have been made as to the date. Sergeyev (1970, pp. 57–9) even supposes it the oldest document of all, written in 1592–93, basing his view on the belief that only an eyewitness would have used certain phrases. This contention will require further evidence in support before it can be accepted. The style is quite different from Remezov's, and the subject matter is, to say the least, an awkward fit. The fifth insertion is probably not from the same source, but is no less awkward. Can we ascertain when the insertions were stuck in? Andreyev (1960, pp. 254–8) produces two facts which may be relevant. Remezov and his son Leontey are known to have visited Kungur (a

[1] L. A. Gol'denberg, *Semen Ul'yanovich Remezov* (Moscow, 1965), pp. 113–15.
[2] The curious fate of these, effectively the first Russian atlases, is told by Gol'denberg (1965, pp. 82–110). The most complete one, *Chertezhnaya kniga Sibiri*, was published in Russia in 1882, while its unfinished predecessor, *Khorograficheskaya chertezhnaya kniga*, was published by L. Bagrow as *The atlas of Siberia by Semyon U. Remezov* in 1958.

town 600 km to the west of Tobol'sk, across the Urals) in 1703, and could have obtained the account then; and one of the inserted sections (chapter 5) contains the phrase *slovo i delo*, translated here as 'words of command', which Andreyev says became well-known in the 1730's. He therefore argues that the sticking-in was done between 1730 and 1734, when Müller took the document away. This seems to me a weak argument, for the *Slovo i delo Gosudarevo* principle (of reporting and punishing persons suspected of plotting against the tsar) was widespread in Peter the Great's time, and known since the first half of the 17th century; and it is not certain that Müller took the document in 1734. Gol'denberg (1965, pp. 119–20) offers the view that the Short Kungur Siberian chronicle insertions were made by Remezov himself about 1709–10, and that they are in his own handwriting, which changed as he grew older. The authorship of the material is still unknown, but Gol'denberg agrees that it may well have come from Kungur in 1703.

The Remezov chronicle was Müller's find. It is not surprising that he used it much more than he used the others when he was writing his history, which was first published as *Opisaniye Sibirskago tsarstva* in 1750; and since Müller's history was the standard work for a long time (J. E. Fischer's, published in 1774, is generally regarded as simply a continuation of Müller's), the Remezov chronicle was part of the foundation of many other accounts of the events of Yermak's time.

The New chronicle (*Novyy letopisets*), as it continues to be called, is in effect a compendium of many manuscripts. The editors of the 1910 edition decided against trying to sort it all out into versions, on the grounds that this would be very hard and would not serve a useful purpose, for most of the material in it is repeated elsewhere. It covers events between 1580 and 1630 in Muscovy as a whole, and Platonov, one of the editors, believes that it was written in 1630 (Bakhrushin, 1955, p. 21). Only the first two of its 422 paragraphs concern Yermak, but, if the dating suggestion is correct, it is older than the three longer accounts. N. A. Dvoretskaya[1] records the location of 25 versions of these two paragraphs.

The Siberian chronicles have been the subject of detailed study over a long period. The foregoing paragraphs outline just a few of the views expressed and the conclusions reached. The best modern summaries of the work done are to be found in the books already quoted by Bakhrushin (1955, pp. 19–52) and Andreyev (1960, pp. 195–259), where references are given. The chronicles translated in this book are the most important surviving accounts of these events, but not by any means the only ones. Besides the other versions of the three major chronicles printed in *Sibirskiye letopisi* of 1907, there have been later discoveries of still further versions (Dvoretskaya, 1957). It must also be remembered – indeed, it is quite evident when reading the texts – that these chronicles

---

[1] N. A. Dvoretskaya, 'Arkheograficheskiy obzor spiskov povestey o pokhode Yermaka', *Trudy Otdela drevnerusskoy literatury*, Tom XIII (1957), pp. 478–9.

are not just historical records, but have a considerable element of literary pretension. A new edition is at present in preparation by groups of Academy of Sciences scholars at the Siberian Division at Novosibirsk and at the Institute of History in Moscow (Preobrazhenskiy, 1972, p. 29).

Finally, the texts of seven charters and letters relevant to the events described in the chronicles have been included. The gist of some of these is given in the Stroganov chronicle, as already mentioned. Müller quotes them all in his *Opisaniye Sibirskago tsarstva* of 1750, and they re-appear, re-edited, in the 1937 edition of his book. In Müller's time they seem all to have been in the Stroganov family archives, but by 1937 they were in various other places; some had been lost, but other versions were used.

Translation has of course posed a number of problems. It is not easy, and perhaps not always possible, to give an impression in English of the rather special character of the language used in these chronicles. In general, no attempt has been made in the English version to improve on the often clumsy and sometimes obscure Russian original. The printed texts used are full scholarly editions, giving variant words and spellings: these variant forms are not carried over into the translation, but in certain cases a variant form has been silently introduced. Linguistic problems in general, including difficulties of corrupt text, are mentioned in footnotes where this seems necessary. But detailed attention has not been given to linguistic matters here, since the printed originals are relatively easily available, and there have been, in addition, several recent works in Russian concerned specifically with these matters.[1]

The illustrations

As mentioned above, the Mirovich version of the Remezov chronicle is illustrated. The pictures are all reproduced here, so they need not be described, but some general remarks about them are called for.

The reader's first impression is that there must have been at least two artists – one for the main chronicle and another for the interpolations, for the pictorial styles are rather markedly different. Gol'denberg (1965, p. 117) believes the main chronicle was illustrated by one of S. U. Remezov's sons, probably Leontey but possibly Semen, for the pictures are not like other known pictures by S. U. Remezov. Gol'denberg notes that the only coloured objects are the trees, which are yellow-green or

[1] Yu. V. Fomenko, 'K voprosu ob imennom sklonenii v russkoy pis'mennosti XVII veka (na materiale sibirskikh letopisey)', *Uchenyye zapiski Moskovskogo gosudarstvennogo pedagogicheskogo instituta*, Tom CXLVIII (1960), pp. 392–412, and 'Nablyudeniya nad glagol'nymi formami v yazyke sibirskikh letopisey XVII v.' in *Voprosy istorii i dialektologii russkogo yazyka* (Magnitogorsk, 1961), pp. 35–51; O. G. Porokhova, 'Vzaimodeystviye russkoy i staroslavyanskoy (po proiskhozhdeniyu) leksiki v russkom pis'mennom yazyke XVII v. (na materiale sibirskikh letopisey)', in *Istoricheskaya grammatika i leksikologiya russkogo yazyka* (Moscow, 1962), pp. 115–37, and *Leksika sibirskikh letopisey XVII veka* (Leningrad, 1969).

brown in the original, and are very similar to trees in S. U. Remezov's atlases. He therefore suggests that Leontey drew the pictures and wrote out the text, and that his father (who was the author of the text) added the trees afterwards. This seems a slightly curious reversal of expected roles, with the man in charge doing the menial job, but perhaps is less odd if we imagine that the father was seeking to give his son an opportunity. On the other hand, the pictures in the interpolated sections may, Gol'denberg thinks, have been by the father, for they somewhat resemble other pictures of his. It will be recalled that the handwriting of these sections is also thought by Gol'denberg to be the father's.

V. N. Alekseyev, the most recent writer on the subject, advances a rather different view.[1] He believes that the main chronicle was illustrated by three artists: most of the drawings were done by S. U. Remezov himself, but about 40, which seem to show a lesser degree of skill, were done by his father, U. M. Remezov, and another ten, which exhibit least influence of the icon-type style, were done by the son Leontey. Alekseyev finds his reasons for this attribution in a study of the style, and also in a close comparison of the pictures and the text. He agrees with Gol'denberg, however, in believing that the pictures in the interpolated sections are by S. U. Remezov, and accounts for their difference in style from the others that he attributes to the same man by arguing that S. U. Remezov had spent some time in Moscow before he did them and had absorbed influences there. Although Alekseyev has written the most detailed analysis that has yet appeared, I find his arguments on the subject of the main chronicle pictures interesting rather than compelling. There is general agreement, however, that all the pictures are by members of the Remezov family.

The pictures therefore date from about 1700; so the information they give about Russian life is more likely to relate to that time than to the period of the events described. If that is borne in mind, they are a very valuable source. Andreyev (1960, p. 258) maintains that these pictures are the only 17th-century drawings of indisputably Russian origin – an exaggeration, as a history of Russian art shows[2], but not such a very great exaggeration.

Andreyev is right to emphasise the Russian-ness. The artist of the main chronicle was thoroughly familiar with traditional Russian style – that of 16th-century illustrated chronicles and of the later icon-painting. But certain western influences are apparent, especially in pictures near the end of the chronicle, and one must imagine that the artist had seen engravings in western books (chapters 136, 152 and 156, for instance). Alekseyev (1974, p. 189) suggests that one such influence may have been *Kronika Sarmacyey Europeyskiey* by Alexander Gwagnin (Guagninus),

[1] V. N. Alekseyev, 'Risunki "Istorii Sibirskoy" S. U. Remezova (problemy attributsii)'. *Drevnerusskoye iskusstvo. Rukopisnaya kniga. Sbornik vtoroy* (Moscow, 1974), pp. 175–96.
[2] A. A. Sidorov, *Risunok starykh russkikh masterov* (Moscow, 1956), pp. 44–64.

published in Kraków in 1611, which contains a number of battle scenes[1]; but his argument is not concerned with the chapters mentioned above, and in any case fails to convince me that this particular book, rather than many others like it, was the one the Remezovs used. Stylistically, there is some affinity with western European work of two centuries earlier – for instance, with the Berner Chronik of Bendicht Tschachtlan.[2] This was not published and could scarcely have influenced the Remezovs; but no doubt there were other chronicles which were somewhat similar and of which they might have seen copies or reproductions. The artist of the interpolated sections, however, had a less studied, more natural style, and, it seems to me, despite Alekseyev's view, betrayed no obvious western influence. Much remains to be explained about the pictures, and it is hoped that their reproduction here will stimulate examination by art historians.

A notable feature of the pictures is their closeness to the subject-matter described in the text. There can be no doubt that text and pictures were done at the same time; there is indeed physical evidence of this, in that the writing often overlaps the pictures, and this is part of the argument that this manuscript was a father-and-son production. Almost every important incident described in the text is illustrated. Often a 'multiple narrative' technique is used, whereby one picture will show several incidents which did not take place simultaneously, but consecutively. One may wonder if this closeness of illustration to text is designed, at least in part, to help those unable to read. They could follow the story (with a small amount of help) simply by looking at the pictures. But one must also recall that the chronicle was not a book. The illustrated version has existed, as far as we know, in only one copy. That would not have circulated much, and certainly not among illiterates.

Yet the closeness is relative. If one examines the text and pictures carefully, there are discrepancies. Some small details occurring in the pictures are not mentioned, but are perhaps implied, in the text. This aspect has been studied by Alekseyev (1974, pp. 179–80), who uses the discrepancies to help identify the chronicler's sources, and who postulates a visual tradition which is distinct from the oral or written tradition.

In the original, the drawings are in pairs, one pair to a page, and the used area of each page measures about 17 by 27 cm. Each picture is thus about 17 by 13 cm. The illustrations in this edition are reduced by almost half. Apart from the colouring already mentioned, the material used for the drawings as well as the text was brown ink containing iron salts. All the pictures were reproduced in A. Zost's edition of this chronicle (1880) – itself a rare book even when *Sibirskiye letopisi* was

---

[1] Earlier editions, in Latin (*Sarmatiae Europeae descriptio*, Kraków, 1578, and Speier, 1581), do not contain the relevant pictures.
[2] E. A. Gessler, *Die schweizer Bilderchroniken des 15./16. Jahrhunderts* (Zürich, 1941), plates 6 and 7.

published in 1907 – and a few of them have also appeared as illustrations in other works, such as Müller, 1937, Gol'denberg, 1965, and Alekseyev, 1974.

Later published accounts

While the chronicles are the main source for these events, other published books by persons who studied or visited the area might be expected to contain prime source material. The authors of many such were foreigners, all of them knowing Russia well and some knowing Siberia too.

First may be mentioned the ambassadors of Queen Elizabeth of England, Sir Jerome Bowes (in Moscow 1583–84), Giles Fletcher (in Moscow 1588–89), and Sir Jerome Horsey (who held many other positions too, including that of Russian Ambassador to England, and was resident in Russia, on and off, from 1573 to 1591). All these might have met in Moscow participants of the campaign, and certainly must have measured its effect on the court. But their attention was fully occupied with matters of more immediate concern, and they merely show themselves aware of the conquests (thus Horsey took note that Ivan IV 'conquered the kingdom of Siberia'[1]).

Nikolay Gavrilovich Spafariy (Spathary) was a Moldavian of Greek descent who headed a Russian embassy to China in 1675. He travelled out by way of Tobol'sk, the Irtysh and the Ob', and he noticed the remains of a settlement, which he believed to be Kuchum's, near Abalak on the Irtysh.[2] Evert Ysbrantszoon Ides was a Netherlander who also served as Russian ambassador to China, making his outward journey by much the same route in 1692[3]. In his book he describes the taking of Sibir' – but quite inaccurately: he has Yermak defeating a twelve-year-old prince of Tobol'sk, Altanai Kuchumovich. He evidently confused Kuchum with his son, or with Mametkul.

Much more relevant is the account of Siberia, as it was then known, by Nicolaas Witsen, published as *Noord en Oost Tartarye* in Amsterdam in 1698. Witsen was an outstanding person, who became a burgomaster of Amsterdam, and was in Russia as a diplomat in 1664–5 and 1667. His book is large and is packed with miscellaneous information about 'north and east Tartary'. Unfortunately there is no English translation. Witsen expressed views on many of the points raised in this introduction – the importance of the Stroganovs, the role of Yermak; but he did not visit the area, as far as we know, and was of course much too late to pick up even echoes of stories by participants.

A Swedish officer, captured by the Russians at Poltava, was sent to

[1] In his 'Travels', printed in L. E. Berry and R. O. Crummey, ed., *Rude and barbarous kingdom* (Madison, 1968), pp. 262–369.
[2] An English translation is in J. Baddeley, *Russia, Mongolia, China* (London, 1919), Vol. II, pp. 244–54.
[3] *Driejaarige reize naar China* . . . (Amsterdam, 1710), p. 15.

western Siberia where he spent the years 1709–22. His name was Philipp Johann von Strahlenberg, and he wrote a book about his experiences.[1] While he was observant, and in particular collected materials for a map of the region, he had no special interest in history, and his book adds nothing to the story of Yermak. I mention him here because his book circulated widely and became accepted as a standard source; in fact it is less accurate and much less compendious than Witsen's – but it is, of course, an eye-witness account.

Finally, the latest in time and the most important in content is Müller's history (1750), already mentioned. Müller was a professional historian commissioned to write a history of Siberia. He travelled very widely in the country, and must have spent quite some time in Yermak's area of operations. He identified many of the places mentioned in the chronicles, though signs of habitation had often already almost disappeared, and his account gains greatly from this first-hand description of the scene of the events. Müller's more important observations, therefore, have been referred to in footnotes to the translations which follow, and the map facing p. 18 owes much to his identifications.

[1] *An historico-geographical description of the north and eastern parts of Europe and Asia* (London, 1738).

THE STROGANOV CHRONICLE

according to the Spasskiy manuscript[1]

On the taking of the Siberian land, how to the Pious Sovereign, the Tsar and Great Prince Ivan Vasil'yevich of all Russia,[2] God granted the Siberian state for the sovereign to rule over, and granted that he should defeat the Sultan of Sibir', Kuchyum son of Murtaza[3] and capture alive his son, the khan's heir Mametkul, and how God enlightened that Siberian land by holy baptism and by the holy churches of God and established in it a bishop's throne for an archiepiscopacy.

[1] News came to the hearing of the Pious Sovereign, the Tsar and Great Prince Ivan Vasil'yevich of all Russia, concerning the frequent warlike incursions of infidels from the Siberian peoples into the sovereign's land of Perm', and how the godless ones by their incursion had brought much captivity and desolation on the sovereign's cities and settlements and villages of the land of Perm'. God inspired the Pious Sovereign, the Tsar, to question the men of his state who had knowledge concerning that land. The sovereign ordered that Yakov and Grigorey Stroganov should be brought before him, and he questioned them how the land of Perm' might be protected from attack by the Siberian peoples and by what means restraint could be exercised on Sultan Kuchyum. They related everything in detail to the sovereign, and their words were pleasing to the sovereign. He granted them his favour and commanded that they should be given according to their wishes what was needed, howsoever the land of Perm' might be protected by them from the Siberian peoples. He commanded concerning this that in all matters the sovereign's charters should be granted to them for trade among the Siberian peoples and the peoples of other hordes and lands.

---

[1] The text translated is printed in *Sibirskiye letopisi*, 1907, pp. 1–46. The manuscript is now held at the Saltykov-Shchedrin State Public Library in Leningrad (accession no. 13 for 1930), and was originally written some time between 1621 and 1673 (see Introduction, pp. 24–5).

[2] The tsar during all this period (though he died in 1584, before the final outcome was clear) was Ivan IV, known as Groznyy. The epithet is commonly translated as 'The Terrible', but might be more accurately rendered as 'The Awe-Inspiring'; it was not pejorative.

[3] The form given is Murtazeliyev. The Yesipov chronicle has Martazeyev. Kuchum's father's name was certainly Murtaza, perhaps Murtaza Ali, which could lead to Murtazeliyev.

35

[2] On the establishment of the stronghold of Kankor on the Pyskorskiy headland, where was the monastery of our All-Merciful Saviour, called Pyskor.

In the year 7066 [1558] on the 4th day of April[1] the Pious Sovereign, the Tsar and Great Prince Ivan Vasil'yevich of all Russia, granted Grigorey son of Anika Stroganov the empty lands below Great Perm' for 88 versts down the river Kama, along its right bank from the mouth of the stream Lysva, and along the left bank below the Pyznovskaya backwaters, along both banks of the Kama to the river Chyusovaya. In those regions where Grigorey Stroganov might choose a strong and well guarded place, we have commanded him to establish a stronghold and build fortresses and to appoint by his own authority cannoneers and fortress gunners and musketeers and artillery-men[2] for defence against the Siberian peoples and the Nagay peoples and the peoples of other hordes.[3] We have also commanded this same Grigorey to recruit freely to himself those who are untaxed and unregistered in those lands.[4] The sovereign's charter for the township of Kankor[5] was granted with the subscript[6] of the secretary Petr Danilov. It was decreed by the courtiers[7] Fedor Ivanovich Umnoy and Aleksey Fedorovich Adashev and the treasurer Fedor Ivanovich Sukin and Khozyain Yur'yevich Tyutin. The secretary Tret'yak Karacharov signed the decree.[8]

[3] On the establishment of another stronghold on the Orlovskiy water meadow, called Kergedan, but now called Orlov.

In the year 7072 [1564], on the 2nd of January, the Sovereign, the Tsar and Great Prince Ivan Vasil'yevich of all Russia, granted to Grigorey son of Onika Stroganov a grant charter in the same lands as he had granted him before this, decreeing that he should choose a place on the Orlovskiy water meadow, twenty versts below the previous township

[1] The year was reckoned from the creation of the world, which was believed to be in 5508 B.C. 5508 years should therefore be deducted to give the modern date; but for days between 1 September and 31 December, 5509 must be deducted, because the new year began on 1 September. Days and months are Old Style. By our present calendar, all the dates given in these chronicles would be 10 days later; this would be 14 April.

[2] Russ. *vorotniki*, which normally means gatekeepers, but in the specialised usage of the documents of this kind and period, means persons serving artillery detachments (Porokhova, 1969, p. 127). The list already contains gunners (*pushkari*), and the distinction between the two is not clear.

[3] See Introduction, pp. 20–4. A horde (Russ. *orda*) was not only the people (who might or might not be an ethnic unit), but also the territory they occupied.

[4] Russ. *ne tyaglyye i ne pismyannyye*. These are categories of peasant, and the meaning is that Grigoriy Stroganov should collect the unattached peasants, who had no doubt run away from their masters into this frontier area.

[5] On the Kama, near modern Solikamsk, some 200 km upstream from Perm'. For this and other place-names, see Map 1, facing p. 18.

[6] Russ. *pripis'*, meaning something added in writing, probably more than a signature (which the word can mean); perhaps like the end of the next chapter.

[7] Russ. *okolnich'i*, a rank at court, the next below boyar.

[8] The full text of this charter is given on pp. 281–4.

of Kankor. To Grigorey it was also enjoined that he should by his own authority establish walls of thirty sazhens,[1] and on the side of access from below he should wall up the place with stone in the clay, and should by his own authority appoint musketeers and guards in that stronghold and maintain rapid-firing artillery in both of those strongholds; he should cause to be made cannons, muskets, fortress guns and hand-guns by the services of an unrecorded gunsmith of those whom Grigorey should hire for himself, and Grigorey should maintain that artillery with himself. The sovereign's charter for that stronghold was granted; the subscript to the charter was by the sovereign's great secretary Yuriy Bashanin: the Tsar and Great Prince Ivan Vasil'yevich of all Russia; in another place was the subscript of Senya Nepein: by the decree of the Sovereign, the Tsar and Great Prince Ivan Vasil'yevich of all Russia; in a third place was the subscript of Kozma Romantsov: it was decreed according to the word of the Tsar and Great Prince by the treasurer Nikita Afonas'yevich Funikov, according to the memorandum with the subscript of the secretary Ivan Bulgakov.[2]

[4] On the establishment of the Chyusovaya strongholds.

In the year 7076 [1568] on the 25th of March the Sovereign, the Tsar and Great Prince Ivan Vasil'yevich of all Russia, granted Yakov son of Onika Stroganov a charter from the mouth of the river Chyusovaya upstream on both sides and to the height of the land and to the head-waters of the stream. In those lands from the Kama upstream along the Chyusovaya for eighty versts on the right and the left side he was to establish strongholds for fortification and defence against the Siberian and the Nagay people and other hordes, and to cause to be made for the strongholds rapid-firing artillery, cannons and fortress guns and hand-guns, and all necessary fortifications, and he was to recruit men to those strongholds freely and to maintain them there, cannoneers and fortress gunners and musketeers and guards and artillery-men.[3] The sovereign's charter was granted with the subscript of the secretary, Druzhina Volodimerov.[4]

[1] A sazhen' is a measure of distance generally translated as fathom. On land it was normally 2·134 m (three arshins), at sea 1·83 m, or equal to the English fathom. Thirty sazhens would therefore be about 64 m, and so presumably the length of one side of the defensive square.
[2] The full text of this charter has not been located.
[3] The exact whereabouts of these strongholds is not now known in all cases. Besides Kankor and Kergedan, there were Yayvenskiy Gorodok and Nizhne-Chusovskiy Gorodok, on the Yayva and Chusovaya (Bakhrushin, 1955, pp. 99–100).
[4] The full text of this charter is given on pp. 284–7.

[5] On the establishment of the Sylva and Yayva forts, how they were established against the advances of the Siberian and Nagay peoples.

In the year 7078 [1570], according to the command of the Pious Sovereign, the Tsar and Great Prince Ivan Vasil'yevich of all Russia, in order to prevent the Siberian and Nagay peoples from crossing the rivers, so that they should not have a way to the sovereign's towns of Perm', and in order to contain the Sylva and Iren Tatars and Ostyaks and the Chyusovaya and Yayva and Inva and Kosva Voguls, Yakov Stroganov established forts above the Sylva and above the Yayva rivers, and appointed in those forts rapid-firing artillery and cannons and fortress guns and muskets and hand-guns, and cannoneers and fortress gunners and musketeers and artillery-men.

[6] On the killing of Russian trading men and fishermen by the Cheremis and the Bashkirs.

In the year 7080 [1572] on the 15th of July, by divine dispensation, the Cheremis came to the river Kama and they incited to come with them a great number of Ostyaks and Bashkirs and Buintsy.[1] Near the previously mentioned strongholds of Kankor and Kergedan they killed Russian trading men, 87 in number. Concerning this the Pious Sovereign, the Tsar and Great Prince Ivan Vasil'yevich of all Russia, sent his royal charter, with the subscript of the secretary Kirey Gorin, to Yakov and to Grigorey Stroganov. He commanded that they should gather their men and send them out from the strongholds after those who were traitors to him, the sovereign, of the Cheremis, the Ostyaks, the Bashkirs and the Buintsy.[2] So they, Yakov and Grigorey, selected a leader in their strongholds and gave him fighting men, cossacks and volunteers from among their men, and sent them after them, against the traitors to the sovereign, who had proved treacherous to the sovereign. Those who were sent out killed some of the accursed pagans and captured others alive and brought all of these to take an oath that they would be true to the sovereign in all things and be subject to him and give taxes to the sovereign and stand for the sovereign against the enemies who opposed the sovereign, without treachery. They seized hostages from among them and sent them to their strongholds and to Perm' to the sovereign's *voyevodas*.

[1] See section on non-Russian peoples in the Introduction. It is not clear, however, who the Buintsy were; but there are two modern towns called Buinsk, both near the Volga below Kazan', so the Buintsy were perhaps, like the, Cheremis and the Chuvash, subjects of the khanate.
[2] This sentence gives the gist of the charter of 6 August 1572 (see pp. 288–9).

[7] On the coming of the khan's heir Mametkul, son of the Siberian Sultan Kuchyum, to the river Chyusovaya and on the capture of Russians.

In the year 7081 [1573] on the 20th of July, sacred to the memory of the holy prophet Elias, Mametkul, son of Khan Kuchyum,[1] the Siberian sultan, came out of the Siberian land from the river Tobol to the river Chyusovaya to make war, having prepared himself with his *murzas*[2] and princes, to spy out roads by which he could go to war against the strongholds of Yakov and Grigorey Stroganov and against Perm' the Great. On his advance they killed many Ostyak subjects and took their wives and children into captivity. They killed the sovereign's envoy, Tret'yak Chebukov, and all the Tatars serving with him, who were going with him to Kazan' against the Kazan' Horde, and took others into captivity. He did not go up to the Chyusovaya strongholds, halting five versts off, since the Russian prisoners told him that there was a multitude of fighting men in the strongholds and that they were waiting for him to come upon them. He was alarmed by that and turned back. But Yakov and Grigorey did not dare to send their hired cossacks from the strongholds after the Siberian forces without the sovereign's command. Even before this the Siberian sultan with his army had killed the Ostyak subjects, Chagir' with his comrades, and had taken into captivity others who lived near the Chyusovaya strongholds. Concerning that Yakov and Grigorey wrote to Moscow to the Pious Sovereign, the Tsar and Great Prince Ivan Vasil'yevich of all Russia, requesting that the sovereign should make them a grant and should order them to pursue them without penalty and avenge the injuries done to them. For that the sovereign made a grant to Yakov and Grigorey and ordered that his sovereign's charter should be given to them, decreeing for them that in the Siberian land beyond the Yugrian range in Tagchei[3] and on the river Tobol and on the Irtysh and on the Ob' and on other rivers, where it was useful for protection and as rest-houses for the volunteers, they should build forts and keep fire-arms and gunners and musketeers and guards against the Siberian and Nagay people and against other hordes. They should put up buildings near the fortresses, at fishing places

---

[1] Most scholars today believe Alliy (Ali) was Kuchum's son and Mametkul (Mahmet-Kul) was his nephew. As Müller (1750, p. 173) notes, Mametkul later became a military leader in the service of Boris Godunov, and is referred to as Mametkul Altaulovich. Thus he could be neither Kuchum's son nor brother (Kuchum's father being Murtaza), but Altaul might have been Kuchum's brother. Kuchum's title in the Russian is sometimes tsar (as here), but also khan or sultan. To avoid possible confusion, the word tsar has been used in these translations only for the tsar of Moscow. For the same reason Mametkul's title tsarevich is translated here as khan's heir.

[2] Tatar nobles.

[3] Also Takhchei. A rather vague term apparently signifying the Tura basin (Bakhrushin, 1955, p. 142). The Yugrian range (Russ. *Yugorskiy kamen'*) was the ordinary phrase for the Urals.

and at plough-lands, on both sides of the river Tobol and along rivers and lakes and up to the headwaters and should be strongly fortified with all necessary fortifications. Whichever Ostyaks and Voguls and Yugrians abandoned the Siberian sultan, and would be under his sovereign's hand, and would give tribute to the sovereign, these men they should send with tribute to Moscow and pay the tribute in to the sovereign's treasury, and Yakov and Grigorey should protect in their strongholds those tributary Ostyaks and Voguls and Yugrians and their wives and children from the advance of the fighting men of Sibir'. And Yakov and Grigorey should assemble volunteers and their own men and the Ostyaks and Voguls and Yugrians and Samoyeds, together with the hired cossacks and the artillery, and should send them to wage war on the Siberian sultan and to make the Siberians prisoner and to bring them to give tribute for the sovereign. If there should come to those fortresses to Yakov and Grigorey merchants from Bukhara and the Kazakh Horde and other lands with any merchandise, they should trade freely with them without duty. The sovereign's charter for those lands in the Siberian border country beyond the Yugrian range, for Tagchei and for the Tobol and for the Irtysh and along the Ob' for the fortress lands, was granted in the year 7082 [1574], on the 30th of May, with the subscript of the secretary Petr Grigor'yev.[1]

[8] On the summoning of the Volga *atamans* and cossacks, Yermak son of Timofey and his comrades, from the great river Volga to the Chyusovaya strongholds to give aid against the un-believers.

In the year 7087 [1579] on the 6th of April, Semen and Maksim and Nikita Stroganov heard these reports from trustworthy men concerning the daring and bravery of the Volga cossacks and *atamans*, Yermak son of Timofey and his comrades, how on the Volga crossings they were killing the Nagay and despoiling and killing the Ardobazartsy.[2] Having heard this concerning their daring and bravery, they sent some of their men with a letter and with many gifts to them, inviting them to come to them at their ancestral estates in the Chyusovaya strongholds and in the forts to give them aid. The cossacks greatly rejoiced at this, that messengers had come to them from honourable men and summoned them to give them help. Thereupon the *atamans* and cossacks, Yermak son of Timofey and his comrades, Ivan Koltso, Yakov Mikhaylov, Nikita Pan

---

[1] The whole of this chapter is a not very exact summary of the charter of this date (see pp. 289–92).

[2] Also Ordobazartsy. The meaning is not altogether clear; perhaps a composite and pejorative term meaning 'members of hordes and inhabitants of bazaars'. The chronicler, being a Stroganov man, is polite about Yermak's former occupation. No doubt his band were despoiling and killing anyone with worthwhile spoils, whether they were Tatars or not.

and Matfey Meshcheryak,[1] assembled with their faithful and excellent company, 540 men in number, and soon set out to their lands.

[9] On the coming of the Volga *atamans* and cossacks, Yermak son of Timofey and his comrades, to the Chyusovaya strongholds.

In the same year on the 28th of June, sacred to the memory of Cyrus and John, the miracle-working and selfless saints, the *atamans* and cossacks, Yermak son of Timofey Povolskoy[2] and his comrades, came from the Volga to the Chyusovaya strongholds. And they, Semen and Maksim and Nikita Stroganov, received them with honour and gave them many gifts and provided food and drink in abundance for their enjoyment. The *atamans* and cossacks stood against the godless infidels,[3] daring and united, together with the men living there in the strongholds, and they fought the godless infidels fiercely and unmercifully and stood firm and spurred themselves on against the unbelievers. Those *atamans* and cossacks lived in their strongholds for two years and about two months.

[10] On the coming of the Voguls up to the Chyusovaya strongholds and up to the Sylva fort to make war.

In the year 7089 [1581], on the 22nd of July, the malicious Devil, who from time immemorial has hated good done to the human race, incited the evil and godless Vogul *murza*, Begbeliy Agtakov, with his Vogul and Ostyak company, which numbered 680 men. They came up to the Chyusovaya strongholds and up to the Sylva fort, unnoticed and by stealth, and laid waste and burnt down the villages and hamlets of those living around there, and took many people into captivity, men, women and children. But merciful God did not permit the accursed ones to succeed. The Russian troops soon achieved a victory over those godless men, coming from their strongholds, and seized many near the strongholds, and killed many at the crossings according to those reports. They

[1] These four comrades were the *sotniks* (commanders of 100) in Yermak's army. If total numbers are correct, each *sotnya* was rather over-strength. The family names may indicate non-Russian background in some cases. Nikita Pan sounds Polish, but he might have been Ukrainian, and Matfey Meshcheryak might have been a member of the Turkicised Finnic people on the Oka, the Meschera.

[2] Meaning from the Volga. The epithet here seems to be midway between a descriptive adjective and a family name – a common way for family names to arise. Although the family name does not seem to have survived – in any case Yermak, as far as we know, had no children – it links up with the idea that the correct family name was Alenin (see Introduction, p. 11); for Yermak's grandfather (according to that idea) was Afonasiy Grigor'yevich Alenin, who died at Yur'yevets Povol'skoy.

[3] Russ. *Agaryan*, Hagarenes: the descendants of Hagar and her son Ishmael who 'dwelt in the wilderness of Paran' (*Genesis*, xxi, 21). In Russian the word came to mean Moslems. The word used more frequently in these chronicles is *busurmany*, also translated as infidels.

seized many others and captured alive their *murza*, Begbeliy Agtakov. Those godless men, seeing their own exhaustion, since God had granted victory over them to the sovereign, on this account gave their submission and admitted their fault, undertaking that they would pay tribute to the Sovereign, the Tsar and Great Prince Ivan Vasil'yevich of all Russia, and would not go to war against the Russian land.

[11] On the sending of the Volga *atamans* and cossacks, Yermak son of Timofey and his comrades, and of the troops of the Stroganovs to Sibir' against the Siberian sultan.

In the year 7090 [1581] on the first of September, sacred to the memory of our holy father St Simeon Stylites, Semen and Maksim and Nikita Stroganov sent from their strongholds the Volga *atamans* and cossacks, Yermak son of Timofey and his comrades, to Sibir' against the Siberian sultan. Together with them they had assembled from their strongholds their troops, men of Lithuania, foreigners,[1] Tatars and Russians, daring, brave and valiant soldiers, three hundred in number. They sent them out together with the Volga *atamans* and cossacks, and from them they formed that gathering of eight hundred and forty daring and brave men.[2] Assembling together they offered up hymns of prayer to all-merciful God, glorified in the Trinity, and to his most pure Mother, Mother of God, and to all the powers of heaven and to His holy saints. They paid them a satisfactory reward, attired them in clothing and supplied them with fire-arms, cannons and rapid-firing guns and seven-span muskets and many provisions and all these things in sufficiency. They gave them guides, who knew that road to Sibir', and interpreters of the infidel language, and sent them in peace to the Siberian land. Those *atamans* and cossacks together with the hired troops advanced gladly into the Siberian land against the Siberian sultan, with their formation of companies, appointed for clearing the country of Sibir', to make clean the land and to drive out the godless barbarian. The *atamans* and cossacks went for four days up the river Chyusovaya to the mouth of the river Serebryanaya, and along the river Serebryanaya for two days. Yermak came to the Siberian road, and there they built a stronghold fortified with walls of earth, naming it Yermak's stronghold Kokuy.[3]

---

[1] Russ. *nemets*, lit. dumb, meaning then any western European. The word later came to mean German.

[2] The chronicles disagree about numbers in Yermak's army (see Introduction, p. 13). Most scholars go along with the figure 540, but Vvedenskiy (1962, pp. 98–9) is inclined to think the 300 men who joined on the Chusovaya an over-statement, for there were not too many available males on the Stroganov estates at that time.

[3] This camp was evidently still in existence at the time of G. F. Müller, the historian who published in 1750 (Müller, 1937, p. 220 – this information was not printed in the first edition). The Kokuy is a tributary of the Serebryanka, or Serebryanaya.

From that place he crossed 17 versts[1] across the portage to the river called Zharavlya, and they went down that river and came out on the river Tura. Here was the Siberian land.

[12] On the coming of the Siberian troops of the prince of Pelym to the towns of Perm' and to Kankor and to Kergedan and to the Chyusovaya strongholds and up to the Sylva and Yayva forts.

At the same time in the year 7090 [1581], and on the day sacred to the memory of our holy father St Simeon Stylites, the impious and godless prince of Pelym was filled with great fury.[2] Still more was he possessed by wild ferocity, and plotted evil trickery in his heart. He began to contrive deception with cunning, but it all resulted for the godless man in his own destruction. Then that impious prince assembled his troops, who numbered 700 men, and called to his aid the daring, brave and powerful murzas and princes of the Siberian land together with a great number of troops. That evil man by compulsion also took with him a great number of the Sylva, Kosva, Iren, Inva and Obva Tatars and Ostyaks and Voguls and Votyaks and Bashkirs. He advanced with his troops, unleashing his fury against the towns round Perm', against Cherdyn'. They captured those places and burnt them down. He came up even to the walls of the city, with much violence and ferocity approaching the city, which narrowly escaped being captured. But almighty God did not permit the accursed ones to succeed. They soon left that place and advanced up to the stronghold of Kay and there did great damage. From there the accursed ones advanced to Kam'skoye Usol'ye,[3] and there burnt down the villages and town settlements and captured the inhabitants. They advanced to the strongholds of Kankor and Kergedan, and from there they advanced to the Chyusovaya strongholds and to the Sylva and Yayva forts. Suddenly the accursed ones fell upon the Chyusovaya strongholds and cut down a great number of the Christians living around there and burnt down their villages and dwellings. They savagely took captive the Orthodox Christians, with many captured and made prisoner. The Volga *atamans* and cossacks were not there in the strongholds. Before the coming of that accursed and godless prince of

---

[1] The Russian term used is *poprishche*, which has designated, like the English league, several different measures of length: equivalence to two-thirds, one, one and a half, four and twenty versts are all found (Porokhova, 1969, p. 178; H. G. Lunt, *Concise dictionary of old Russian* (Munich, 1970), *sub nomine*). The verst also varied in length, and at this time was equal to 1000 *sazhens* or 2·13 km (Bakhrushin, 1955, p. 99). The distance from Moscow to the land of Sibir' is given in chapter 1 of the Yesipov chronicle as nearly 2000 *poprishche*; in order for this distance not to be grossly exaggerated – it is nearly 1400 km as the crow flies, and perhaps twice that much by water – the smallest value of *poprishche*, two-thirds of a verst, seems likeliest here. So 25 *poprishche* equal 17 versts.
[2] The prince of Pelym was a Vogul chieftain, who was a thorn in the Russian flesh for another decade. Probably identifiable with Begbeliy Agtakov of chapter 10.
[3] Now Solikamsk, 'the salt works on the Kama'.

Pelym, in the same year, Semen and Maksim and Mikita[1] sent them to the Siberian land against the Siberian sultan. The men who remained behind in their strongholds and forts narrowly escaped death at the hands of the accursed and godless Tatars, from their evil harassment, being saved not by their own strength, but by the help of God. Thenceforth they suffered many afflictions and harassments from the accursed ones. But Semen and Maksim and Mikita together with their valiant and brave men summoned to their aid all-merciful God, glorified in the Trinity, and his most pure Mother, Mother of God, and all His saints. Even more they advanced against the enemy, and valiantly and with one accord stood firm amid this great harassment by the accursed ones. They fought strongly and valiantly with the accursed ones, and a great number fell on both sides. The accursed ones learnt that Russian troops had gone to war against their Siberian land, and were alarmed at this. And so, by the help of God, the accursed barbarians were defeated, and their Russian prisoners were released. Those godless ones withdrew, covered in shame, like curs, to their own lands. Concerning that attack of the prince of Pelym, the *voyevoda* Vasiley Pelepelitsyn[2] wrote from Cherdyn' to the Sovereign, the Tsar and Great Prince Ivan Vasil'yevich of all Russia, advising that the enemy had made war on the land of Perm', and set fire to the villages and church buildings and town settlements; that Semen and Maksim and Mikita Stroganov did not give help to the sovereign's towns and did not send their men to give aid, and did not dispatch the Volga *atamans* and cossacks, Yermak son of Timofey and his comrades, to him to give aid. Concerning that there was sent from Moscow to the Chyusovaya stronghold to them, Semen[3] and Maksim and Mikita Stroganov, a decree of the Sovereign, the Tsar and Great Prince Ivan Vasil'yevich of all Russia, with the subscript of the secretary Andrey Shchelkalov, on the 6th of November[4] of the year 7091 [1582]. In the sovereign's decree it was written: Vasiley Pelepelitsyn has written to us from Perm' that you have sent out from your forts the Volga *atamans* and cossacks, Yermak with his comrades, to make war on the Votyaks and the Voguls and the Tatars and the lands of Pelym and Sibir' in the year 7091 [1582] on the 1st day of September; that on the same day the prince of Pelym assembled with his Siberian troops and Voguls and went to war against our lands of Perm', attacked the town of Cherdyn' and the fort and killed our men and caused grievous harm to

---

[1] The usual form is Nikita, but in this chronicle Mikita is used almost as frequently.

[2] A secretary (*d'yak*) in the tsar's service. Before becoming *voyevoda* at Cherdyn' in 1580 he had held other high administrative positions.

[3] The original of this charter (see p. 293) does not mention Semen. For the possibly rather considerable significance of this evident insertion, see Introduction, p. 25. Much of the rest of the charter, it will be noticed, is reasonably accurately copied.

[4] The chronicler is confused. The date of the charter was 16 November 1582, as he writes correctly some lines lower. But there had been another charter, also addressed to the Stroganovs, and on generally related matters, on 6 November 1581 (see pp. 292–3).

our people. And this was done through your treachery. You have estranged the Voguls and Votyaks and the Pelym people from our favour and provoked them and gone to war against them. By this provocation you have made mischief between the Siberian sultan and us, and by calling in the Volga *atamans* you have hired robbers to serve in your forts without our permission. These *atamans* and cossacks before this brought us into conflict with the Nagay Horde, they killed Nagay envoys on the Volga crossings, and robbed and killed Ardobazartsy, and many robberies and losses were inflicted on our people. They could have redeemed their guilt by guarding our land of Perm', but they acted in concert with you since they have committed acts and robberies such as they did on the Volga. On the day when the Voguls marched on Cherdyn' in Perm', on that same day Yermak and his comrades set out from your forts and went to make war on the Voguls, the Ostyaks and the Tatars, and gave no aid whatsoever to Perm'. We have sent to Perm' Voin Anichkov, and have commanded that those cossacks, Yermak with his comrades, should be taken and brought to Perm' and to Usol'ye Kamskoye, and we have commanded that they should stay there, separately, and that you should under no circumstances keep cossacks with you. If until their return you cannot remain in the fort, retain a few men, up to a hundred with an *ataman*, and send away all the rest to Cherdyn' without fail immediately. But if you do not send out of your forts the Volga cossacks, the *ataman* Yermak son of Timofey and his comrades, and keep them with you, and do not defend the lands of Perm', and if by that treachery of yours any harm comes henceforth to the lands of Perm' at the hands of the Voguls and the men of Pelym and the troops of the Siberian sultan, then you will fall into our great disfavour, and the *atamans* and cossacks who have obeyed you and served you and betrayed our land, we shall order to be hanged. And you should without fail send those cossacks away from you to Perm'. Written in Moscow, in the year 7091 [1582] on the 16th day of November.[1] After this Semen and Maksim and Nikita were greatly distressed that previously it was the command of the Sovereign, the Tsar and Great Prince Ivan Vasil'yevich of all Russia, according to his previous charters that they should establish strongholds and hire troops against the Siberian sultan, but now the sovereign's decree was that it was commanded not to send out the Volga *atamans* and cossacks. But their cossacks, Yermak and his comrades, had been sent out to Sibir'.

---

[1] The full text is given on pp. 293–4. It is interesting that of all the charters summarised in this chronicle, this one, a broadside directed at the Stroganovs, is given at greatest length. Perhaps this is to bring out the point that later events showed the Stroganovs to have been fully justified.

[13] On the coming of the Volga cossacks and *atamans*, Yermak and
his comrades, to the river Tavda in the Siberian land.

In the year 7090 [1581] on the 9th of September, sacred to the memory
of the ancestors of our Lord, Joachim and Anna, the warriors came
unflinching to that land of Sibir' and waged war on many Tatar strongholds and encampments down the valley of the Tura. They came in all
their valour to the river Tavda, and at the mouth of that river they captured some Tatars. There was one of them, Tauzak by name, who was of
the khan's court, and who told them everything in order concerning the
Siberian khans and rulers, *murzas* and princes, and concerning Khan
Kuchyum. They had reliable intelligence from him concerning everything and let him go to tell Sultan Kuchyum of their arrival and of their
valour and bravery. From this Tauzak Khan Kuchyum heard of the
coming of the Russian troops and of their valour and bravery. They also
told him: 'The Russian troops are so powerful: when they shoot from
their bows, then there is a flash of fire and a great smoke issues and there
is a loud report like thunder in the sky. One does not see arrows coming
out of them. They inflict wounds and injure fatally, and it is impossible
to shield oneself from them by any trappings of war. Our scale-armour,
armour of plates and rings, cuirasses and chain-mail do not hold them;
they pierce all of them right through.' Khan Kuchyum was very greatly
disturbed and distressed concerning this, and moreover was in great
perplexity. He sent orders throughout all his realm to the cities and
encampments for men to come to his aid and to take up arms against the
powerful Russian troops. In a short time there assembled before him all
the great number of his troops, the native rulers, *murzas* and princes,
the Tatars, Ostyaks and Voguls and all the other tribes under his rule.

[14] On the khans and princes of that Siberian land, how and from
where they originated.

There was in the Siberian land on the river Ishim a certain khan of the
law of Mohammed, Ivan by name, a Tatar by birth. There arose
against him a Tatar from the common people of his realm, Chingis by
name, who came upon him like a robber, calling up others like himself,
and slew him, and himself became khan. A certain man of the servants of
Khan Ivan saved his son, the khan's heir Taybuga, from Chingis'
slaughter. After some years Chingis learnt concerning Taybuga that he
was the son of Khan Ivan, whom he had slain and whose khanate he had
seized. He bestowed great honour on him and gave him the title of
Prince Taybuga and commanded others to call him by this title. After
this Taybuga began to ask that he should be sent out on a campaign.
Chingis assembled an army for him and sent him out. He came to the
river called the Irtish, where the Chud'[1] lived, and then by his power

[1] A general term meaning non-Russian tribes found in the northern regions.
See Introduction, p. 22.

THE STROGANOV CHRONICLE

made subject to himself many peoples living along the river Irtish and
the great Ob', after which he returned home. After being with Chingis a
short time, he again began to ask him to send him out. Chingis sent him
out, saying that he could remain wherever he wished. Coming to the
river Tura he established a city and called it Chingiy, where now is the
Christian city called Tyumen'. After him there reigned in that city his
son Khodzha. After Khodzha there reigned his son Mar, and this Mar
was married to the sister of Upak, the Khan of Kazan'.[1] This Upak
killed his brother-in-law Mar and had possession of that city many years.
After this Mamet, the son of Ader, killed Khan Upak. The children of
Mar were Ader and Yabolak, and the son of Ader was Mamet. This
Mamet killed Khan Upak and established a city above the river Irtish
and named it Sibir', and reigned in that city.[2] After him Agash, the son
of Yabolak, reigned. After him Kazy, the son of Mamet, reigned, and
after him his children Yetiger and Bekbulat Khan Kuchyum son of
Murtaza together with many troops came against them out of the
steppe from the wild country. Kuchyum killed Yetiger and Bekbulat
and from then onwards called himself Khan of Sibir'. The son of
Bekbulat was Seydek, whom they took away to Bukhara at an early age.
Khan Kuchyum had two sons, one called Mametkul and the second
called Alliy.[3]

[15] On the sending by Khan Kuchyum of his son Mametkul to
battle with the Russian troops.

The ungodly Khan Kuchyum sent out his son Mametkul with a
number of his troops, and commanded them to take up arms manfully
against those Russian troops who had come against them. Kuchyum
himself ordered a barricade[4] to be built for him by the side of the river
Irtish, at Chyuvashiye,[5] and to be heaped up with earth. They strength-
ened it with many fortifications and, to describe it briefly, it was suitable
for fortification. Mametkul with many of his troops advanced to a

[1] Howorth (1876–88, p. 1062) identifies Upak with Ibak, who had relations,
both friendly and unfriendly, with Ivan III of Moscow. He died in 1493 or soon
after. But the index of *Sibirskiye letopisi* (1907) disagrees.
[2] The town of Sibir', as it concerns us for the rest of the chronicles, was about
20 km above the site later chosen for Tobol'sk, on the Irtysh, at a point originally
called Kashlyk by the Ostyaks and Voguls, but called Isker by the Tatars. The
word Sibir', which refers to the region as well as the town, has been derived in
various ways. The most plausible is that it is Turco-Tatar, and comes from the
Mongol word *shibir* meaning a dense forest on a marsh (Vasmer, *Russiches
etymologisches Wörterbuch, sub nomine*). See also p. 64, note 1.
[3] This genealogy is similar to that in the Yesipov chronicle, chapters 2–5.
Here the head of the line of khans is ludicrously called Ivan, while Yesipov calls
him On. But he was probably not a historical character in any case.
[4] Russ. *zaseka*, a defensive work made of felled trees, with the branches
pointing towards the enemy. The most exact rendering would be abatis, but this
word is hardly current now. But see also Remezov chronicle, chapter 42, and
note.
[5] Also Chyuvashevo (or Chuvashevo). Now called Mys Podchevash (Okladnikov, 1968, p. 28), a headland on the Irtysh near Tobol'sk.

47

certain natural boundary, which is named Babasan. The Russian troops, the *atamans* and cossacks, seeing such a gathering of the pagans, were not in the least alarmed at it, and placed their hope in God. They advanced swiftly from their forts and fell upon the pagans. The pagans on horseback made a strong and ruthless attack on their assailants, and inflicted many wounds on the cossacks by spear thrusts and sharp arrows. The Russian troops began to fire from their muskets, their rapid-firing small cannons, their small-shot guns, their fortress guns, their Spanish guns and arquebuses, and with these they killed countless numbers of the pagans. There was at that time a fierce battle with the Tatar troops and those who fell on both sides were very many in number. The pagans saw many of their troops fall in action against the Russian troops and gave themselves up to flight. The Russian cossacks again proceeded along the river Tobol and came up to a mountain. The pagans began to shoot at them from the mountain, and their arrows fell from above on the Russians' boats like rain. But the Russians passed by these places, unharmed in any way by the Tatars.

[16] On the coming of the Russian army to the encampment of Karacha, the councillor of the khan.

The cossacks came up to the encampment of Karacha and there waged a second battle with Karacha, the councillor of the khan.[1] They captured his encampment and in it the khan's mead and the khan's wealth, which they took to their boats. The pagans overtook them near the river Irtish, some on horseback and others on foot. The *atamans* and cossacks fought a battle with them there on the bank and manfully attacked the pagans. There was at that time a great battle waged to the death on both sides. Then the pagans saw many of their men falling in action against the Russian troops and gave themselves up to headlong flight. In that battle few of the Russian troops in Yermak's company were killed; but every one of them was wounded. Khan Kuchyum seeing that his troops were defeated went out with many of his men and took his stand on a high place on the mountain called Chyuvashevo. His son Mametkul remained at the barricade with many troops. Meanwhile the cossacks proceeded up the river Irtish.

[17] On the capture of the stronghold of Atik *murza*.

The Russian army came up to the stronghold of Atik *murza*,[2] captured it and settled down in it. Already night had come and darkness had

---

[1] Russ. *karach* means minister or high official, from the Uighur *karachu* (Vasmer, *sub nomine*). This no doubt led Lantzeff and Pierce (1973, p. 98) to follow Bakhrushin (in Müller, 1937, p. 487) in thinking that Karacha was the rank and not the name. But this is not necessarily so. English is not the only language to have family names like King and Prince.

[2] Evidently a minor chief, probably Tatar but possibly Vogul.

descended, and the cossacks having seen such a great gathering of the pagans at the barricade were alarmed at it and said among themselves: 'How can we stand against such a great gathering?' They began to deliberate among themselves, forming an assembly, and they took good counsel concerning this and said one to another: 'Should we leave this place, or stand fast?' Some began to reflect and to say: 'It would be better for us if we went away from them in retreat.' Others spoke sternly and firmly against them. 'O like-minded brothers, where can we flee to, since autumn has already come upon us and ice is freezing over the rivers? Let us not give ourselves up to flight and bring such ill repute upon ourselves, nor have such censure put on ourselves. But let us place our hope in God. For not from many troops does victory come, but help is given from God above. For God can help even the helpless. We have ourselves heard, brothers, how much evil those godless and accursed infidels of the Siberian land and Sultan Kuchyum did, how they brought desolation on our sovereign's towns in our Russian land of Perm', how they brought death and much captivity on the Orthodox Christians and how much harm they did to the Stroganovs' forts. Because of this almighty God is bringing vengeance on these accursed men for this Christian blood. Let us remember, brothers, our promise, how we gave our word and our vows to honourable men before God, and how we pledged ourselves by kissing the cross, so far as almighty God should grant to aid us, on no account to flee, although death should come on all to the last man. We cannot go back because of the disgrace and because it would violate our word, which we pledged on oath. If almighty God, glorified in the Trinity, aids us, then even after our death our memory will not fade in these lands and our fame will be eternal.' After this the *atamans* and cossacks all took heart and their courage was reaffirmed and they pledged themselves to the last man, all saying with one accord: 'Together we are ready to die for the holy churches of God and to suffer for the true Orthodox faith. We shall serve the Pious Sovereign, the Tsar and Great Prince Ivan Vasil'yevich of all Russia, and we shall stand firm against the pagans until blood is shed and until death itself comes. And so, brothers, we shall not betray our vow and shall with one accord stand firm in that resolve.' To all of them this good counsel commended itself. As night had already passed and day was dawning and the sun had shone out, the clouds were illuminated with brilliant light. Yermak was greatly concerned about his affairs and said to his company with tears: 'O friends and brothers, let us pray to God and to His most pure Mother, Mother of God, and to all the heavenly powers and to His saints, that we may be saved from the attacks of our ungodly and accursed enemies.' They came out of the stronghold to battle on the 23rd of October, sacred to the memory of the holy apostle James, the brother of our Lord. They proclaimed all together as if with one voice: 'God is with us!' And again: 'O Lord, help us Your servants!' They began to make an advance on the barricade most bravely and fiercely, and there was a great battle with the pagans. The pagans shot innumerable arrows from the top of the barricade and from loop-holes. They laid low many daring men of Yermak's company, wounding some and despatching others to death. The pagans seeing that brave men had fallen, themselves broke through their barricade in three places and came out on a sortie, hoping to put the cossacks to headlong flight. During the sortie a great battle then took place, and they fought ruthlessly until in hand to hand fighting they cut each other down. The cossacks all together fell upon the pagans, displaying their bravery and ferocity before the impious and godless infidels. In a short time the pagans began to fail in their strength. God granted the cossacks victory over the pagans. The cossacks gained ground, overcame them and killed innumerable pagans. They drove them from the barricade and planted their banners on the barricade. They wounded the khan's heir Mametkul, but his troops carried him off in a small boat across the river Irtish. Khan Kuchyum, standing on a lofty place, saw that his Tatars had fallen and that his son Mametkul had been wounded and had fled. He swiftly commanded his mullahs to call out their abominable infidel prayer. They began to summon to their aid their abominable gods, but there was not even a little aid granted to them. At that time the Ostyak princes departed with their men, each to his home. Khan Kuchyum, seeing his ruin and the loss of his kingdom and riches, said to all his men with bitter lamentation: 'O *murzas* and princes, let us flee without delaying. We see ourselves the loss of our kingdom. Our strong ones are exhausted, and our brave warriors have all been slain. O woe is me, what shall I do or where shall I flee? Shame covers my face! Who is it who defeated me and deprived me of my kingdom? The Stroganovs sent men of the common people against me from their forts to avenge on me the evil I had inflicted; they sent the *atamans* and cossacks, Yermak and his comrades, with not many of their men. He came upon us, defeated us and did us such great harm. They killed my troops and wounded my son, who was taken away from them barely alive. He brought shame upon me myself and drove me from my kingdom. My sickness has returned upon my head, and my iniquity has descended upon me. For I with joy seized what was not mine, I waged war on the Russian land, Perm' the Great and the Stroganovs' forts. But now I have been deprived of all I had and I have myself been defeated. For there is no gladness on earth that does not turn to grief.' The accursed khan hastened to the city of Sibir' and took with him some small part of his treasures. They then turned to headlong flight and left the city of Sibir' deserted. The brave Yermak and his company came to the city of Sibir', later called Tobolesk, on the 26th of October, sacred to the memory of the holy and great martyr Demetrius of Salonika. They glorified God, who had granted them victory over the pagans and the accursed infidels and rejoiced with great rejoicing. They captured and divided among themselves much wealth of gold and silver and golden fabrics and precious stones and very costly skins of sable, marten and fox. It was indeed marvellous to hear and it was fitting in truth to praise almighty God, glorified in the Trinity, who had granted them victory over their pagan enemies. It was not because of the great number of the valiant Russian troops that they defeated the proud Khan Kuchyum, for Khan Kuchyum assembled so many of his troops that one could say that one cossack had to contend with ten or twenty or thirty pagans. The accursed khan lamented exceedingly for the great number of his men who had perished. But God opposes the proud and gives his grace to the humble Christians. On the fourth day the Ostyak prince, Boyar by name, came with many Ostyaks to the city of Yermak and his company; they brought with them many gifts and provisions. After this many Tatars with their wives and children began to arrive and began to live in their former tents.

[18] On the killing of cossacks while fishing near Yabolak.

In the same winter, on the 5th of December, when Volga cossacks of Yermak's company without apprehension went fishing at a certain natural boundary, which is called Yabolak,[1] and while the cossacks were in their camp, the khan's heir Mametkul came suddenly and killed them without any surviving. A report concerning their killing was heard in that city. Yermak was very much outraged at this and was moved to anger. In his heart he was greatly enraged; he commanded his company to gird themselves with arms and went to battle. They pursued the pagans from behind and overtook them near Yabolak. The troops thus carried out Yermak's command, manfully fell upon the pagans and launched an attack. On both sides the troops sprang upon each other savagely and unmercifully. Laid low by these mortal battles, the corpses of the dead fell on both sides. Now already the darkness of night had fallen, and the battle ceased. The pagans fled, and Yermak with his company returned to the city.

[19] How they captured alive the khan's heir Mametkul, the son of Kuchyum.

In that spring, at the time of flooding, a Tatar called Seibokhta[2] came to the city and said that the khan's heir Mametkul was stationed at the river Vogay. Certain men of Yermak's company went to the Vogay and came to that place. At night time they fell upon the camp of the khan's heir and killed many pagans. They captured alive the khan's heir Mametkul and brought him to their city. Khan Kuchyum long remained at the river Ishim, waiting for his son Mametkul. Not long after this messengers came to him and informed him of everything in succession,

---

[1] Now called Abalak (see Map 1). Many place-names have changed somewhat, but most are recognisably the same.
[2] Senbakhta in the Yesipov chronicle.

51

and told him that the cossacks had made his son prisoner. Khan Kuchyum was not a little afflicted at this, and was much possessed by great sorrow concerning his son Mametkul.

[20] On the coming of Prince Seydek, son of Bekbulat, against Khan Kuchyum.

After a short time other messengers came to him and announced to him that Prince Seydek, son of Bekbulat, was coming against him with many troops.[1] Khan Kuchyum, hearing this, was very much alarmed, and after this his councillor Karacha, together with his men, departed from him. Khan Kuchyum lamented bitterly and said to himself: 'When God does not show grace to a man, then honour turns to dishonour for him, and even dear friends desert him.' Karacha came to the Lyniskaya land and began to live near a large lake, above the river Tara, near the river Osma.

[21] On the daring and bravery of Yermak and on the capture of the city of Kazym, and on the killing of Nikita Pan, the Volga *ataman*, with his company.

In the same year, when Yermak with his company displayed his valour, they unsheathed their swords against the ungodly ones, and trusting so much in the strength of their swords, they captured many strongholds and encampments of the Tatars along the river Irtish and along the Great Ob' and also the Ostyak city of Kazym[2] with their prince. During their advance the pagans killed the *ataman* Nikita Pan with his company, during the assault on their strongholds. Yermak with his troops returned to the city of Sibir'. Concerning this the *atamans* and cossacks, Yermak son of Timofey with his comrades, wrote from Sibir' to those honourable men Semen and Maksim and Nikita in their strongholds that the Lord God, glorified in the Trinity, was pleased to defeat Sultan Kuchyum for them and to capture his capital city in his land of Sibir', and that they had captured alive his son, the khan's heir Mametkul. Then according to the reports of those *atamans* and cossacks Semen and Maksim and Mikita Stroganov wrote from their strongholds to Moscow to the Pious Sovereign, the Tsar and Great Prince Ivan

[1] It will be remembered that Kuchum had seized power by killing Bekbulat (chapter 14).
[2] There is a river and a settlement called Kazym some 700 km downstream from Sibir'. Although this district would have been known to Russians, being near one of the more northerly routes across the Urals (see Introduction, p. 18), it seems likelier that Yermak ventured less far than that, to the river and settlement called Nazym, near the Ob'-Irtysh confluence and only 300 km from Sibir'. Some versions of this chronicle have Nazym, and so do the other chronicles. S. M. Seredonin in his historical essay in *Aziatskaya Rossiya* (St Petersburg, 1914), Tom I, map opp. p. 4, seems to favour Kazym.

Vasil'yevich of all Russia, concerning the capture and conquest of the Siberian land and the taking of the khan's heir Mametkul. Not long after this they themselves went to Moscow, and concerning all of this they informed the sovereign of everything in succession, how they had sent from their strongholds the Volga cossacks with their men to the Siberian land to make war on the Siberian Khan Kuchyum. They made known to the sovereign everything concerning the capture of the khan's heir Mametkul, the son of Kuchyum, and the taking of his capital city of Sibir' and the expulsion of Khan Kuchyum and the pacification of the Siberian land. The Sovereign, the Tsar and Great Prince Ivan Vasil'yevich of all Russia, because of their service and zeal granted the towns of Sol' Bol'shaya, which is on the Volga, and Sol' Malaya. He granted his royal charter for those lands to Semen Stroganov with a red seal with the subscript of the secretary Andrey Shcholkalov, by which he should possess those towns. But to Maksim and Nikita Stroganov he granted that in their townships and strongholds they and all their men should trade exempt from duties.

[22] On the sending of cossacks to the sovereign in Moscow with reports, to make obeisance to the sovereign, the tsar, and to make known their service.

At that time the Volga *atamans* and cossacks, Yermak son of Timofey with his company, wrote from Sibir' to Moscow to the Sovereign, the Tsar and Great Prince Ivan Vasil'yevich of all Russia, concerning the capture of the capital city of Sibir' and the expulsion of Khan Kuchyum and the taking of the khan's heir Mametkul and the pacification of the Siberian land. When the sovereign heard of God's grace, how God had conquered for him, the sovereign, the Siberian land and caused the khan's heir Mametkul to be captured alive, then to those cossacks who had come to the sovereign with that news, he granted his great favour, money and clothes and damasks. To those *atamans* and cossacks who were in Sibir', the sovereign also made a grant and commanded that the sovereign's full great favour should be sent to them. He also commanded that *voyevodas* should be sent, together with men in state service, to the Siberian towns, which God had entrusted to him, the sovereign. The sovereign also decreed that the khan's heir Mametkul should be sent to Moscow.

[23] On the sending from Moscow to Sibir' of the sovereign's *voyevodas*, Prince Semen Bolkhovskiy and Ivan Glukhov.

In the second year after the capture of the Siberian land the Sovereign, the Tsar and Great Prince Ivan Vasil'yevich of all Russia, sent from Moscow to Sibir' the *voyevodas*, Prince Semen Bolkhovskiy and Ivan

Glukhov, with many troops.[1] The *atamans* and cossacks received them with great honour. The sovereign's *voyevodas* according to the sovereign's inventory made known to them the sovereign's favour, and arriving at the city of Sibir' presented it to them. Those *atamans* and cossacks gave to the sovereign's *voyevodas* costly sable skins and fox skins and all kinds of furs, as much as each one could. They were filled with joy and were greatly gladdened, giving thanks to God, seeing that there was conferred on them the sovereign's favour, which the sovereign had granted and sent them for their service as *atamans* and cossacks.

[24] How there was a famine among the people in Sibir'.

During that winter, when the troops from Moscow came to Sibir' to the cossacks, they consumed the provisions which they had brought with them. The cossacks had prepared provisions, the amount being calculated for their own men, and not knowing of the arrival among them of the men of the Moscow force. Because of this there was a great lack of all provisions, and many died of famine, both the troops from Moscow and the cossacks. The *voyevoda* Prince Semen Bolkhovskiy also died and was buried at that time in Sibir'. After this the winter time passed, the frost and cold were relieved by the warmth of the sun, a frozen crust formed on the snow, and it was the time for hunting wild beasts, elk and deer. Then those men were provided with food and the famine eased. When spring arrived and the snow was melted by the warmth of the air, every creature grew fat, the trees and herbs were sprouting and the waters were spread out. Then every living creature rejoiced, birds flew to those lands because of their fruits, and in the rivers fish were swimming because of their fruitfulness, and there was much hunting of fish and birds. By this hunting they were fed, and there was no famine among the people. Those tribes who lived around that place, Tatars and Ostyaks and Voguls, who were under the sovereign's hand, both far and near, brought to them provisions in great quantity of wild beasts, birds, fish and cattle, and costly goods, and all kinds of furs. Then the men of Moscow and the cossacks by the grace of God were abundantly supplied with all foods and acquired much wealth for themselves from trading in furs. And being in such joy and gladness, they gave thanks to almighty God, since God had granted to the sovereign such a land blessed with abundance.

[1] This despatch of troops was the first direct action of the Moscow government in the whole campaign. Only when Moscow heard that things were going well, and saw the promise of great gain, did the government move to support what had up to then been an essentially private venture of the Stroganov family. The venture had been known to, perhaps even instigated by, the tsar – but no material assistance had up to now been given.

[25] On the sending of the khan's heir Mametkul, son of Kuchyum, to Moscow.

According to the command of the Sovereign, the Tsar and Great Prince Ivan Vasil'yevich of all Russia, the *voyevoda* Ivan Glukhov and the Siberian *atamans* and cossacks sent to the Pious Sovereign, the Tsar and Great Prince Ivan Vasil'yevich of all Russia, in the reigning city of Moscow the Siberian khan's heir Mametkul, son of Kuchyum, with many of his men.[1] Then for the second time was the tsar's great favour sent from Moscow to Sibir' to the *atamans* and cossacks.

[26] On the killing of the *atamans* Ivan Koltso and Yakov Mikhaylov with their companies.

In that year envoys from Karacha came to the city to Yermak and his company to ask for men to protect them from the Nagay Horde, and took an oath that they would neither do nor plan any evil against the cossacks. Yermak and his company trusted in their faithless oath, but they, the evil infidels, formed a plan not favourable to the Christians. The cossacks were enfeebled in their wits and did not remember the saying of the prophet: do not trust in every spirit, but enquire into all spirits, for not every spirit is from God. For there is a spirit of God and a spirit of falsehood.[2] They did not discern the falsehoods and deceptions of these accursed men and did not know their custom, that they held their hostages to be beyond their oath because of the evil cunning and inconstancy of the wily Karacha. They could not conceive of it, and they sent to him the *ataman* Ivan Koltso together with 40 men. These men gave themselves into the hands of the accursed ones and into the keeping of their impious enemies, the godless infidels, and there they were all killed by the impious Karacha. News was heard in the city by the *atamans* and cossacks, that the *ataman* Ivan Koltso with his company had been slain, and all their brothers wept bitterly for them, lamenting from the bottom of their hearts. It came to the hearing of the pagan infidels, who lived near that town, that the *ataman* Ivan Koltso together with his company had been slain. Then the *ataman* Yakov Mikhaylov, wishing to carry on trade among the accursed ones, went up to them to make observations. But those accursed ones seized him and killed him; and so those good and brave soldiers, the *atamans*, passed away.

[1] Mametkul remained to enter the Russian service (see p. 39, note 1). The year after his arrival in Moscow the English Ambassador Giles Fletcher reported him to be 'with the Emperour at Mosco and well interteyned' (*Of the Russe Common Wealth*, London, 1591, p. 64ᵛ).
[2] Presumably the passage referred to is *1 John* iv, 1: Beloved, believe not every spirit, but try the spirits, whether they are of God: because many false prophets have gone out into the world.

[27] On the advance of Karacha to the city and on the defeat and killing of his sons.

In the same year at the time of holy Lent, when the month of March had come, at that time Karacha advanced with many of his men in all his might and power. They encircled all the city with their baggage trains. Karacha himself remained at a certain place called Sauskan, about two versts from the city. The cossacks were kept under siege for a long time. Winter had already passed and the early signs of spring came. When spring arrived and summer followed on, the earth was bringing forth its verdure and scattering abroad its seeds, with birds pouring forth their song. To speak briefly, all things were made new. Karacha did not withdraw even a little, but remained at the investment of the city, wishing to kill them by famine; and like a viper breathing fury against the cossacks, he deviated in his accursed purpose, and wished to carry them away. The accursed one stretched out his hands to put the cossacks to death and to take to himself their company. He remained near the city for a long time. When the month of June came and the 12th day arrived,[1] the solstice turning back to winter, on one night at that time the *ataman* Matfey Meshcheryak together with cossacks came out of the city in secret, and there was no word or sound from any one of them. They came to the camp of Karacha and planned to fall upon them, wishing to take vengeance for the grievous injuries inflicted upon them by Karacha. They came against their impious and deceitful enemy, and there they endeavoured to wreak on him a severe and merciless vengeance. Yermak remained in the city with not many men. The other cossacks came up to Karacha at Sauskan and fell upon their camps manfully and bravely, while the pagans were sleeping without any apprehension. By the grace of God and the aid of the most pure Mother of God, the cossacks cut down a great multitude of the pagans, and coming near the camp of Karacha they killed two of his sons. The pagans fled hither and yon away from the cossacks. Karacha himself and not many men with him fled to the other side of a lake. Others fled to where the pagans were stationed at the investment of the city. Already after the coming of night day was dawning, and the pagans hearing what had happened all hastened from the city to Sauskan. They were hoping to put the cossacks to death. They came up to them and began to join battle. The cossacks were not at all alarmed at this, but were even more fortified. The pagans attacked them fiercely. The cossacks defended themselves against the enemy in Sauskan, and so there was a battle until midday, and then the armies' conflict ceased. The pagans retreated from the Russians, while the cossacks returned to their city, rejoicing and gladdened and rendering praise to almighty God. But Karacha, seeing that he could not defeat the cossacks, departed to his home covered in shame.

[1] Old Style; 22 June by the Gregorian calendar.

[28] On the killing of the brave *ataman* Yermak, together with Russian warriors.

In that year, on the 5th of August, on the eve of the Transfiguration of our Lord, sacred to the memory of the holy martyr Eusignius, messengers came from Bukharans, men engaged in trade, to the *atamans* and cossacks, to Yermak and his company, and said that Khan Kuchyum would not admit them. Yermak with not many men went to meet them along the river Irtish, and coming to the Vagay did not find the Bukharans. They went as far as the place called Atbash and returned from there. As already day had passed and the darkness of night had fallen, the cossacks had wearied themselves greatly by the long journey. They came up to a cross-channel[1] and encamped there for the night. Khan Kuchyum spied them out, sent around for many Tatars and commanded a strict watch to be kept. During that night there was heavy rain. The pagans, like a viper breathing fury against Yermak and his company, were preparing their swords for vengeance, were hoping to regain their inheritance, and wished to achieve the end of their desired aim. The time was about midnight. Yermak and his company were sleeping in their camps, beneath the curtains of their beds. The pagans, breathing fury as if mad, prepared themselves for the shedding of blood, and understood that it was already time to achieve their wish. Swiftly they unsheathed their arms, fell upon their camp and slew them with their drawn swords. And so they were all killed there, and only one escaped; and the most wise, brave and eloquent[2] Yermak was killed. Some men remaining of the tribes say that your brave soldier Yermak started up there from his sleep and saw his company being slain by us and could have no hope for his own life; that he fled to his boat but could not reach it, since the distance was so great, and here he fell in the river and was drowned. But sent by God, death came suddenly to the brave troops and valiant cossacks, and so they ended their lives. A report was heard in the city by the *ataman* Matfey Meshcheryak and his company that the chief *ataman*, the most wise Yermak, and his company had been slain, and those in the city lamented bitterly for them.

[29] On the departure of the cossacks to Russia.

Not many days afterwards the *ataman* Matfey Meshcheryak together with the remaining cossacks went to Russia, leaving the city of Sibir' deserted.

[1] Russ. *perekop*; an artificial short-cut across a loop in the river, dug on Yermak's orders and later seen by Müller. See Remezov chronicle, chapter 98.
[2] Russ. *ritor*, an orator. It seems entirely likely, from some of his reported adventures, that Yermak had a persuasive tongue.

[30] On the coming of the khan's heir Alliy, son of Kuchyum, to the city.

When the cossacks had departed from the city, then the khan's heir Alliy, son of Kuchyum, saw that the cossacks had left the city, and he came with his men to the city. After this his father, Khan Kuchyum, also came there, to his capital city of Sibir', full of rejoicing.

[31] On the coming of Seydek

This news came to the hearing of Prince Seydek, son of Bekbulat, that the leader and commander of the cossacks, the *ataman* Yermak, had been killed, and that the other cossacks had departed from the city. The Tatars very much rejoiced and were glad of this, since they had a great fear of them. Then Prince Seydek, son of Bekbulat, fearlessly came to the city of Sibir', defeated Khan Kuchyum and took possession of the city of Sibir'.

[32] On the second coming from Moscow of the *voyevoda* Ivan Mansurov and on the return of the Volga cossacks, the *ataman* Matfey Meshcheryak with his comrades and with the other remaining troops, who had previously been at war in the Siberian land.

In the second year after the killing of Yermak, in the year 7094 [1585][1] after the day sacred to St Simeon Stylites, the sovereign sent from the reigning city of Moscow the *voyevoda* Ivan Mansurov with many troops. He came to the river Tura, and there they met the Volga *ataman* Matfey Meshcheryak with his company.[2] The cossacks rejoiced and were glad at the arrival of the *voyevoda* in the Siberian land. From there they all returned together with one accord to fight against the godless infidels. Together they went down the Tura and the Irtish and reached the Tobol, where is now the Russian city of Tobolesk, protected by God. The pagans assembled in an agreed place near the river Irtish on its bank. When the *voyevoda* saw such a gathering of the pagans, he and his troops were much alarmed and did not approach the bank. They again went down the Irtish and reached the great river Ob'. For it was then already autumn and the winter time drew near. The air in the sky changed to cold, there was snow, and ice was congealing on the river. The *voyevoda* saw the change in the air, as the winter drew near, and together with all his men he wintered there, established a stronghold above the river Ob'

---

[1] Actually only a month after Yermak's death, which was on 5 August 1585; but since the new year began on 1 September, it could be said to be 'in the second year'.

[2] According to the other chronicles, Meshcheryak retreated by a more northerly route; but he still could have met Mansurov somewhere.

at the mouth of the Irtish and settled in it. With them there were also the Volga cossacks, Matfey Mescheryak and his company.

[33] On the coming of the Ostyaks to the stronghold.

After some days a great number of the Ostyaks came up to the stronghold and began to attack it from all sides. The men from that stronghold opposed the attackers from the walls of the stronghold. When the darkness of night fell, the pagans withdrew. On the following morning the pagans again came to the stronghold and brought their idol, which they revered. They set it up near the stronghold beneath a tree on a low place and began to make offerings before it, believing that this ungodly helper would conquer the Christians for them and put them to the sword. That idol was renowned and famous among the pagans, and many pagans brought it a great many offerings from distant towns during all that day. At that time the cossacks fired from their cannon in the stronghold. They smashed into many pieces that tree, beneath which the pagans were making offerings to the idol, and shattered their idol. The pagan infidels were terrified at this, not knowing of it, and they believed that someone had fired from a bow. They said to each other: 'The Russian troops fire powerfully indeed. They have smashed such a large tree and shattered our god.' From that time onwards the Ostyaks no longer came to the stronghold.

[34] On the third coming from Moscow of the *voyevoda* Danilo Chyulkov.

After some time the Pious Sovereign, the Tsar and Great Prince Feodor Ivanovich of all Russia sent from Moscow to Sibir' the *voyevoda* Danilo Chyulkov[1] with many troops and with artillery. He came to the Siberian land. News of his arrival was heard among the infidel tribes of Sibir'. The Tatars were alarmed at this, fearing the frequent arrival of Russian troops, and fled from the city, which before this was their Tatar capital city in Sibir', situated at the mouth of the Tobol and the Irtish and named Sibir'. They left this city deserted. The Russian troops arrived, settled in it and fortified the city strongly; it is now the city called Tobolesk, protected by God.

[35] On the coming of Prince Seydek, son of Bekbulat, with Siberian troops to make war on the city of Tobolesk.

This accursed Mohammedan Prince Seydek planned to assemble a great army with Siberian troops for himself, and he came to make war on

[1] A Danilo Chulkov (ours is spelt in both ways), described as a 'well-born man from the nobility of Ryazan'', was said by Prince A. M. Kurbskiy to have been executed about 1568–70 by Ivan IV (J. L. I. Fennell, *Prince A. M. Kurbsky's history of Ivan IV*, Cambridge, 1965, pp. 224–5). A relative, perhaps; or conceivably Kurbskiy got it wrong.

the city of Tobolesk, wishing to capture it and to kill the people in it, so that Russians would not settle in their land. He professed to the sovereign's *voyevodas* that he had come to trade. He placed his fighting men in concealment, and traded with the Russians for a day. On the following morning he came stealthily up to the city to make an attack with all his men and he invested the city and began to attack it. The troops from Moscow and the Volga cossacks saw their shameless conduct and this violent attack on the city, and allowed them to approach the walls of the city. They began to fire among them from the city and killed many. Some came out of the city on a sortie against them and killed many infidels and captured others alive. In that battle they seized Prince Seydek himself, who had been wounded. Those accursed troops took to flight and fled to their camps. The Russian troops pursued them, cutting them down, even up to their camps. The enemy left their camps and all their wealth in their camps and barely escaped themselves. In that battle the Volga *ataman* Matfey Meshcheryak was killed. Henceforth there was great fear among all the infidels of the Siberian land, and all the Tatars, both near and far, did not dare to go to war against the sovereign's cities.

[36] On the establishment of cities and forts in the Siberian land.

According to the command of the Sovereign, the Tsar and Great Prince Ivan Vasil'yevich of all Russia, and after him according to the command of his son, the Sovereign, the Tsar and Great Prince Fedor Ivanovich of all Russia, there began to be established in the Siberian land cities and forts and there began to be propagated in the Siberian land the Christian Orthodox faith. Churches to God were raised up, and the preaching of the Gospel teaching spread to every end of the Siberian land, and the thunder of psalms resounded. In many places by the command of those sovereigns Christian cities and strongholds were established, and in them churches to God were raised up, and monasteries were constituted to the glory of the Father and of the Son and of the Holy Ghost. The unbelievers saw such grace shining forth in their land and the sovereign's imperial hand raised over them, and many submitted themselves under the sovereign's hand and left their impious faith. Many unbelievers came to baptism and were baptised, living in the Orthodox faith. Everywhere indeed was the grace of God spread abroad and poured out abundantly throughout the length of the Siberian land.

[37] On the collection of fur tribute.

After the capture and purification of all the Siberian land and after the pacification of the infidel people, the Siberian Tatars and the Ostyaks and Voguls, by the trading of the honourable men, Semen and Maksim and Mikita Stroganov, and by the aid, bravery and valour of the good troops of good birth, the *atamans* and cossacks, Yermak son of

Timofey Povolskoy and his comrades, then those honourable men also won over in addition the infidels living near their strongholds and forts along the Kama, the Chyusovaya, the Usva, the Sylva, the Yayva, the Obva, the Inva, the Kosva and other rivers. They brought all those infidels to take an oath, that they would serve the Sovereign, the Tsar and Great Prince Ivan Vasil'yevich of all Russia, without treachery, and in all things to act uprightly and to be well disposed to the sovereign, and to give fur tribute[1] from themselves. And henceforth Semen and Maksim and Nikita began to send their men to collect that fur tribute from their strongholds and forts along the rivers to the encampments of the Tatars, Ostyaks and Voguls and to collect fur tribute from those infidels and to send it with their men to Moscow to the Novgorod treasury.[2] And afterwards by the command of the Sovereign, the Tsar and Great Prince Fedor Ivanovich of all Russia, from those infidels the collections of tribute began to be made by the *voyevodas* among the towns, where those tribes lived at various places, at Cherdyn', Ufa and Verkhotur'ye and among other Siberian towns, where those tribes lived around near the towns.

This narrative is set forth concerning the establishment of strongholds and forts in the Siberian lands, the despatch of the *atamans* and cossacks, Yermak son of Timofey and his comrades, to Sibir', the journeying of those cossacks in the Siberian lands, the defeat of Khan Kuchyum, the capture of his son, the khan's heir Mametkul, and the taking possession of the Siberian land by the troops of the Russian state. These words on this theme have come to the close of this narrative. For so every reader will understand and will not forget the achievement of such great things. I wrote this account for a commemoration, so that the accomplishment of such great things will not be forgotten.

[1] Russ. *yasak*, a word of Turkic origin meaning tribute of any kind, but in Siberia it came to mean fur tribute. It acquired great importance, and indeed was one of the driving forces behind the whole Russian advance across Siberia. Fur tribute had been levied on the northern peoples by Tatars and Mongols before the arrival of the Russians, who took over many points in the existing collection system. For detailed examination of the system, see Bakhrushin, 1955a, pp. 49–85 and Fisher, 1943, pp. 49–61.

[2] Russ. *chet'*, meaning in the 16th and 17th centuries an office of the central government concerned with the taxable peasantry (*tyagloye naseleniye*) from a financial and administrative point of view. There were six offices of this kind in the early 17th century, each in a different town, and the Novgorod office evidently dealt with this particular levy – perhaps because of its earlier association with the fur trade.

THE YESIPOV CHRONICLE

according to the Sychevskiy manuscript[1]

On Sibir' and the capture of Sibir'.

On the Siberian land, how by the will of God it was captured by a Russian army, assembled and led by the *ataman* Yermak son of Timofey and his valiant, excellent and single-minded company.

The infidel kingdom began in Sibir', and that is why it was called Sibir', and how by the will of God it was captured by Orthodox Christians, by a Russian army, as a heritage for the Russian Crown; how they defeated Khan Kuchyum son of Martazey,[2] and on the courage and bravery of the Russian army, assembled and led by the *ataman* Yermak son of Timofey; on the establishing of cities in the Siberian land and on the building of Orthodox churches; likewise concerning the miracles of our Most Holy Lady the Virgin Mary, Mother of God, where they were performed during our day and generation: all these and other matters I have set forth each in chapters, so that they can all be traced without difficulty.

Concerning the Siberian khanate and princedom I have taken some things from the Tatar Chronicle,[3] and others by questioning reliable men who personally informed me well and readily.

[1] The text translated is printed in *Sibirskiye letopisi*, 1907, pp. 105–70. The manuscript is now held at the Saltykov-Shchedrin State Public Library in Leningrad (call no. Q.XVII.33), and was originally written in 1636 (see Introduction, p. 26).

[2] The Stroganov chronicle calls Kuchum's father Murtaza, which is closer to the correct form.

[3] Nothing is known of this chronicle, presumably now lost. Mr David Wileman has suggested that if it described, as seems plausible, the genealogy of the Taibugids given in chapter 2, it might have been written by one of Taibuga's descendants who were captured by the Russians and sent to Moscow (see chapter 33 below), where they apparently flourished (see Remezov chronicle chapter 126).

Chapter 36 On the rectification of this chronicle, having such additions.
Chapter 37 The book of names for the commemoration of the dead cossacks Yermak with his brethren, that is to say with his company, and how prayers for their souls, greater, intermediate and lesser, were to be read for them.

Chapter 1
On the Siberian land[1].

This Siberian land lies towards the north-eastern[2] regions a great distance from Moscow, the reigning city of Russia, almost thirteen hundred versts.[3] Between these kingdoms of Russia and the Siberian land there lies a mountain range of exceeding great height, so as to reach with some of its peaks up to the clouds of heaven; for thus has it been set up by God's decrees, like the fortified wall of a city.[4] On this range grow various trees: cedars and pines and others; and among them various wild beasts have their dwelling places, some fit for consumption by men, others for adornment and vestments. And the ones fit for consumption, these are clean: that is, the deer, the elk, and the hare; the others are those which are fit for attire and the adornment of vestments, that is the fox, the sable, the beaver, the glutton, the squirrel and others like them.[5] There is an abundance of sweet-singing birds, and even more an abundance of various flowering grasses. From this range many rivers issue, some flow towards the Russian tsardom, others to the Siberian land. It is wonderful, indeed, how by God's decrees there are rivers there; the water wore away hard rock, and there are vast and most beautiful rivers, and in

[1] The name Sibir' (for derivation see p. 47, note 2) had been applied to an area between the Urals and the Irtysh-Tobol confluence probably since the 13th century (Vasmer, sub nomine). Even when the area had been expanded to include Kuchum's khanate, it was, of course, very much smaller than the vast territory the name came later to connote (see Map 1). Yermak, the 'conqueror of Siberia', is an interesting case of a reputation growing through changing word use.
[2] Russ. polunoshchiye, literally midnight, by extension northern, but in more exact usage north-eastern (Dal', Tolkovyy slovar' zhivogo velikorusskogo yazyka, Moscow, 1956, sub nomine).
[3] Russ. poprishche, see p. 43, note 1. 2000 poprishche equal 1330 versts, or about 2850 km, which is plausible.
[4] The Urals always made a great impression on dwellers in the Russian plain. In fact they are not at all impressive to anyone who has seen the Caucasus or the Alps. The most Alpine-looking section is the Polar Urals, far to the north of the crossing places used by most contemporaries of Yermak; but the northern routes were used by the early travellers, whose tales no doubt lived on. See Introduction, p. 18.
[5] The animals are the same now as then, except that the deer in the 16th century is likely to have been red deer (Cervus elaphus), whereas today, at least in the north, it would be more likely to be reindeer (Rangifer tarandus). Among the fur-bearing animals, the sable (Martes zibellina) was over-hunted and nearly became extinct, but protective legislation has now brought it back.

them the freshest waters and an abundance of various fishes. Where these waters issue there are forests fruitful for harvesting and most extensive grazing lands for cattle.[1]

The first river which issues into the Siberian land is called the Tura. On this river a people called the Voguls have their dwelling places; they speak in a language of their own and worship idols. Into this river, the Tura, there flows another river, the Tagil, and yet another, the Nitsa, and the three rivers combine into one confluence, and although the rivers combine in this way, the name Tura is still used by reason of greater antiquity. From here the river Tura flows within the Siberian land; on it live the Tatars. The river Tura flows into a river called the Tobol, and the river Tobol flows into a river called the Irtish. This river Irtish at its mouth flows into a great river called the Ob'. On these rivers many tribes have their dwelling places: the Tatars, the Kalmucks, the Mongols, the Skewbald Horde,[2] the Ostyaks, the Samoyeds and other tribes. The Tatars keep the law of Mohammed. I do not know what law or traditional belief of their fathers the Kalmucks keep, since I have not found any writings on this and was unable to find out by enquiry. The Skewbald Horde and the Ostyaks and Samoyeds do not have a religion, but worship idols and make sacrifices, as if to God, in vain ordering their houses by magical craft; since when they make offerings to their idols, they pray as though to God. For this reason a man makes offerings, so that that idol will grant him all the many things to his house.

In truth, these people did not make themselves like animals, for if an animal is even something without the faculty of speech, God did not command it to eat or not to eat wild beasts or birds or hay. These men did not make themselves like them, since not knowing God, who is in heaven, nor His Law, and not receiving what comes from those who bid them to listen, they became eaters of raw flesh; consuming the meat of wild beasts and reptiles, they drank abominable things and blood, like water, from animals, and ate grass and roots.

The Ostyaks have clothing made from fish, and the Samoyeds from reindeer. The Ostyaks travel by dogs, and the Samoyeds by reindeer. This great river, the Ob', at its mouth enters by the bay of Mangazeya. This enters the ocean by two mouths directly towards the north. In

---

[1] This is important cattle country today. Cereal crops are also grown here, but arable farming becomes more important rather further south. Observations of the natural world, as found in this paragraph, are not common in the chronicles, so may be taken as evidence that this section at least derives from an eye-witness account.

[2] The Skewbald Horde (also called the Piebald Horde) is shown in Remezov's *Atlas* of 1701 as occupying the area round the town of Surgut on the middle Ob'. Nikolay Spafariy mentions the Horde when he describes his visit to Surgut in 1675; this is recorded in the English account by Baddeley (1919, p. 251), who also (p. cxlii) quotes Lehrberg as identifying this group with a people who bred piebald horses of giant size. Okladnikov (1968, p. 34) says that the Skewbald Horde was an alliance of Sel'kup (then called Samoyed) tribes round Surgut.

65

these mouths ice has endured from time immemorial, never melted by
the sun, and this is an impassable place and unknown to men.[1]

Chapter 2
On the Siberian khans and princes.

The river called Ishim at its mouth enters the river Irtish, which I
have previously named. On this river, the Ishim, there lived a khan of
the law of Mohammed called On. And there arose against him a man
from the common people of his realm, called Chingis, and he attacked
him with others, like a robber, and killed Khan On, and Chingis took the
khanate himself. One of the servants of Khan On saved from Chingis'
slaughter the son of Khan On, whose name was Taibuga.[2] After some
years it became known to Khan Chingis concerning Taibuga, that he
was the son of Khan On, and he received him and paid him great honour,
and granted him princedom and power among the people. After this
Prince Taibuga asked Khan Chingis to send him forth: wherever the
Khan wished, there he would go with troops. Khan Chingis assembled
many armed troops and sent him forth along the river Irtish, where
the Chud' lived. Prince Taibuga departed with the troops, conquered
for the khan many of those living there along the river Irtish and along
the great Ob', and from there returned home with rejoicing. Khan
Chingis, hearing from Taibuga that he had conquered many for him and
made them subject, bestowed even more honour upon him. Again
Taibuga asked Khan Chingis that he would let him go, to stay wherever
he would wish. So the khan let him go. 'Wherever', he said, 'you wish,
there you may remain.' Prince Taibuga departed with all his household
to the river Tura, and there built a city and called it Chingiden;[3] and at
this place there is now the city of Tyumen'. Taibuga lived in this city
many years; there also he died. After him his son Khodzha reigned, and
after this Khodzha's son Mar. The children of Mar were Ader and
Yabalak. Prince Mar was married to the sister of the Khan of Kazan,
Upak. This Khan of Kazan, Upak, killed his brother-in-law, Mar, and
took possession of the city, and ruled many years. The children of Mar,
Ader and Yabalak, died a natural death. After this Mamet, the son of
Ader, killed Upak, the Khan of Kazan, and destroyed his city of
Chingiden and went away from there within the Siberian land, and

[1] Untrue, of course, although it no doubt seemed like this. In fact there is open
water for several months, and ships often went there. Perhaps the chronicler is
being deliberately discouraging, for in the early 17th century there was sensiti-
vity about foreign infiltration (see Belov, 1956, pp. 116–19).

[2] Howorth (1876–88, p. 1062) believes that this story about On and Chingis is a
dim legend, based on Chingis Khan himself. Taibuga, he thinks, is the real stem-
father of the Siberian khans. His dates are not known.

[3] Also called Chingi-Tura. It was the Siberian khanate's first capital, which
later moved to Kyzyl-Tura (now Ust' Ishim), and finally to Isker, where it came
to be known to Russians as Sibir' (V. V. Khramova in *The peoples of Siberia*,
Chicago, 1964, p. 424).

established a city for himself on the river Irtish, and named his city Sibir', that is to say, the most important.[1] And the khan lived in it for many years and died; and from that time onwards the kingdom on the river Ishim was ended.

Chapter 3
On Sibir', why all this land was called Sibir'.

So when Mamet had defeated the khan of Kazan and commanded a city to be established, because he had defeated the khan, bearing witness to his valour, he also commanded that it should be called the superior city;[2] from this time onwards all this land was also called Sibir'. The Siberian cities are named each of them according to aspect, according to occasion and according to the ancient name; all together the land is named Sibir', just as the Roman land also is called Italia from a certain Italus, who ruled over the Hesperian lands, as the Latin chronicle testifies. The cities of all the Roman land have a variety of names, but all together it is called Italia. What it was called before this I do not know, since many years have passed since the city of Sibir' was built and I have been unable to find out by enquiry. For previously the Chud' lived throughout all the Siberian land, but what it was called has been remembered by no-one, nor have I found any writing on this.

Chapter 4
The princedom of the other Siberian princes.

After Prince Mamet there reigned in Sibir' the son of Yabalak, Agish; after him the son of Mamet, Kazym; after him the children of Kazym, Yetiger and Bekbulat; the son of Bekbulat was Seydyak.[3]

Chapter 5
On Khan Kuchyum.

Khan Kuchyum son of Murtazey[4] came over the steppe from the Kazakh Horde[5] with many troops, and arrived at the city of Sibir'. He

[1] This was at the second location, Kyzyl-Tura. 'Sibir', that is to say, the most important': this seems to be based on an attempt, which modern philologists will not countenance, to derive Sibir' from the Turco-Tatar *bir*, meaning one.
[2] Another reference to the questionable derivation.
[3] Other spellings found for these names in Russian accounts: Mamut, Makhmet; Abalak, Agalak, Yabolak; Aguish; Kasim; Yediger, Yadiger, Idiger; Seidiak, Seydek.
[4] Kuchum, who was grandson of Upak, or Ibak, and son of Murtazey, or Murtaza, claimed descent from Chingis; the princes whom he deposed (the date was 1563) were descended from Taibuga. There was thus no relationship, except by marriage two generations earlier.
[5] See Introduction, p. 22.

captured the city and killed the princes Yetiger and Bekbulat, and proclaimed himself khan of Sibir'. He made many tribes subject to himself, and his mind was full of self-exaltation, and for this reason he perished according to the saying: 'God resisteth the proud, but giveth grace unto the humble'.[1] The son of Bekbulat, Seydyak, was saved from Khan Kuchyum's slaughter and taken away to the Bukharan land. Khan Kuchyum reigned in Sibir' for full many a year, in abundance, gladness and rejoicing; he had tribute and taxes from many tribes, even to the year of the Lord's command, when God wished to destroy his kingdom and to give it up to the Orthodox Christians.

Chapter 6
On the religion of Khan Kuchyum.

The law of Khan Kuchyum and which those who were under his rule keep is that of the accursed Mohammed, and some worship idols and sacrifice to them, as though to God. Concerning this the holy fathers wrote in their canons and gave them to the world, for what they said is: if anyone adheres to the commandments of Mohammed and gives heed to his teaching, then he will be anathema, that is to say accursed. Moreover, for idolaters also a canon is set forth: when men are judged deserving to be accursed, there is unrighteousness among rulers, and discord in the army, among all the people strife and many revolts, the arising of warfare, no heritage of children; the people mourn because of misfortunes and disasters. I think that it was for this reason that God sent his wrath upon this Khan Kuchyum and those who were under his rule, because they did not know God's Law and worshipped idols and sacrificed to devils, not to God, but to gods whom they knew not,[2] as in ancient days in the time of the law-giver Moses the people of Israel made a calf and worshipped it instead of God and said: 'These be thy gods, O Israel'.[3] And for this reason the Lord sent his wrath upon them, and commanded a serpent to bite them, and each of them being wounded by a serpent died. And again the Lord had mercy upon them and put a thought into the heart of the blessed Moses. He being moved by God's sign made a serpent of brass and lifted it up on a pole, pre-figuring the crucifix of Christ.[4] Those wounded by the serpent looked upon that serpent and were healed. He commanded them not to hold that serpent in place of God, but he acted thus making allowance for their infirmity. But they worshipped this serpent also and began to praise it, as if it were God, and for this reason they were destroyed in their thousands, by famine and plagues, by captivity and war and by various ravages, as the same blessed Moses says in the song in Deuteronomy, prophesying for

---

[1] *James* iv, 6; *1 Peter* v, 5.
[2] 'They sacrificed unto devils, not to God; to gods whom they knew not' – *Deuteronomy* xxxii, 17.
[3] *Exodus* xxxii, 4.   [4] *Numbers* xxi, 8.9; *John* iii, 14.

their future to the disobedient Jews in their latest afflictions. And the Lord saw and was jealous and was moved with wrath because their sons and daughters made these sacrifices to devils, and God said: 'I will turn my face from them, since they have angered me in their idols'.[1] And again let us know His divine fatherly care, with which He cares for us and shields us, as a bird does its fledgelings. Thus also from these idolaters God turned His face because of their idols and bloody sacrifices, and put them to death, not by famine, nor by plague, nor by burning fire, nor slaying them by stoning, but He sent against them His two-edged sword, cutting down and devouring and giving up to destruction the devilish sacrifices to idols and their worshippers and votaries.

Chapter 7
On the coming of Yermak and the others to Sibir'.

God sent his chosen to purify the land and to conquer the infidel Khan Kuchyum and to destroy the abominable gods and their unholy temples, which were still a nesting place for wild beasts and a habitation for owls.[2] God chose a leader not from famous men, the *voyevodas* of the Tsar's command, but armed with glory and martial valour the *ataman* Yermak son of Timofey and with him 540 men. They forgot the honour and glory of this world, they changed death into life, taking up the shield of the true faith and fortifying themselves manfully and displaying bravery before the godless ones. For they grieved not over vain things, they rejected a life of sweetness and repose, and loved arms and shields, a savage and bitter undertaking. They gave their heads no rest and their eyes no sleep, until by the help of God they won victory over the accursed infidels. For they suffered an abundant outpouring of their blood by increasing wounds from arrow shots from the accursed infidels, and they retreated from these attacks. For they, the accursed ones, with fury threatened them and were more arrogant than the centaurs, and like Antaeus. But they were saved by God's hands, for it is written: he will not fear giants, or be afraid of wild beasts, or tremble before iron weapons or the mouths of crocodiles, for he has a champion in God more than any rock or stronghold. Thus even these soldiers placed their hopes firmly in the Lord and they all said: 'We are worthy to die for the true faith and to suffer for the Orthodox religion and to serve the most pious tsar'. For not from many soldiers does victory ensue, but from God from on high, for true in truth are these words: not by many soldiers did they

---

[1] The first phrase is from *Deuteronomy* xxxii, 20. The earlier reference to sons and daughters seems to derive from the previous verse. For all his learning, and his ecclesiastical background, Yesipov does not always get his biblical quotations right; either his memory or the text he used was at fault, and it has not been possible to determine which. The same question arises, and is not solved, in the Remezov chronicle, chapters 136 and 138.

[2] Russ. *sirini*, which also means a mythological bird with a woman's face and breast.

overcome the battle cries of the pagans and abase their lofty brows. And they humbled the proud and through all the Siberian land they triumphed with free steps, and they were not hindered by any man. And by these men there were established cities and God's holy churches were erected. If in ancient times the Siberian land was darkened by idolatry, now it is shining with devotion to God; the service of devils has disappeared and the altars of idols are shattered. Knowledge of God was implanted, the consubstantial Trinity and the uncreated Godhead are glorified according to the saying: 'Their sound went into all the earth and their words unto the ends of the world.'[1] For even if God did not grant to the blessed apostles to go forth to these lands, yet their preachings have gone forth everywhere.

Chapter 8
On the coming of Yermak and the other cossacks to Sibir'.

In the year 7089 [1581],[2] in the reign of the Pious Tsar and Great Prince Ivan Vasil'yevich, Autocrat of all Russia, these warriors came from the Volga to Sibir'. They came to Sibir' by the Chyusovaya river, and reached the river Tagil, and sailed on the Tagil and the Tura, and sailed to the river Tavda.[3] At the mouth of that river they captured a Tatar, named Tauzak, of the court of Khan Kuchyum; and he told them everything concerning Khan Kuchyum. Hearing of the coming of the Russian troops and of their courage and bravery, Khan Kuchyum was greatly afflicted concerning this and increasingly exerted his mind. Swiftly he sent into all his realm to command troops to come to him at the city of Sibir' and to arm themselves against the Russian warriors. In a little time there assembled before him a great number of Tatars and Ostyaks and Voguls and other tribes who were under his rule. The khan sent out his son Mametkul[4] with a great number of troops, and commanded them to oppose strongly those who attacked them. He himself ordered a barricade to be built by the side of the river Irtish at Chyuvashevo and to be heaped up with earth and to be fortified with many defences, as is the case with suitable fortifications. Mametkul together with his troops came to a certain natural boundary,[5] called the river Bobasan. The cossacks, seeing such an assembly of the pagans, were not in the least frightened by it. There was a great battle there, and they killed a great number of the pagans; the pagans fled headlong. Again

---

[1] *Romans* x, 18.
[2] Since the month is not stated, this could be 1580 if it was in the autumn. But see Introduction, p. 7.
[3] From the headwaters of the Chusovaya, or rather of its tributary the Serebryanka, there was a portage of about 30 km to the Tagil, a tributary of the Tura. The Tavda must have got in by mistake, for it is on another route.
[4] Probably nephew rather than son. See p. 39, note 1.
[5] Russ. *urochishche*, which can also mean a nomad camping ground, but that seems less likely here. The river, whether Bobasan, Babasan (Stroganov chapter 15) or Babasany (Remezov chapter 42), has not been exactly located.

the cossacks sailed in their boats[1] along the river Tobol. The Tatars began to shoot from behind a mountain at their boats; but they sailed past that place totally unscathed.

Chapter 9
On Karacha's encampment.

The cossacks came to Karacha's encampment;[2] this Karacha was the councillor of Khan Kuchyum. Battle was joined with Karacha and they captured his encampment and acquired a great quantity of wealth and carried down the khan's mead to their boats. They then sailed to the river Irtish. The pagans came to the bank, some on horseback and others on foot. The cossacks disembarked and valiantly attacked the pagans; there was then a fatal defeat for the pagans, and the pagans gave themselves up to headlong flight.

Chapter 10
On the deliberation of the cossacks.

Khan Kuchyum saw the downfall of his men, and went out with many of his people, and took his stand on a lofty place, on a hill called Chyuvashevo. At the barricade was his son, Mametkul, with many of his people. The cossacks went upstream along the Irtish, and captured the stronghold of Atik *murza*, and occupied it. Night came, and they were all in deliberation after seeing such a gathering of the pagans, which meant odds of ten or twenty to one, and they feared and were terrified. They wished to flee that night, but others did not wish to do this, since it was already autumn. But they placed their hopes in God, and they fortified the others also to go against the pagans the next morning, placing their hopes in God.

Chapter 11
On the battle at Chyuvashevo by the barricade.

On the 23rd of October all the Russian troops went out from the stronghold to battle, all proclaiming: 'God is with us'. And again they added: 'O God, help us Your servants'. They began to make an advance towards the barricade, and there was a great battle. These unconquerable heroes spread slaughter around them and displayed fierce-hearted daring, and were as though having the points of spears in their entrails,

[1] Russ. *strugi*, flat-bottomed river boats, propelled by oars or sail. See Introduction, pp. 19–20.
[2] Russ. *ulus*, a word of Turkic origin meaning nomadic encampment, but also people or tribe. The first seems more appropriate here.

for they armed themselves strongly with their valour and were all breathing with rage and fury, clad in iron, holding copper shields, bearing spears and firing iron shot. Battle was joined from both sides. The pagans shot innumerable arrows, and against them the cossacks fired from fire-breathing harquebuses, and there was dire slaughter; in hand to hand fighting they cut each other down. By the help of God the pagans gradually began to diminish and to weaken. The cossacks drove them onwards, slaying them in their tracks. The fields were stained with blood then, and covered with the corpses of the dead, and swamps were formed by the blood which flowed then, as in ancient times from the bodies at the city of Troy by the river Scamander, captured by Achilles. Thus they conquered the accursed infidels, for the wrath of God came upon them for their lawlessness and idolatry, since they knew not God their creator. The khan's heir Mametkul was wounded by the Russian warriors and would have been captured then, but his men bore him away to the opposite side of the river Irtish.

Chapter 12

On the flight of Khan Kuchyum.

Khan Kuchyum, standing on the lofty mountain which I have previously named, saw the downfall of his men, and commanded his mullahs to call out their abominable prayer, to invoke their abominable gods – but from these there was no help or aid for them. At that same time the Ostyak princelings with their men departed each to his home. Khan Kuchyum saw the loss of his kingdom, and said to those being with him: 'Let us flee without delaying, we see ourselves that we are bereft of everything; the strong are exhausted, and the valiant have been slain. O bitter fate! O woe is me, alas, alas! What shall I do and where shall I flee? O shame, cover my face! Who is it who has defeated me and unjustly banished me from my kingdom? A man from the common people, Yermak, came without many followers and wrought such evil things, slayed my soldiers and put me to shame. O lawless man, do you not know that even children suffer because of their parents either from fire or from hunger and nakedness, and cattle are devoured by wild beasts? O lawless man, for your abominable deeds may God not wish to see you, and may an unnatural sickness return upon your head, and may your own iniquity descend upon you!' Thus even he himself spoke to these men, and to this he added: 'Lo I conquered in the city of Sibir' the princes Yetiger and Bekbulat and I won great riches; I came and I conquered, sent by none, but in my own name seeking gain and greatness'. Khan Kuchyum fled to his city, and took some small part of his treasures, and gave himself up to headlong flight with all his troops, and left his city of Sibir' deserted.

Chapter 13
On the coming to the city of the *ataman* Yermak
and the others with him.

And when at Chyuvashevo the warrior army stopped, the fighting men laboured valiantly. Already then night had come, and they departed from there and encamped for the night; and set a strong guard against the pagans, so that the accursed ones should not harm them as snakes bite. In the morning all the fighting men prayed to all-merciful God and His Most Holy Mother and approached the city of Sibir' without fear. But as they drew near the city, and there was not to be heard in the city any voice or any sound, they wondered at first if the accursed ones had concealed themselves in the city. The fighting men put their trust in God and went into the city. Yermak with his company entered the city of Sibir' in the year 7089 [1580], on the 26th day of October, sacred to the memory of the saint and great martyr, Demetrius of Salonika. They glorified God, who had given them victory over the accursed idolaters and infidels, and with joy were rejoicing. Worthy in truth is it even for generations coming henceforth to recall this victory, how with not many troops they captured so great a kingdom by the help of God.

Chapter 14
On the coming of Tatars and Ostyaks to the
city of Sibir' to Yermak and his comrades.

On the fourth day after the capture of Sibir' the Ostyak prince named Boyar came to the city of Sibir' with many Ostyaks, and they brought to Yermak and his comrades many gifts and provisions, which supplied their wants. After that many Tatars with their wives and children began to arrive and began to live in their former homes, seeing that God had subjected them to the Orthodox Christians.

Chapter 15
On the killing of cossacks by the Tatars.

In the same year on the 5th of December one of Yermak's companies went to catch fish to a certain river, which is called Basan,[1] without any apprehension. They set up their camp and went to sleep without a guard. The khan's heir Mametkul came upon them by stealth with many men, and slew them. A report was heard in the city concerning the killing of these men. Yermak with his company hastened in pursuit of

[1] Identified in the Stroganov chronicle, chapter 18, as Yabolak, which is the modern Abalak, a lake and village about 25 km from Sibir'.

the pagans and came up with them, and there was a great battle with the pagans for a long time. The pagans fled headlong, and Yermak with his comrades returned to the city of Sibir'.

Chapter 16
On the sending to the tsar in Moscow with a report.

When God was pleased to give up the Siberian land to the Christians, after its capture, in the same year Yermak and his comrades sent to Moscow an *ataman* and cossacks with a report.[1] They wrote to the Pious Tsar and Great Prince Ivan Vasil'yevich, Autocrat of all Russia, to this effect: by the grace of all-merciful God, glorified in the Trinity, and His Mother, the most pure Mother of God, and by the prayers of the great miracle-working saints of all Russia, and by the just prayer to all-merciful God of this same Sovereign, the Tsar and Great Prince Ivan Vasil'yevich of all Russia, and by good fortune, they had captured the Siberian kingdom and had defeated Khan Kuchyum and his troops; they had brought under his royal, exalted hand many alien peoples living there, Tatars and Ostyaks and Voguls and other tribes, and had brought many of them to take an oath according to their faith, to be under his royal, exalted hand for all time, as long as God should be pleased for the universe to endure; and for them to give fur tribute to the sovereign every year without cessation; to contemplate no evil things against the Russians; but whoever should wish to go to the sovereign into his sovereign service, upon them should his sovereign service be conferred, to serve uprightly, and not to pardon the sovereign's enemies, so far as God should grant to aid them; and for themselves it was enjoined not to commit treason, not to desert to Khan Kuchyum and to other hordes and peoples, and not to think any evil things against all the Russians, and to stand fast in all upright constancy. The *atamans* and cossacks arrived in Moscow, and news concerning them was given to the sovereign. The Pious Sovereign, the Tsar and Great Prince Ivan Vasil'yevich, Autocrat of all Russia, heard the news and commanded that their despatch should be accepted and read in his royal presence. When the sovereign heard of the aid and power of God, how the Lord was bestowing a kingdom and was granting a territory, was conquering the unconquered and was rendering his enemies subject, then he glorified God and His most pure Mother, since God had shown such favour; it is not from numerous troops that such a victory comes. He bestowed upon Yermak his royal favour, pronounced in his absence.

[1] Russ. *sounch*, the commoner form of which is *seunch*, meaning a report containing good news. The Stroganov chronicle, chapter 22, has the report being sent to Moscow *after* the events of the next three chapters – the capture of Mametkul, Seydyak's appearance, and the taking of Nazym (or Kazym); on the whole a likelier sequence. The Pogodin version of the Yesipov chronicle (not translated here) mentions the name of one of this party – Cherkas Aleksandrov (*Sibirskiye letopisi*, 1907, p. 281).

The sovereign bestowed upon the cossacks his royal favour, money and clothing, and the sovereign again dismissed them to Sibir' to Yermak and his comrades. To Yermak and to the other *atamans* and cossacks the sovereign sent generous royal gifts for their service to him, the sovereign, and for the shedding of their blood.

Chapter 17
On the coming of the Tatar Senbakhta and on the capture of the khan's heir Mametkul.

After this a Tatar named Senbakhta came to the city to Yermak, and informed him that the khan's heir Mametkul, son of Khan Kuchyum, was stationed at the river Vagay, about seventy versts from the city of Sibir'. Yermak sent some of his company, men young and expert in warfare. These troops went forth and coming up to their encampments fell on them by night, some of them sleeping and others not sleeping but still awake, and they killed many pagans. They came to the tent of the khan's heir and surrounded it and captured the khan's heir Mametkul alive and with all his wealth. They brought him to the city to Yermak and his comrades. Yermak received him, informed him of the tsar's great favour and comforted him with kind words. Khan Kuchyum waited for his son Mametkul for a long time, and then messengers came to him and informed him that his son Mametkul had been taken captive. Hearing this, the khan was afflicted concerning him; and the khan sorely lamented, he and all his household, for a long time.

Chapter 18
On the coming of Prince Seydyak from Bukhara and on the departure from Khan Kuchyum of his councillor Karacha.

Messengers came to Khan Kuchyum and informed him that there was coming against him with a large army Prince Seydyak, the son of Bekbulat, from the land of Bukhara, where escaping from the slaughter he had concealed himself, and recalling his native land wished to regain it as his inheritance; who now desired to avenge the blood of his father, Bekbulat. Khan Kuchyum heard this from those who informed him, and was terrified with a great fear; for still there was much in him of his first fear, which was caused by the Russian army. After this his councillor Karacha together with his men, who were of his household, departed from Khan Kuchyum and did not wish to be in subjection to him. Hearing this, the khan began to lament with great lamentation and said: 'That man for whom God has no mercy, him even dear friends desert and are as his enemies'. Karacha reached lake Yulmyskoye,[1]

[1] Not exactly identified. This part of the country has a very large number of lakes.

which is on the upper reaches of the river Irtish, between the river Tara and the river Om′, and remained there.

Chapter 19
On the capture of strongholds and encampments.

Yermak with his company displayed his valour through all the Siberian land, stepping out freely and fearing no man, for the fear of God was on all those living there, like a two-edged sword going before the face of the Russian army, mowing down and destroying and spreading terror. He took many strongholds and encampments on the river Irtish, and on the great Ob′ they captured the stronghold of Nazim[1] with its prince and with all its wealth. After which he returned to the city of Sibir′ with great rejoicing and booty.

Chapter 20
On the coming of *voyevodas* and troops from Moscow to Sibir′.

In the year 7091 [1583] the Pious Tsar and Great Prince of all Russia, Ivan Vasil′yevich, sent to his dominion in Sibir′ his *voyevodas*, Prince Semen Bolkhovskoy and Ivan Glukhov, with many troops. At that same time there was a great famine in the city of Sibir′. When the troops arrived,[2] the famine increased, many died of hunger and Prince Semen died and was buried there.[3] The famine occurred in the winter time. When spring came, then the Tatars and Ostyaks began to bring to the city many supplies acquired by their hunting. Again there were in the city many supplies, abounding with grain and vegetables and other things, which provided for their needs.

Chapter 21
On the sending of the khan's heir Mametkul to Moscow.

In the same year they sent the khan's heir Mametkul, son of Kuchyum, from Sibir′ to the reigning city of Moscow together with many troops. Before they arrived in Moscow, by the will of God the Pious Sovereign, the Tsar and Great Prince Ivan Vasil′yevich of all Russia departed to the Lord to eternal rest;[4] he had commanded that after his decease there

[1] Nazym is a river and village near the Ob′-Irtysh confluence. The Stroganov chronicle in some versions has Kazym, which is further downstream. Bakhrushin (1955, p. 27) favours Nazym.
[2] It is probable that although the troops left Moscow in 1583, they did not arrive at Sibir′ until 1584. The charter of 7 January 1584 (see pp. 294–5) seems to make this quite clear.
[3] The new arrivals had brought no food.
[4] Ivan IV died in March 1584.

should be raised to his royal throne his son, Feodor Ivanovich, the Pious Tsar and Great Prince, Autocrat of all Russia, which was even so. And the troops brought the khan's heir Mametkul to the reigning city of Moscow, and by the command of the Tsar and Great Prince Feodor Ivanovich of all Russia he was honourably received, and on his arrival the Sovereign granted to the khan's heir Mametkul his royal favour in great measure; thus also did the Sovereign grant to the serving men, who were sent with him, money and food and pieces of cloth.

Chapter 22
On the envoys from Karacha and on the killing of cossacks by the godless Karacha.

In the same year[1] envoys from Karacha came to Yermak and his comrades and asked for men to protect them from the Kazakh Horde; they took an oath according to their faith that they would meditate no evil against the cossacks. Yermak and his comrades took counsel, and they had faith in their ungodly and wily oath, and they sent to him an *ataman*, Ivan Koltso by name, and forty men with him. And when these troops came to the godless Karacha, on a sudden they were all killed by the godless Karacha. It was heard in the city that these troops had been slain by the godless Karacha, and Yermak and the cossacks, their company, wept for a great time, as for their own children. It came to the ears of the pagans that they had slain the *ataman*, Ivan Koltso, and others, and they began to slay the cossacks in many places, wherever they were found, in the districts and encampments.

Chapter 23
On the coming of the Tatar Karacha and other Tatars to the city of Sibir'.

In the same year at the time of Lent Karacha came with many troops and besieged the city of Sibir' with waggon trains and set up camps. Karacha himself stayed in a certain place which is called Sauskan, two versts from the city; he caused much hardship to the people of the city, and he remained thus until the spring. When it was the month of June, at that time cossacks secretly came out of the city, and they came to the encampments of Karacha in Sauskan; they fell upon them by night while some were sleeping without any apprehension, and they slew a great number of the ungodly Tatars and killed two sons of Karacha. The other Tatars disappeared in different directions. Karacha and a few men with him fled away beyond a lake. Some ran to other Tatars standing at the way out from the city and informed them of all that had befallen them. Hearing these things, those who were standing at the way

[1] Presumably 1584.

out of the city also ran to Sauskan; they were hoping to put the cossacks to death, and they fell upon them. The cossacks were hiding from them in the bushes, and they came out in a sortie and fought valiantly with the pagans. There was a battle until mid-day, and then the fighting ceased. The Tatars retreated from them, and the cossacks returned to the city. Karacha, seeing that it was impossible to vanquish the cossacks, departed home in shame.

Chapter 24
On the killing of Yermak and the other cossacks with him by Khan Kuchyum.

In the year 7092 [1584],[1] the hour was appointed by God, and death came upon the warriors. Messengers from Bukharans, men engaged in trade, came to Sibir' to Yermak and his comrades, and informed them that Khan Kuchyum would not let them in to Sibir'. Yermak with not many fighting men went to meet these pagans along the river Irtish in their boats. On reaching the river Vagay he did not find the Bukharans, and continuing along the Vagay up to the place which is called Atbash, he did not find them either and returned from there. As night had come on, the cossacks, tired by the long journey, went as far as a cross-channel, and there spent the night and set up their camp; they did not post a strong guard, since their wits were enfeebled as the hour of death was approaching. The khan, having seen them, gave orders to guard strongly against them that night and sent many Tatars to station themselves at many points. That night there was a great rainfall. At midnight a large number of the pagans came up, while the cossacks were sleeping without any apprehension, and fell upon them and slew them. Only one cossack escaped. When Yermak saw his troops slain by the pagans and saw no one from whom he might have help for his life, he fled to his boat but was unable to reach it, since he was clad in iron and the boat had floated away from the bank; and failing to reach it he drowned. For by the judgement of God death came upon the warriors, and thus did they lose their lives, and they were slain on the 5th of August. When those who had remained in the city heard that the *ataman* Yermak had been killed together with the others, they lamented for them with great lamentation, grievously for a great time.

Chapter 25
On the flight of the remaining cossacks after the killing of Yermak and the others.

After the killing of Yermak and his company those who had remained in the city of Sibir', seeing that the ungodly Tatars had killed their leader together with his company, the other cossacks, feared to live in

[1] Most scholars now accept that this should be 1585. See Introduction, p. 7.

the city. They departed from the city secretly, and sailed down the Irtish and the great Ob' and fled across the mountain range to Russia, leaving the city of Sibir' deserted.

Chapter 26
On the khan's heir Aley, son of Kuchyum.

When the cossacks had fled from the city, then the khan's heir Aley,[1] son of Kuchyum, learned that the cossacks had fled and had left the city deserted, and he came up with troops and entered the city and settled himself there. When Prince Seydyak, son of Bekbulat, heard these things, that the *ataman* Yermak with his comrades had been killed at the cross-channel, that the others had fled from the city, and that the khan's heir Aley, son of Kuchyum, was in possession of the city, he set out with all his household and troops, and came to the city of Sibir'; he captured the city and conquered the khan's heir Aley and the others and drove them from the city. He was taking possession of the patrimony of his father Bekbulat, and thus he remained in the city.

Chapter 27
On the coming from Moscow to Sibir' of the
voyevoda Ivan Mansurov and troops.

In the second year after the killing of Yermak the *voyevoda* Ivan Mansurov came with troops from Moscow to Sibir', and sailed to the river Irtish.[2] A great number of Tatars had assembled in an appointed place near the Irtish on its bank. The *voyevoda*, seeing so great an assembly of pagans, and hearing that the cossacks had fled from the city, was afraid and did not approach the bank, but sailed down along the Irtish and reached the great Ob'. It was then autumn and ice was congealing on the rivers; Ivan Mansurov saw that winter was approaching and gave orders for a stronghold to be built above the river Ob' opposite the mouth of the Irtish. He installed himself there with the troops and so passed the winter.

Chapter 28
On the coming of the Ostyaks to the stronghold.

After some days a great number of Ostyaks who lived along the great Ob' and the Irtish came up to the stronghold and began to attack the stronghold from all sides. Men from the stronghold opposed them, and

---

[1] The Stroganov chronicle's Alliy – no doubt Ali. It is thought he really was Kuchum's son (see p. 39, note 1).

[2] Mansurov left Moscow in 1585 and arrived on the Irtysh in 1586. 'The second year' can be taken to mean 1585 after 1 September, as in the Stroganov chronicle chapter 32, and it referred to the time Mansurov left.

thus they stood and fought for a whole day. When night came, the pagans withdrew from the stronghold.

Chapter 29
On the idol of the Ostyaks.

In the morning the Ostyaks came up to the stronghold and brought with them an idol. They had this instead of a god, and this idol was famed in their land. They set up this idol beneath a tree and began to sacrifice before it. They expected that by its aid they would capture the Christians and put them to death. At the same time as they were sacrificing, the Russians fired a cannon from the stronghold, and smashed into many pieces that tree, beneath which was the idol, and this idol itself. The pagans were terrified, not knowing what this was, and they thought that someone had let fly from a bow, and they said to each other: 'These are indeed powerful archers, as they have smashed such a tree'. And from this hour they returned to their homes.

Chapter 30
On the coming of *voyevodas*.

In the year 7093 [1585][1] the *voyevodas* Vasiley Sukin and Ivan Myasnoy came from Russia, and with them were many Russian men. They established the city of Tyumen', which was formerly the city of Chingiy, and built houses for themselves, and they erected churches as a refuge for themselves and other Orthodox Christians.

Chapter 31
On the city of Tobol'sk and on its building and
on the establishment of a church and on its primacy,
how it was called the principal city.

In the year 7095 [1587], in the reign of the Pious Sovereign, the Tsar and Great Prince Feodor Ivanovich of all Russia and according to his royal will, there was sent from Moscow the sovereign's *voyevoda* Danilo Chyulkov with many troops. According to the sovereign's command they went as far as the river Irtish, ten versts from the city of Sibir'; it was his pleasure to enlighten the land there to the glory of the Father and the Son and the Holy Ghost. It replaced Sibir' as the main city. This city of Tobol'sk was the leading one, since it was there that victory and conquest of the accursed infidels occurred, and so it took the place of Sibir' as the reigning city.[2]

---

[1] This should be 1586.

[2] Tobol'sk remained the principal city of Russian Siberia certainly until 1764, when it became the capital of Western Siberia, with Irkutsk having equal status as the capital of Eastern Siberia. Tobol'sk was replaced by Omsk only in 1839.

Chapter 32
On the capture of Prince Seydyak and Saltan,
heir of the Kazakh Horde, and Karacha,
and on the killing of others.

After the establishment of the city of Tobolsk, after some days Prince Seidyak came out of the city of Sibir', and with him came Saltan, heir of the Kazakh Horde, and Karacha, the councillor of Khan Kuchyum, and with them were 500 troops. Having reached the place which is called Knyazh Lug, they began to send hawks after birds. The *voyevoda* Danilo Chyulkov with his troops saw them from the city of Tobolsk, and having taken counsel he sent envoys to Prince Seidyak and commanded them to say to Prince Seidyak that he should come to the city to consult on establishing peace. For he was still like a viper breathing fury against the Orthodox Christians, not submitting, but like a snake wishing to wound them. When the envoys arrived they announced these things which Danilo Chyulkov had commanded them to speak. Prince Seidyak heard these words from them, sought counsel with the khan's heir Saltan and Karacha, and immediately after they had taken counsel Prince Seidyak set out, and with him were the khan's heir Saltan and Karacha. A hundred troops came with them according to their command; they left the others outside the city. They came to the city of Tobolsk. The *voyevoda*, Danilo Chyulkov, together with his troops met them at the city gates, and commanded them to lay down their arms outside the city. On entering the house of Danilo Chyulkov they all sat down at the table, for food was already prepared. They spoke much concerning the establishment of peace. Prince Seidyak sitting at the table was sunk in thought and tasted neither the drink nor the food. Danilo Chyulkov saw this and said to Prince Seidyak: 'Prince Seidyak, what evil do you contemplate against the Orthodox Christians, you have tasted neither the drink nor the food?' Prince Seidyak said to him: 'I do not contemplate any evil against you.' Danilo Chyulkov then took a cup of drink and said: 'Prince Seidyak, if you and the khan's heir Saltan and Karacha do not contemplate evil against us, the Orthodox Christians, then drink this cup to our health.' And Prince Seidyak took the cup of drink and began to drink, and it choked him in his throat. After this the khan's heir Saltan took it and began to drink it, and it choked him the same way in his throat, for God was exposing them. The *voyevoda* and his warriors saw that Prince Seidyak and the others were contemplating evil against them and wished to put them to death, and when Danilo Chyulkov waved his hand, his warriors began to kill the pagans. Prince Seidyak rushed to a window and after him came also the khan's heir Saltan and Karacha, but immediately they were seized and bound; the others were slain. When those standing outside the city heard that Prince Seidyak had been overcome, they turned to flight, and so great a

81

terror came upon them that they did not return even to their own city. When those who were in the city heard the news, they also fled from the city, and no one remained in the city.

Chapter 33
On the sending of Prince Seidyak and Saltan and Karacha to Moscow.

After some days they sent Prince Seidyak and Saltan, heir of the Kazakh Horde, and Karacha to the reigning city of Moscow with many warriors.

Chapter 34
On the death of Khan Kuchyum, where he passed away.

When Khan Kuchyum was defeated and fled out of the city and from his realm to the wild country, he came to a place which he found, and stayed there with his remaining men. Many times did he attempt to go to Sibir', to devastate the infidel cities of Sibir' and to take vengeance on the Orthodox Christians, but he was possessed by fear because of his former defeat. At one time he attempted to go there and gathered together his remaining troops, as many as there were, and went to Sibir'. When he came to the river Irtish, still not near the city of Tobolsk, suddenly trembling and terror came upon him, and he did not go to the city of Tobolsk and to the other cities, but devastated a few infidel villages and then fled to the place where he resided. It was reported in the city of Tobolsk that Khan Kuchyum had devastated the Tatar villages, and the Russian soldiers assembled and hastened in pursuit. They overtook him near the open country and fell upon him, and by the help of God they killed the troops of Khan Kuchyum and captured two of his queens and his son, the heir, and gained a great quantity of riches. Khan Kuchyum escaped with not many men and came to his encampment. He took his remaining men and went secretly to the land and camps of the Kalmucks. After spying out their herds of horses, he fell upon them and drove them away. Having perceived him, the Kalmucks pursued him and overtook them. They killed many of his troops and took back their horses. Khan Kuchyum fled to the Nagays and was slain there by the Nagays, for they said: 'If the Russian warriors learn that you are staying here, they will do the same to us as to you.' And there he ended his life.

Chapter 35
Thanksgiving to God.

Thenceforth the sun of the Gospels illuminated the Siberian land, and the thunder of psalms resounded, and above all in many places cities were established, and God's holy churches and monasteries were built to the glory of the Father and the Son and the Holy Ghost, as a refuge for the Orthodox Christians. Many unbelievers, witnessing the Christian faith, were baptized in the name of the Father and the Son and the Holy Ghost, and from unbelief became believers, and everywhere the grace of God was poured out in the Siberian land, as it is written: 'Thou hast visited the earth, and watered it, multiplied it and enriched it.'[1] In places that no one had heard of, there now are cities and villages and dwellings within them, and a great number of Orthodox Christians have spread over the face of all the Siberian land. Concerning these things I have spoken up to here; now, however, I have come to the rectification.

Chapter 36

You should have assistance for rectifying the account of this chronicle concerning the capture of Sibir' and such a conquest:

In the year 7129 [1621] by the will of God and the command of the Pious and Christian Sovereign, the Tsar and Great Prince Mikhail Fedorovich of all Russia, and with the blessing of the most eminent bishop Filaret Nikitich, patriarch of Moscow and of all Russia, there was installed in Sibir' in Tobolsk the first archbishop, Kipriyan, who had previously been an archimandrite in Khutyn.[2] In the second year of his installation he remembered the *ataman* Yermak together with his company and commanded that Yermak's cossacks should be asked how they came to Sibir', and where were the battles with the pagans, and whom the pagans killed in the fighting and where. The cossacks brought to him a written account[3] of how they came to Sibir', and where they had battles with the pagans, and where cossacks were killed, with their names. He, being a good pastor and having concern for them, commanded the names of the slain to be entered in the book of names for the commemoration of the dead in the church of Sofia of Divine Wisdom and to be read out during the prayers to the eternal memory of the dead on Orthodox Sunday in the cathedral together with those of all who had suffered for Orthodoxy.

[1] Psalm lxv, 9. The Authorised Version reads 'Thou visitest the earth and waterest it: thou greatly enrichest it'.

[2] That is, in Novgorod. Kipriyan was a major figure in the Church of that time. He remained Archbishop of Tobol'sk until 1624, and died in 1635 as Metropolitan of Novgorod. The writer of this chronicle, Savva Yesipov, was one of his staff at Tobol'sk.

[3] This document, the cossacks' own *napisaniye* or relation, has not survived, but is assumed to be the main source of the chronicles.

Chapter 37
The book of names for the commemoration of the dead cossacks[1].

In the year 7089 [1581] in the reign of the Pious Tsar and Great Prince Ivan Vasil'yevich of all Russia God chose and sent a man not from among the famous nor from the *voyevodas* of the Tsar's command to cleanse the land and defeat the infidel Khan Kuchyum and destroy their impious and ungodly temples. They were still a nesting place for wild beasts and an abode for owls, but in these places cities were established and God's holy churches were erected as a refuge for the Orthodox Christians, to the glory of the Father and the Son and the Holy Ghost. But God chose from among the simple people and armed with glory, a warrior's skills and liberty the *ataman* Yermak son of Timofey Povolskoy together with his single-minded and excellent company of proved valour. They forgot all the honour, glory and carnal pleasure of this world and turned death into life. They took up the shield of the true faith, fortified themselves manfully and displayed their valour before the ungodly ones, all proclaiming : 'We are worthy to die for the true, holy churches of God and to suffer for the true faith and to serve the Pious Tsar'. They placed all their hope firmly in the Lord, since not from many troops does victory come, but from above from God, for He can give help even to the helpless against the opposing infidels. All these things were accomplished by Divine Providence, and these warriors came fearless to the Siberian land to their ungodly encampments. Their opponents assembled at an appointed place near the river Irtish on its bank at Chyuvashevo, and a great number of them were spread round, like the grass of the field. There was a great battle with them on the 23rd of October, and the Orthodox army by the help of God struck down the ungodly ones, like ears of corn. To those slain at that place[2] the great commemoration.

That same winter when Yermak's company went up to Yabalak without apprehension to catch fish, the pagans suddenly fell upon their encampments and killed them. To those slain in that action[3] the intermediate commemoration.

[1] Russ. *sinodik*, book of names for the commemoration of the dead. This list, compiled on the basis of the lost *napisaniye*, was written, as the previous chapter makes clear, in Kipriyan's second year, i.e. 1622, and was probably the starting point of this chronicler, Yesipov (see Bakhrushin, 1955, pp. 18–20). Sections of it are repeated in the earlier chapters. A fuller version of the *sinodik* has recently been found in the State Historical Museum in Moscow (Uvarov collection, No. 931(370)(540). See Ye. K. Romodanovskaya, 'Sinodik yermakovym kazakam', *Izvestiya Sibirskogo otdeleniya Akademii Nauk SSSR*, No. 11 (1970), pp. 14–21). The most important additional information it provides is the names of the persons being commemorated – a rather glaring omission in Yesipov's abbreviated version.
[2] The names in the fuller version (see previous footnote) are Okol, Ivan, Karchiga, Bogdan Bryazga and their company.
[3] There is confusion about the names given here. Two consecutive paragraphs in the fuller version refer to the Abalak action, which is also dated in both as

In the second year after the capture of Sibir', when Yermak together with his company displayed his valour, they drew their swords on the ungodly ones and waged war along the river Irtish and along the great Ob'. They captured Nazim, stronghold of the Ostyaks, together with their prince and many Ostyaks. To those slain in that action[1] on their march the great commemoration.

In the third year after the capture of Sibir' Karacha, the councillor of Khan Kuchyum, sent his envoys to Yermak and his comrades for men to protect him from the Kazakh Horde. Yermak according to the counsel of his comrades trusted in their ungodly and faithless oath and sent to this same Karacha an *ataman* named Ivan Koltso, and 40 men with him. These men gave themselves into the hands of the ungodly ones, and were all slain there. To those slain in that action[2] the great commemoration.

In the fourth year after the capture of Sibir', on the 5th of August, messengers came to Yermak and his comrades from Bukharans, men engaged in trade, informing them that Khan Kuchyum would not let them in. Yermak went to meet the Bukharans, and they went up to the river Vagay and spent the night at the cross-channel. The pagans spied them out and fell upon their encampments by night. But by God's will the appointed hour arrived, and death came upon the warriors, and they were all killed there. To those slain in that action[3] and to Yermak, as God was pleased to end their lives, the great commemoration and the great extolment.[4] The names of those who were slain, and where, are written down in the book of names for the commemoration of the dead. Here I have ceased writing concerning this, and behold I have written this down to rectify my own account. An end is now set to this chronicle.

December 5th. The first paragraph has Sergey, Ivan, Andrey, Timofey and their company; but the second has the same names as those given for the Chuvashevo battle – Okol, Ivan, Karchiga, Bogdan Bryazga and their company. The confusion is further confounded by the fact that the Remezov chronicle, chapters 73–80, mentions Bogdan Bryazga's exploits *after* both these battles.

[1] The names given here are Ataman Nikita [Pan], Timofey, Ivan, Anana, Antsyfor, Ivan, Grigoriy, Andrey, Aleksey, Nikon, Mikhail, Tita, Feodor, Ivan, Artemiy, Login, and others of their company. The commemoration is also downgraded to intermediate.

[2] The names given here are Ataman Ivan Koltso, Vladimer, Vasiliy 2, Lukiyan, with all their company.

[3] The names given here are Yakov, Roman, Petr 2, Mikhail, Ivan, Ivan and Yermak. Further identification of most of these persons is not possible. The names given in this and the four immediately preceding footnotes represent almost all the names we know of participants in the campaign. Three others only are not listed here: the *atamans* Ivan Groza and Matvey Meshcheryak, and the cossack Cherkas Aleksandrov. The Stroganov chronicle, chapter 35, reports Meshcheryak's death, but perhaps the other two were still alive when the *sinodik* was compiled.

[4] Russ. *vozglas*, meaning the concluding section of a prayer, when the priest, sometimes after a silence, raises his voice and thus emphasises the particular purpose of the prayer (F. A. Brokgauz and I. A. Efron, *Entsiklopedicheskiy slovar'*, St Petersburg, 1890–1907, *sub nomine*).

This chronicle: the Siberian kingdom and principality and concerning its capture, was composed in the city of Tobolsk in the year 7145 [1636], on the first of September.

The compiler of this chronicle is a sinful man. His personal name is made known by four letters: twice a hundred with one and two with one. His family name is indicated by six letters: the first letter as a simple letter is the same as E. There are five other letters: twice a hundred with twice four, eightfold ten with sevenfold ten, twice one, and a hard sign completes it.[1] Some things I wrote down from a document which I had previously composed;[2] certain things were curtailed in speech, and I enlarged upon them, conversing for the love of you, who will deign to read through this chronicle. Other things I ascertained by enquiry from trustworthy men, who saw them with their own eyes and were there in those years. Concerning this my words have come to an end.

Let us, brethren, celebrate once more the miracles of God, which have been accomplished in our day in lands newly enlightened concerning Jesus Christ, our Lord, and glory to Him and to the Father and to the Holy Ghost, as you are blessed for ever and ever. Amen.

---

[1] Russian letters had numerical values based on the Greek system (before the 18th century Russian numerals were expressed alphabetically), so simple ciphers could be devised whereby the number represented by each letter was broken down into smaller numbers and then expressed in other letters. This was commonly done, as here, to conceal the names of authors or copyists – in this case the numbers spell Sava Yesipov. See L. V. Cherepnin, *Russkaya paleografiya*, Moscow, 1965, pp. 391–4, for explanation of the system, and W. K. Matthews, *Russian historical grammar*, London, 1960, pp. 71–2, for table of numerical values.

[2] This document has not been found.

THE REMEZOV CHRONICLE

according to the Mirovich manuscript[1]

[1] The text translated is printed in *Sibirskiye letopisi* 1907, pp. 312–66. The manuscript was originally written about 1700 (see Introduction, p. 27). The illustrations reproduced here comprise the whole of the Mirovich version, except for the front and back covers. The original is in the library of the Academy of Sciences, Leningrad (call no. 16.16.5). The text written into the top of each picture is printed in translation underneath or opposite its picture.

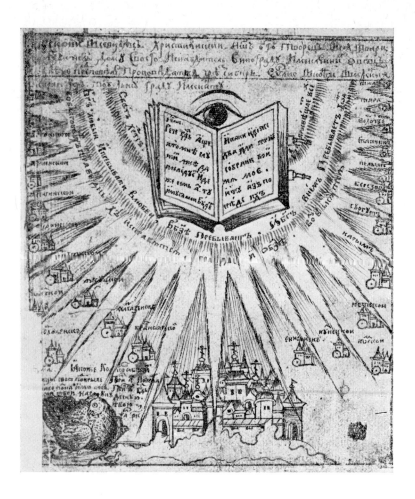

The history of Sibir'

1. From the beginning of time our Christian God, the All-Seer, Creator of all creatures, Founder of his house, and Provider of the vine and of spiritual sheep, decreed for the Gospels to be preached throughout Sibir' to the ends of the universe and the limit of the mountains to the famous city of Tobol'sk.[1]

---

[1] In the picture, the words in the open book read: 'The Gospel. The Lord said, If any man serve me, let him follow me; and where I am there shall also my servant be. And again, where two or three are gathered together in my name, there am I in the midst of them.' These words come from *John* xii, 26, and *Matthew* xviii, 20.

The words in concentric semi-circles round the book read:
'Christ the light enlightens all.'

'God is love; and he that dwelleth in love dwelleth in God, and God in him. Joh.'

'And he will dwell in righteousness, and towns will arise to the Lord.'

The middle sentence, attributed to John, comes from *I John* iv, 16. The other two appear not to be biblical quotations, but the first echoes the meaning of *John* I. 9.

The outer semicircle shows a series of towns, from left to right: '[first four illegible], Irkutskoy, Yakutskoy, Mangazeysko, Krasnoyarskoy, Verkhoyansk, Yeniseysk, Kuznetskoy, Tomskoy, Ketskoy, Narym, Surgut, Berezov, Pelym, Yepanchin, Verkhotur'ye, Tara, Tyumen'.' They are the Siberian towns of Remezov's time, not of Yermak's. The large town at the bottom, though un-named, is no doubt Tobol'sk.

The words in the bottom left corner read: 'Just as a hen gathers its [chicks] under its wing, so shall I . . . my name. The Lord is thy shade upon thy right hand. Ps. cxx.' The last sentence is the second half of verse 5 of the Psalm mentioned (which is numbered cxxi in our Bible), but the first sentence, which is not wholly legible, seems not to be a direct quotation from the Bible.

2. As our great Christian Lord God who endows his servants from birth endowed Samson with the strength of a giant, so he gave Yerman, son of Timofey Povolskoy, strength, success and valour from an early age to be of sturdy heart and mighty deeds.[1]

[1] The words on the face of the picture read (top) 'The brave one is learning to shoot at the target', and (bottom) 'Yermak fighting'.

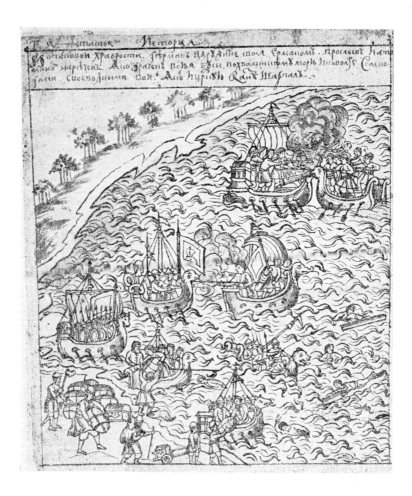

3. And for such valour German became known as Yermak[1] among his fighting men who chose him as *ataman*, he being famed for attacking ships on the Caspian sea and on the Volga together with many free warriors, even plundering the royal treasure.

[1] Yermak is not a common Christian name. It may be a nickname, which is the view taken by those who think his original Christian name was Vasiliy (see Introduction, p. 11), or it may be a diminutive, as implied here – but the more usual derivation (see Vasmer, *sub nomine*) is from Yermolay.

91

4. On hearing of this the Pious Tsar Ivan Vasil'yevich sent against
them a strong troop of his men with orders to kill every one of them and
put to death the captured leaders so that they should not loot his treasure
and block the roads.

The Short Kungur Siberian chronicle[1]

5. Beginning of the depredations of Yermak son of Timofey Povolskoy. In the years 7085 and 7086 [1577 & 1578] he warred on the Oka and the Volga and destroyed ships and barges and merchant caravans in

[1] This chronicle is an insertion into Remezov's own account, and can easily be identified, from external appearance, as consisting of chapters 5–8, 49–52, 73–80 and 99–102. Chapters 140–7 are also an insertion, but not from this source. The writer is unknown, but the insertion was probably made about 1700, perhaps by Remezov himself.

company with 5000 men,[1] intending to go on with men from the Don and the Yaik to conquer the Kizilbash.[2] Before that and in those same years rumours of his misdeeds had spread in Russia, in Kazan and in Astrakhan, one of which was that Kizilbash envoys had been robbed by one named Yermachko with many men and that he had gathered 7000 men on the sea. And in the same year 86 [1578], on the first day of October the great sovereign sent the boyar Ivan Murashkin along the roads to Astrakhan with this order: wherever these robbers were found they were to be tortured, executed and hanged on the spot. When Yermak in council with his company learnt these terrible words of command[3] on August the 29th, they decided to flee to Sibir' to conquer it, turning their boats upstream along the Volga and the Kama. And that royal order no longer found them in their encampments, but those who got caught were put to death. As for those with whom Yermak was supposed to be, them the commanders did not even think to capture but themselves took to flight. On the 26th day of September[4] Yermak's company missed their way and did not reach Sibir' by the Chyusovaya but rowed up the Sylva coming with the first frosts to the boundary now called Yermak's stronghold. They collected grain and provisions from the inhabitants and spent the winter here. Beyond the mountains they fought the Voguls and enriched themselves, while Maksim Stroganov kept them supplied with grain. Three hundred men raided the Voguls and returned with rich booty to their homes and for the expedition to Sibir' for which they prepared many light boats and stores.

[1] Numbers of men in Yermak's company are high throughout this chronicle. A band of 5000 marauders seems large, but was perhaps possible. When Yermak moves into Sibir' (chapters 7, 12, 13, 36 below) the numbers are considerably higher than the other chronicles allow. Müller, the first historian of Siberia, who wrote in the 1740's, evidently thought the higher figures correct (1750, pp. 95–6) – but he discovered the Remezov chronicle and made it his main source. Most modern scholars disagree (see Introduction, p. 13).

[2] Redheads. 'The name given by the Ottoman Turks to the confederation of seven Turkoman tribes who placed the Shaikhs of Ardabil on the throne of Persia and helped Shah Ismail (1487–1524) to found the dynasty of the Safavids. Shah Ismail had given them as headdress the red turban worn by disciples of his ancestors' (W. E. D. Allen, *Russian embassies to the Georgian Kings*, Cambridge, 1970, Vol. I, p. 237). Hence, in a generally pejorative sense, Persians.

[3] Russ. *slovo i delo*, meaning literally 'word and deed'. The phrase connoted a highly repressive system of encouraging citizens to denounce suspected subversives to the authorities. The system, and therefore the phrase, were in wide use in the time of Peter the Great (1682–1725). The words would have been almost meaningless in this context at the time of the events described, so their use here is evidence that the inserted material cannot be much, if at all, older than the Remezov material (see Introduction, p. 28).

[4] Probably not the September following the August of a few lines higher, for it would imply moving 1800 km, upstream, in 27 days. There are severe dating problems in this chronicle (see Introduction, p. 7).

6. On the 9th day of May they finished building in the stronghold the promised chapel dedicated to St Nicholas the Miracle Worker. Some went with Yermak down the Sylva to the mouth of the Chyusovaya, while others remained in the stronghold with their wives and children, settling there permanently. As for Yermak with his men at the mouth of the Chyusovaya, they took from Maksim provisions for the upkeep of 5000 men and weapons, and sent up prayers. In 7087 [1579], on the 12th day of June they went up the Chyusovaya to the Tagil portage, fighting all the way. Their guides were Zyrians. Many died, others deserted, and not knowing the way they did not find the mouth of the Serebrenka but passed higher up to the headwaters and had many delays in turning till the very autumn. On reaching the Serebrenka they left their heavy boats on the river and dragged the light boats over the portage on to the Tagil river. They spent the winter in the Buya encampment and were

fed by the Voguls with birds, fish and beasts, the same as they ate themselves. In many encounters Yermak and his men plundered their encampments and seized a quantity of furs. Many light boats were built in sufficient quantity while the old ones, where they now lie, have trees growing through their bottoms.

7. In 87 [1579] the Sovereign Lord Ivan Vasil'yevich heard that Maksim Stroganov had let go those notorious robbers Yermachek Povolskoy with his comrades and had provided them with stores and arms. And so the following letter was written to Maksim about his letting the robbers go free: 'Man, remember with what a great and powerful neighbour you are provoking a quarrel, and if some unnecessary hostility is aroused between us, you do not know what I shall do to you for this. But if something good comes harmlessly out of this, you do not know what you and yours will receive as a favour in your apprehension'.[1] And Maksim received this missive with joy and sorrow and read it with tears. He did not dare to write openly to Yermak about

[1] This seems to be a highly condensed, not to say garbled, version of the royal charter of 16 November 1582 (full text on pp. 293–4), which is also summarised in the Stroganov chronicle, chapter 12. If it is, the date in the chronicle is three years too early.

the bloodshed he was causing but gave it out as though men had come bringing news how in fighting and in everything he was successful, which gladdened him because not in vain had he provided them with provisions and arms, and help, and let them go free. Yet for his expedition with his men in the boats what Yermak took from Maksim was with threats, and not as an honour or a loan, and he wanted to kill him, plunder his stores, utterly ruin his house and his dependants, and confronted Maksim with menaces. Maksim besought them in God's and in the sovereign's name to have the issued provisions accounted for with the undertaking that on their return he should know from whom to take the price of the provisions, and who would pay the exact price or somewhat more. Of that army Ivan Koltsev[1] and his captains shouted the loudest: 'O man, you do not know that even now you are dead, we shall take you and shoot you to bits. Give us against a receipt by roll of names on to the boats, by companies for 5000 men in all, 3 pounds of gunpowder and lead and a gun for each man by name, and three regimental cannon, 3 poods[2] of rye flour, one pood of dried bread, 2 poods of cereals and oatmeal, one pood of salt, two half-carcasses of meat, and some poods of oil, and regimental banners with icons, one banner to every hundred men'.

[1] Koltso in the Stroganov and Yesipov chronicles.
[2] One pood equals 36 lb or 16·38 kg.

8. Maksim was seized with fear,[1] and with his dependants opened the granaries, and day and night issued the demanded quantity on to the boats according to the names and weights given by the regimental scribes. The boats could not hold all the loads and began to sink near the bank. So they raised the sides of the boats, lightened the quantity of stores in each boat, and having completed this task and taken council among themselves set out on their way on the 13th day of June, peacefully and all of them promising Maksim: 'If God sets us on the way of acquiring booty and of remaining in good health, on our return we

---

[1] It is this sentiment, as expressed in the preceding chapter and this one, that provides the basis for the theory (see Introduction, p. 5) that the Stroganovs did not 'summon' the cossacks, but were used by them. But the unknown author of these chapters, who was writing about a century after the events, might have had anti-Stroganov or pro-cossack views. From the last part of this chapter, he sounds as if he might have been a cossack.

shall pay and reward you. But if we are killed may your love have a service said for our eternal rest, yet we hope to return to our fathers and mothers'. And in Yermak's stronghold there are Zyrians with their wives, and the books of their scribes; and the record of their having lived there, with the names and patronymics of the families is to be found even today in the Stroganovs' treasury. Yermak had two comrades of the same age as himself – Ivan Koltsev and Ivan Groza, also Bogdan Bryazga and four elected captains, as many regimental scribes, and trumpeters and fifers, kettle-drummers and drummers, commanders of hundreds and fifties, and of tens, and the rank and file and standard bearers, and three priests, and a wandering monk who did not wear black robes but kept to the rules, and cooked porridge, and knew about the stores, and about church services all the year round.[1] Punishment for crimes was whipping; and for whoever might think of leaving them and betraying them, not wanting to stay, there was the Don law: his shirt was filled with sand, he was tied up in a sack and thrown into the river. This made all Yermak's men staunch, though more than twenty were drowned with sand and stones in the Sylva. Lechery and foulness were severely forbidden and held in detestation among them, and a sinner, after having been washed, was to be kept three days chained up.[2]

[1] The Christianity versus paganism aspect of the campaign was always prominent; it was not just thought up later by Savva Yesipov. This picture shows (as do many others) a banner carrying the image of the Virgin or of a Saint.

[2] The first insertion from the Short Kungur Siberian chronicle ends here.

9. Yermak heard from many of the Chyusovaya people about Sibir´, said to belong to a king; beyond the mountain[1] rivers flow in two directions – into Russia and into Sibir´; beyond the portage, the rivers Nitsa, Tagil and Tura flow into the Tobol. Along them live the Voguls who travel by reindeer; on the Tura and Tobol also live Tatars who travel in boats and on horseback. And the Tobol flows into the Yrtysh, and on the Irtysh is a kingdom near its mouth and many Tatars. The Irtysh empties into the Ob´; and the river Ob´ empties into the sea by two estuaries.[2] Along it live Ostyaks and Samoyeds who drive with reindeer

---

[1] Russ. *kamen´*, rock – the usual word for the Urals.
[2] In the picture, north is at the bottom (the normal practice for Russian maps of the period), but it is still not quite clear whether the big river on the left is the Ob´ or the Irtysh.

and dogs and feed on fish.[1] On the steppe there are Kalmucks and Mongols and the Kazakh Horde who ride on camels and feed from their cattle.

[1] The reindeer sledges are of course Samoyed. But the man mounted on a reindeer may be the artist's fancy, for that practice has been observed only much further east, among the Tungus.

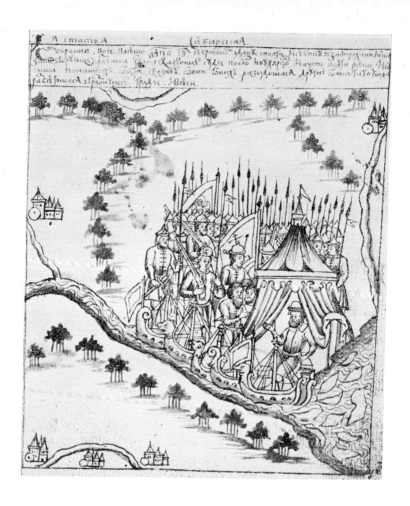

10. In the years 7086 and 7087 [1578 and 1579] the warriors with Yermak gathered from the Don, the Volga and the Yeik, and Astrakhan' and Kazan', and robbed and destroyed the royal treasure boats, and envoys, and men from Bukhara, at the estuary of the Volga. On hearing about men sent by the tsar to punish them some left, and many others dispersed to various towns and villages.[1]

[1] With this chapter the story begins again, after the insertion. There is some overlap. In the picture, the highly stylised tent, which occurs also in many later pictures, must owe more to some western pictorial influence than to reality.

11. Yermak fled up the Volga and the Kama, and on reaching the stronghold of Orel took from the Stroganovs many supplies and arms, and took guides and fled along the Chyusovaya and the Serebrenka rivers to the portage.[1] They dragged the boats on to the Tagil, the portage taking two days to cover, and abandoned some of the boats on the spot.

[1] Müller reports (1750, pp. 102–3) that local people in his time, i.e. 150 years after the event, recounted the story that Yermak's men had great difficulty with the shallow water; they were said to have temporarily dammed the stream with sails, thus raising the water level enough to float the boats further upstream.

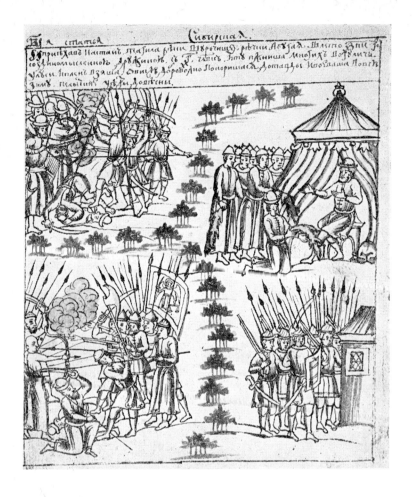

12. In the year 7088 [1580] he arrived with his staunch company of 3000[1] at the encampment on the river Tagil in the valley of the small river Abugay,[2] and there captured many settlements of the Voguls and took prisoners, while others voluntarily submitted as far as the Tavda. They warred in the Pelym districts throughout the entire winter till the spring.

[1] If the numbers are to be taken seriously, one may wonder how 5000 dropped to 3000 just in ascending the Chusovaya.
[2] Müller (1750, p. 106) identifies this with the Barancha, a tributary of the Tagil.

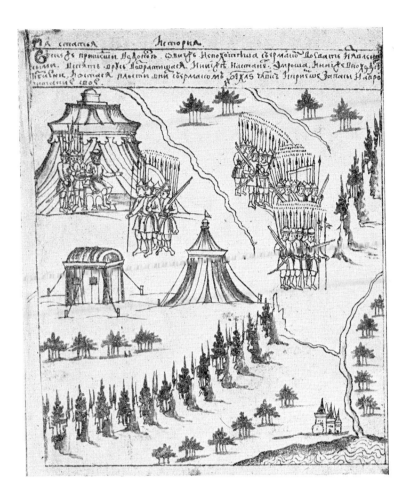

13. With spring came the flood waters, and some did not wish to fight on with Yermak and, covered with wounds, returned to Russia. Others died in the camps, and still others were killed during expeditions, while 1636[1] men remained to sail downstream wih Yermak, having laid in supplies for their subsistence.

[1] This further loss of nearly half the men, before any serious fighting had taken place, seems to discredit this part of the story still more.

14. When spring came the brave cossacks, seeing and realising that the Siberian land was rich and abounding in all things, and that the people there were not warlike, sailed down the Tagil on the first day of May. They plundered boats on the Tura until they reached the first prince Yepancha where now stands Yepanchin Useninovo.[1] Here many infidels had gathered and fighting began that lasted many days, for the river bend is large, three days' travel upstream, and on this river bend they fought till they made their way out, and the cossacks won.

---

[1] Near the later town of Turinsk, which Müller notes (1750, p. 108) was nick-named Yepanchin in his time.

15. They warred throughout the summer. On the first day of August they took Tyumen', which is Chingid[1] and killed the khan Chingyz,[2] and captured great stores and riches. Here they spent the winter because on the Tura they had seen multitudes of pagans and dared not sail to Tobol'sk.[3]

[1] The pre-Russian name; Chingiy or Chingiden in the other chronicles.
[2] The local chief, presumably; probably a Tatar who was not subject to Kuchum (see chapter 30 below).
[3] The site of Tobol'sk is meant, of course. The town was founded after the events described.

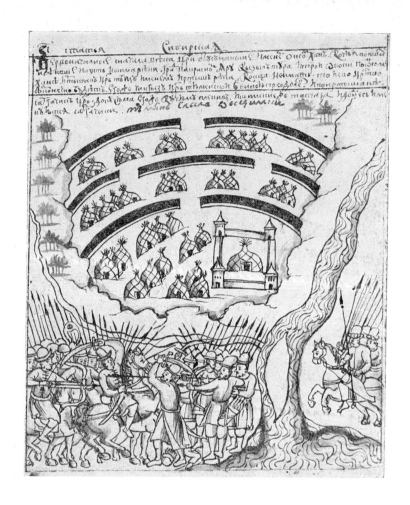

16. From the beginning of time these were the names of the infidel kings: Onsom Khan nomadised along the Ishim and lived at the mouth of this river, with a town on the Krasnyy Yar, Kyzyl Tura,[1] and three earthworks. After Onsom there was Khan Irtyshak: in this name the river Irtysh has no ending, and so would his reign be endless. However Khan Chingyz of Tyumen' defeated him in war.[2] After Irtyshak there was Khan Sargachik till Kuchyum captured him. The Tatars of Ishim are to this day called Sargachiks. Tyumen' was called Ontsimki.[3]

[1] Now Ust' Ishim. The first capital of what the Russians came to call the Khanate of Sibir' was Chingid above, the second was Kyzyl-Tura, the third and last Isker, or Sibir'. A *yar* is the steep bank of a river.

[2] A distant recollection of the great Chingis Khan?

[3] The houses in the picture are clearly Tatar tents, but, as with the Russian ones, stylised. The artist is not consistent. Later, he has Tatars living in 'Russian' tents.

17. Khan Mamet' defeated Alim, the khan of Kazan', and built the
town of Kashlyk at the mouth of the small river Sibirka, extending his
kingdom in Sibir' and bringing the peoples into submission.[1] From that
time greater fame came to Sibir' and to her khans about whom their
infidel history recounts.

[1] The people 'brought into submission' are presenting fur tribute to the conqueror. The Russian artist might have been simply depicting submission in the
way he knew it was practised in his time; but it is also true that the Tatars exacted fur tribute before the Russians arrived. All mentions of tribute in this
chronicle refer to fur tribute.

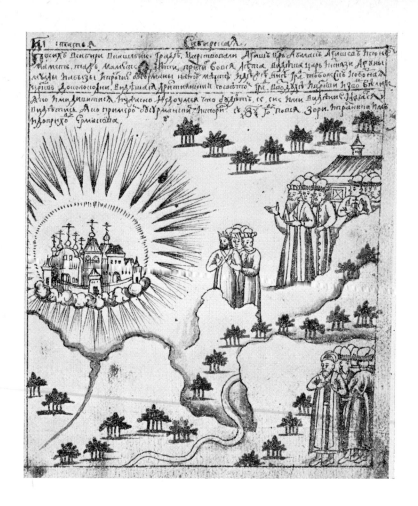

18. After them there reigned in Sibir', in the city of Kashlyk Khan Agish, his son Abalak, and after him Mamet', then the sons of Mamet'. Under them throughout the years the kings and princes, the chanters, the mullahs and preachers and other infidels kept seeing on the site of present day Tobol'sk with its cathedral and bell-tower, a vision of a shining Christian city up in the air, with churches and a great ringing of bells, which aroused wonder and great perplexity about what this might be. According to histories of the infidels they began to see this vision since the year 7060 [1552] every day at dawn and at every festival of theirs before the coming of Yermak.[1]

[1] The chronicler, with the full exercise of hindsight, dates the cracking of morale from the fall of Kazan'. Perhaps he was right.

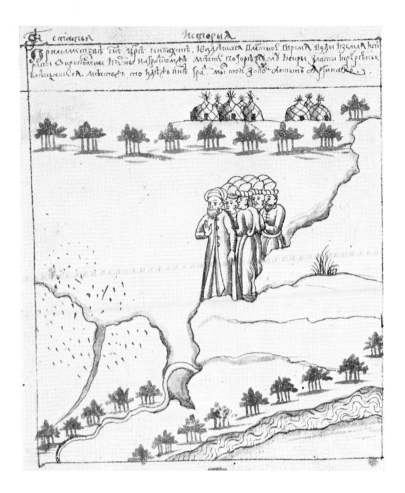

19. Under Senbakht, son of Mamet', there were visions in summer time of waters and land, and grasses, bloodstained and blackened, while on the site of the city hill and dale glistened with sparks of gold and silver, this site being now where the city stands, and the headland is called Altyn Yarginak.[1]

[1] Meaning 'the golden place of judgement'.

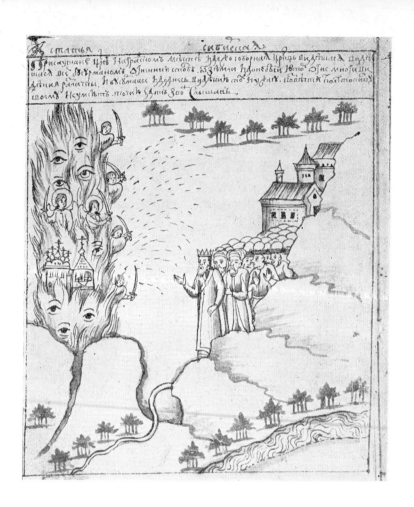

20. Under Khan Sauskan,[1] in the city square where now stands the cathedral, there appeared to all the infidels a pillar of fire reaching from the ground to the sky with various apparitions within the flames.[2] And to this day the infidels, according to their chronicler, are unable to relate about this vision and terror, only that ringing of bells had been heard.

[1] The other chronicles mention a place of this name, just outside Sibir', but not a man. There could have been both, as in the case of Abalak nearby, but there is no other evidence for the man.

[2] Bakhrushin (1955, p. 36) suggests that this was an auroral display; possible, but not specially likely, for at this location the frequency of such displays is only about five times a year (C. Störmer, *The Polar aurora*, Oxford, 1955, p. 15). Some may seek to associate the bell ringing also with aurora; but whether any sound accompanies aurora is still under debate (see D. R. Bates, 'Auroral sound', *Polar Record*, No. 107, 1974, pp. 103–8).

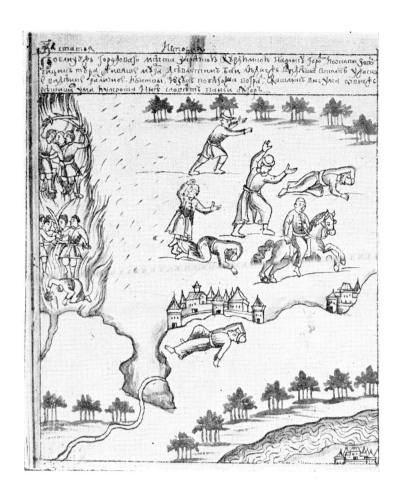

21. Close by the site of the city, beyond the small river Kurdumka, on a headland are a town and earthworks called Batsik-Tura, and there lived *murza* Devletim Bay. The people seeing in the pillar of fire various terrible visions and battles and noise fled into the town of Kashlyk beside themselves, and some lost their minds and died. Today it is called Paney Bugor.

22. Khan Kuchyum came from the Kazakh Horde with many warriors and defeated the king and the princes Yetiger and Bekbulat, and became renowned as the khan of Sibir'. He took much tribute from many peoples of the lowlands, and multiplied his strongholds in many places, naming them as his possessions.

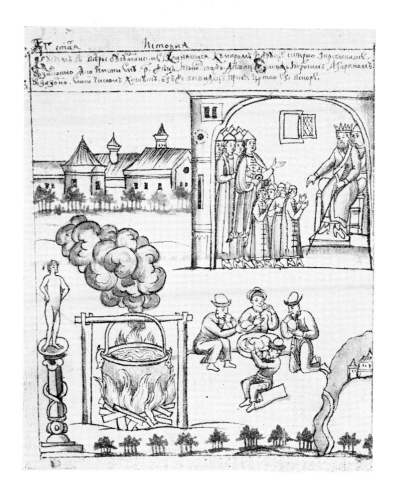

23. Kuchyum was of the infidel faith, worshipping idols and eating unclean foods. He led a sinful life for he had 100 wives, and youths as well as maidens, which is also permissible to the other infidels in whatever number they desire. But God the all-seeing soon put an end to his reign.

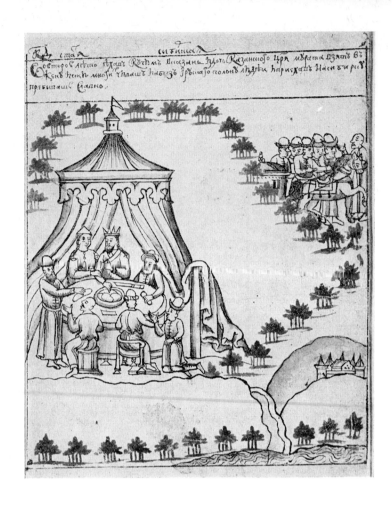

24. In the second year Kuchyum went to Kazan' and took to wife the daughter of Murat, the Khan of Kazan, taking with her many Chuvash and mullahs and Russian captives, and on returning to the Sibirka led a glorious life.

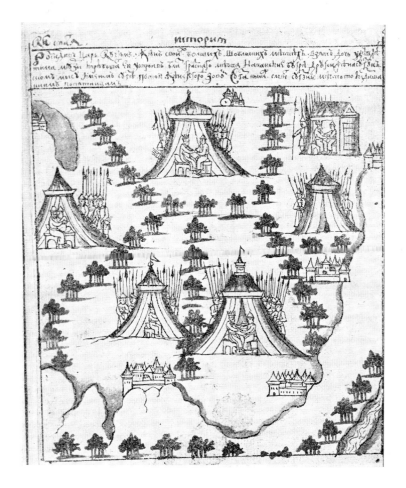

25. Khan Kuchyum placed his principal wives in near-by settlements, and having married the daughter of Devletim *murza* set up a residence for her near the city, on the Pan'in Bugor, and for another one on the Suzgun headland. Her name was Suzga from which the town took its name Suzga. Now this place is called Suzgun. And he visited them on Fridays.[1]

[1] The holy day in the week for Mohammedans. The chronicler probably got this information from a Mohammedan source.

26. Under Kuchyum the above-mentioned vision appeared to the infidels at all times so that such manifestations greatly frightened them. And they began to consult the soothsayers as to what was going to happen and to question the captives about what this vision meant to the Russians. The soothsayers and the captives of one accord foretold to Kuchyum that God would soon give the place to the Christians, and drive him out, and he would come to an evil end. And so it happened. But for this he ordered many to be put to death.

27. Also in Kuchyum's time there was a vision: at the confluence of the great rivers Tobol and Irtysh there is a large sandy island, and often at noon there appeared to the infidels two beasts coming out of the Tobol and the Yrtysh on either side of the island and moving towards the middle where they fought one another in a great fight. The Irtysh beast was white and large and hairy, being the size of an ox and in form like a wolf. The Tobol beast was small and black, like a harrier. It overpowered the large beast, left it for dead and went into the water, while the large beast came to life and went into the water.

28. Many saw this apparition, as well as Kuchyum himself with his men, and he questioned his chanters, mullahs and soothsayers on its meaning. They said to him: 'The great beast is your kingdom while the small one is the Russian warrior, and it will soon happen that he will kill and capture and plunder and seize your towns'. Kuchyum ordered them to be dragged by horses over the fields.

29. Now let us return to the aforesaid, for of that we must speak. Yermak was staying in Chingid and his troops were temporarily reduced by scurvy and stomach disorders. As for Kuchyum, he was campaigning on the Kamysh[1] with all his troops. They thanked God that they had acquired large quantities of dried fish, barley and spelt.[2]

[1] Perhaps identifiable with the river Kamyshlov in chapter 129 below (see Map I opposite p. 18).
[2] *Triticum spelta*, a cereal crop now seldom grown.

30. As spring was drawing near the time had come for Kuchyum to collect the tribute from his subjects, sables and foxes, and other beasts, and fish. He sent his courtier Kutugay to the Tarkhany stronghold to Tarkhan *murza*. Kutugay came to make the collection, and the cossacks captured him in Tarkhany. Tarkhany was a fortified customs stronghold belonging to Kuchyum and not to Chingyz. They brought him to Yermak with the tribute.

31. Yermak questioned him in fitting manner about Khan Kuchyum and all about his people, praising them and saying that he had come as a guest. The cossacks exhibited their prowess and gun-fire, and their five *atamans*. Never having seen cossacks before they were filled with wonder, and told him everything in detail about Kuchyum and the inhabitants. Yermak dismissed him with honour to return to Kuchyum with greetings, and sent a trident,[1] gifts for all the wives, greetings to the princes and *murzas* and other people, and said that he would be returning to Russia.

[1] While the Russian word used (*trezub*) unquestionably means trident, the object in Yermak's hand (and in Kutugay's in the next picture) seems to be more like a sword with a serrated edge. Somewhat similar swords existed in the Middle East about this time. The word trident is no doubt used because it was the symbol of state power; a trident was depicted on the coinage of St Vladimir, Prince of Kiev (died 1015).

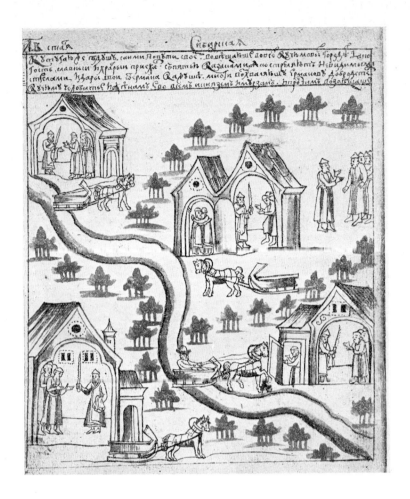

32. Kutugay, travelling by sledge,[1] announced on his way in all Kuchyum's towns that a valiant guest had arrived with five cossacks who shot invisible arrows. He showed his many gifts received from Yermak, praising his virtue and telling about the greetings to Kuchyum, his wives, the princes and *murzas* and the rest.

[1] The sledge type, and the manner of harnessing the horse, appear in the picture to be Russian rather than Tatar.

33. When Kutugay returned to Kuchyum he entered his residence in colourful Russian clothing, but brought no fur tribute, telling how he had been captured by Yermak and questioned. He described the invisible shooting by the five cossacks which he had witnessed, conveyed the greetings and handed over the trident for him and the gifts for the wives, relating all this with wonder and great awe.

34. After hearing him out Kuchyum accepted the trident and the greetings in all honour, but became distressed and very sad and sent orders throughout his possessions to assemble all his subjects living in towns, while he himself with his soothsayers began to question the future as to what was going to happen to them. And all realised that the warrior prince Yermak would not return to Russia but would soon come to them and plunder them.

35. Yermak was living in the town of Chingid, and when navigation
on the rivers was reopened he sailed on the 9th day of May of the year
7089 [1581] down the Tura making speed with all skill. When he
reached the mouth of the Tura six princelings under Maitmas, Kaskar
and Varvarinna were lying in wait there, and they fought for many days.

36. Of Yermak's warriors there remained with him 1060 men. They killed many infidels whom they overcame with God's help. And they took so much booty that the boats could not carry it, so they buried these possessions in the ground at the mouth of the river Tura.

37. After the first battle with Kuchyum's men they sailed on the 8th day of June down the river Tobol, fighting and living on the alert. When they reached the landmark[1] of Berezoviy Yar a great battle was fought lasting many days. The infidels were like sheep rushing out of their folds but with God's help and the manifestation of heavenly hosts they too were defeated.

[1] Russ. *urochishche*, a natural boundary, clearly not a river here (see p. 70, note 5), since *yar* means a steep bank; but possibly a nomad camp ground, the alternative meaning. The same word is used in chapter 38.

131

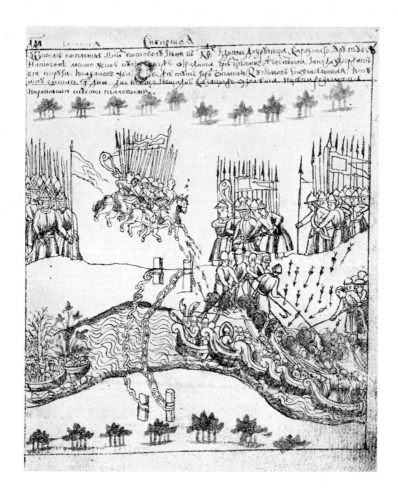

38. From there they sailed down the Tobol on the 29th day of June and reached the landmark of Karaulniy Yar. Here the Tobol is narrow. Kuchyum's men had barred the way with iron chains so as to halt the boats and kill the cossacks. Here, too, was situated a fortified town of Kuchyum, that of the captain Alyshay, and here they fought mercilessly for three days and nights. The cossacks overcame the enemy, broke the chains and sailed through the osiers.[1]

[1] Müller (1750, p. 112) records a story, current among local Russians in his time (c. 1740), of a ruse employed by Yermak to get past this barricade. Sending his boats downstream with dummy figures aboard in cossack clothing, he himself with most of his men went ashore and took the Tatars from the rear. This sounds like the sort of story one might expect to grow up round a popular folk hero – and it is apparently still current (see Introduction, p. 17).

132

39. On reaching the mouth of the Tavda they stayed there a week, deliberating on how to go back with guides up the Tavda and return by way of the mountains and the Voguls.[1]

[1] This statement seems to reflect another crisis in morale – a subject about which the chronicler is rather frank (see chapters 8 and 13 above, 59 below). But one can well understand how some might have thought at this point that the odds against them were just too high.

40. Bearers of news came ceaselessly to Kuchyum telling him of
the great gathering of cossacks and of their own defeat and ruin, and
exhibited their wounds from halberds and swords. Kuchyum com-
miserated with them, and his rage against the cossacks grew.

41. Yermak, together with his adherents, relying on God's help sailed down the Tobol on the 8th day of July and reached Babasan *murza*.[1] Here the infidels seized Yermak's scouting boat about a verst ahead of the others. The cossacks fell upon them in full force, and attacked so splendidly that many of the enemy were killed on the spot while the others soon fled and dispersed; and here they quickly rescued their own men unharmed.

[1] Babasan, or Bobasan, was a river in the other chronicles. But, as in so many other cases, there is also a man of the same name.

42. The assembled forces of the Chuvash, the Kazakh Horde, the
Voguls, the Ostyaks and all the Tatars were sent out of the city by
Kuchyum with his son Mametkul down the Tobol against Yermak, while
he himself had a barrage[1] built near Chyuvashi on the river Irtysh,
strengthening the barriers with trenches and posting a strong guard at
the mouth of the Tobol.

[1] The same word (*zaseka*) is used here as in the Stroganov chronicle, chapter
15, and the Yesipov chronicle, chapters 8 and 11, where it is translated as barricade. There it was apparently thought of as being on land, for it is described as
'by the side of the river' and 'heaped up with earth'. But the picture here, and in
later chapters, shows that this chronicler, or this artist, had in mind a barrier
across the river. This would be quite logical, as it would prevent the Russian
boats from passing; and a shallow enough place could no doubt be found, even on
the broad Irtysh.

136

43. The force sent out under the khan's heir Mametkul came up against Yermak on the 21st day of July at Babasany, at the mouth of a lake on the Tobol. They fought mercilessly hand to hand, slashing one another, so that horses were up to their bellies in the blood and corpses of the unbelievers. The battle lasted five days on the same spot, the boats being prevented from sailing downstream. Then with God's help the cossacks got the upper hand and put the others to flight; the khan's heir also fled. Then at the apparition of St Nicholas the Miracle-Worker he ordered them to venture, and they proceeded downstream.

44. They reached the mouth of the Turba, the limit of Dolgiy Yar,[1] on the 26th day of July at sunrise and saw a multitude of infidels stationed there awaiting Yermak's arrival. The cossacks were much alarmed and halted at an island upstream from the Yar. They deliberated and prayed hopefully to the Holy Trinity, the Blessed Mother of God and to all the saints.

[1] These small natural features, whether tributaries or steep banks, have mostly not been identified.

45. And there appeared the Saviour, whose image on the banner, beloved by the cossacks, moved of its own accord and advanced downstream along the left bank of the Tobol river. Seeing this, Yermak and the cossacks, rowing as one man along that bank, followed it. The pagans shot from the hill at the boats innumerable arrows, like rain, but, saved by God, Yermak and his men sailed past this place without a hair being harmed. And when they had sailed past, the banner took up its usual place by itself.

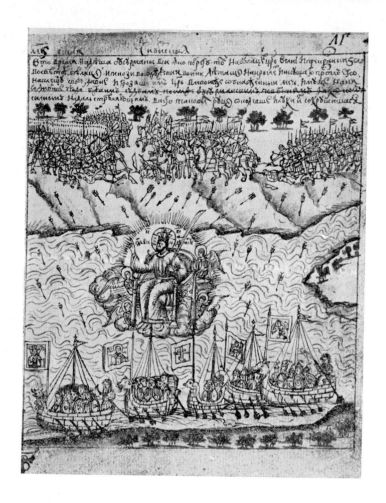

46. Then all the infidels saw how along that bank there appeared on clouds the great and wonderfully beautiful king[1] in a bright light with many winged warriors flying and bearing his throne on their shoulders while the king threatened them with a naked sword in his left hand. O wonderful miracle! According to the infidels' own accounts, the arms of those strong in archery who shot at him from afar went dead by divine fate and their bows were shattered.

[1] The inscription reads 'Jesus Christ Almighty Lord'.

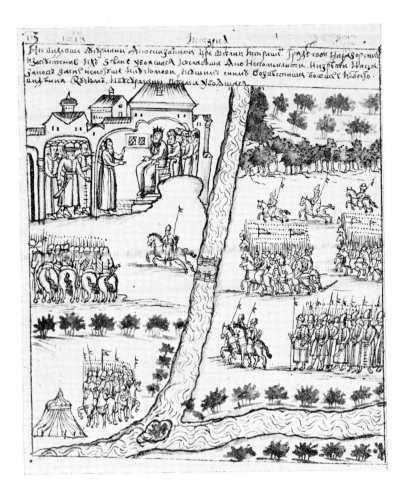

47. When the infidels saw that with the cossacks a great and terrible king was coming with a host to ruin and destroy them, they were terrified and weakened, so that they could no longer plot against the cossacks or look at them. And Kuchyum's men and those with him reported the happening, and Kuchyum and the infidels were filled with a great fear by this vision.

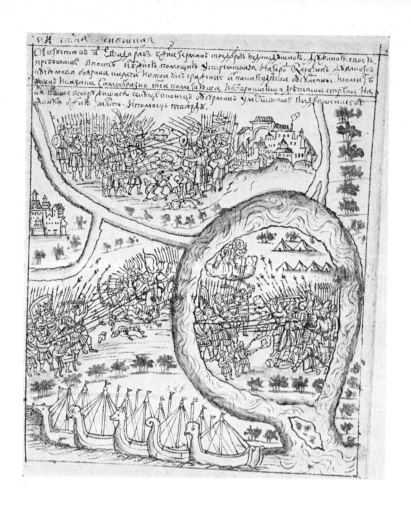

48. On the first day of August God's servant German with his excellent and faithful company, fasting and with God's help, attacked Karacha's town, Karacha being a noble of Kuchyum's council. And in that hour of battle the infidels, as well as German himself and the cossacks, saw the figure of Christ giving assistance and turning aside the arrows flying at them, and with redoubled strength the cossacks fought and killed the infidels, seeing upon themselves the manifest grace of God and his powerful aid.

49. In the year of 87 [1579][1] Yermak was with his company and saw a great number of Kuchyum's men assembled on Karacha's lake and massed like rippling waters. He drove *murza* Karacha from the island on the first day of August, and having formed the desire to return to Russia rowed up the Tavda river, warring all the way from its mouth upstream with the Krasnoyar and the Kalyma districts and with Labutan with other princelings, fighting ceaselessly and without turning back, as far as the Pachenka. Here a great battle took place, and many cossacks were wounded whom the Tatars despatched to the last man, killing also the princeling Pecheneg. They filled with the corpses the lake which is to this day called Bannoye Poganoye[2] and is full of human bones.

[1] Obviously this date is wrong; the other chronicles, and the earlier parts of this one, contradict it. 1582 is likelier. This chapter is the start of another insertion. Remezov's own account of these incidents is in chapters 89 and 90. The excursion up the Tavda was much more likely after the capture of Sibir'.

[2] Meaning 'the unclean bath'.

143

50. From there they rowed up the Tavda, and on the 6th day of
August arrived in Koshuni,[1] to Koshuk, a Vorlyak[2] princeling, and
captured the chief captain Ichimek whom they questioned about whether
there were any fighting men. He informed Yermak about everything.
Yermak killed some of them and levied tribute. They were filled with a
great fear and came submissively with the tribute. All these provinces,
including Chandyr, he subdued by force and by agreement with their
elders. In the stronghold of Chandyr a great worshipping of idols takes
place at which their shaman can perform miracles through demons by
evoking them with sacrifices. They bind the accursed one tightly and
plunge a sword or a knife into his belly right through, and keep him tied
up until he has given answers to everyone. Then they draw the sword or

[1] Koshuki in chapter 90. The man gives his name to the place.
[2] Probably an error for Votyak (see Introduction, p. 23).

144

knife out of his body, and the shaman gets up, fills his cupped hands with his blood, drinks it and smears himself with it and becomes whole again with no wound showing.[1]

[1] Compare what Richard Johnson saw among the Samoyeds in 1556: 'Then hee tooke a sworde of a cubite and a spanne long, (I did mete it my selfe) and put it into his bellie halfeway and sometime lesse, but no wounde was to bee seene, (they continuing in their sweete song still). Then he put the sworde into the fire till it was warme, and so thrust into the slitte of his shirte and thrust it through his bodie, as I thought, in at his navill and out at his fundament; the poynt beeing out of his shirt behind, I layde my finger upon it, then hee pulled out the sworde and sate downe'. Reported by Richard Hakluyt (1598–1600, Vol. I, p. 284).

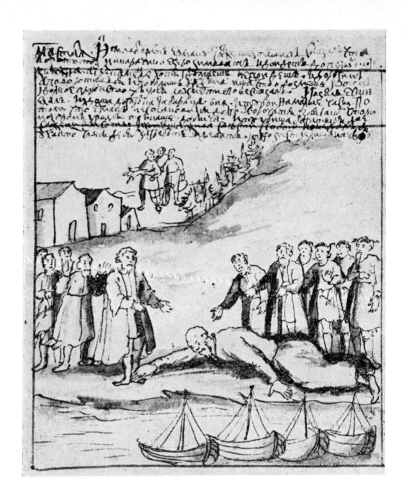

51. And about Yermak's return the shaman said that Yermak would go back to Karacha's lake for the winter, and would go as far as the princeling of Pelym, but 'as for the mountain range, though you have it in mind, you will not cross it, there is no way, so you will turn back and conquer Kuchyum and take the kingdom.' And this prophecy of the idolater was fulfilled but he said nothing about his death. So he took the tribute and left. They reached the town of Tabarintsa Biy but the fighting here was brief for Yermak did not linger even to collect the tribute: what he seized in passing was our spoil.[1] Here he killed a giant warrior two *sazhens* tall. He had wanted to take him away alive but the giant did not surrender: he would seize in his arms some ten men and crush them, so they shot him for a wonder.

[1] Perhaps evidence that this phrase at least came from an eye-witness account.

52. They reached the Pelym princeling Patlik and started a fight with him, great as to numbers and futile noise, for it was only peasants who had gathered to fight, while their wives and children had been taken some distance away beyond the river Konda, to an inaccessible place. Only a few warriors had remained by the fisheries, and these Yermak and his men killed to the last man.[1] Questioning revealed that there was no road across the mountains to Russia. They returned down the Tavda river on the 4th day of October, levied a tribute of corn and arrived at Karacha's winter quarters with many dry provisions, letting those who had brought them go back to their homes. That levy was the first corn tribute in Tobol'sk, and to this day corn and money and furs are collected in the way Yermak had ordered it. And they came to

[1] It is not clear whether this is the same incident as that described in the Stroganov chronicle, chapter 12.

148

Karacha's on the 8th day of November, and always tried to attack Kuchyum, but the hour by God's will had not yet come. All were on their guard, and stopped thinking about their plans and campaign, taking tribute of fish and meat for food, and sheltering themselves in the villages.[1]

[1] The second insertion from the Short Kungur Siberian Chronicle ends here.

53. They seized Karacha's town, and in it countless treasure, gold and silver, and precious stones and pearls, and money in quantity, and cattle, and remained there two weeks of the Assumption fast.[1] They kept fervently praying and fasting, ardently entreating the Lord to keep them alive and grant victory over the infidels so that the Christian race should be exalted and glorified to the ends of the earth and that God's hand should stretch over the true tsar.

[1] 1–15 August, old style.

150

54. As for Kuchyum and his infidels, in his great terror he placed
permanent guards on all the roads up to Karachino[1] so that none of the
cossacks could even fly past like a bird. He thought that seeing such
determination the cossacks would return to Russia in fear of superior
strength, and many spies watched the cossacks in order to kill them and
to see how they lived in their fortified places, but on catching sight of a
mounted cossack patrol on the road they were afraid of them.

[1] or Karacha's town. Because place and man often had the same name, it is
difficult to know whether words like Karachino or Karachin are essentially the
adjective of the man's name, or the true place-name of the geographical feature.

55. A prophetic sign was given to Kuchyum and the entire infidel host over the place where now stand the holy town of Tobolesk and the cathedral: a vision appeared in a bright cloud with sounds and ringing of bells and many apparitions as if showing the destruction of Kuchyum's people by a pillar of fire. Kuchyum greatly feared the Russian warriors after the first warnings of the soothsayers whom he himself had put to death. He understood how it had been no fault of theirs that he had not listened to them, because the signs had been seen daily just before Yermak's coming and not as previously only at festivals and gatherings.[1]

---

[1] The frequency of the reported heavenly signs is another argument against their being an auroral display. See p. 114, note 2.

56. The beasts already mentioned in chapters 23 and 24[1] that came out of the river on to the island were seen a few days before Yermak's coming by the guards placed at the mouth of the Tobol to hold back the cossacks and kill them. As usual the beasts came at noon out of the river on to the island and started a fierce fight, their bodies being torn worse than before. And the small beast having killed the large white one and seen it dead fled from it to a meadow on a spit of land and was seen no more.

[1] Evidently a superseded numbering of paragraphs. Should be 27.

57. The white beast that had been killed lay on the island in the sight of the infidels for three days. On the fourth day they set out in a small boat wishing to take a look at the wonderful beast as it lay dead, but when they were midstream in the Irtysh, preparing to approach the bank, the dead beast suddenly sprang up and with a terrible roar, plunged into the river and sank, while all those who had come to look at it were drowned. This has led the infidels to delude themselves about Sibir' because their shaikhs explained to them in their records that as the small beast was Yermak, and the infidels were the large beast which came back to life after three days, the unbelievers would take Sibir' only for a short time. And they delude themselves about this in Tobol'sk to this day, making attempts to grasp it and causing many difficulties for the inhabitants of Sibir' by their story.

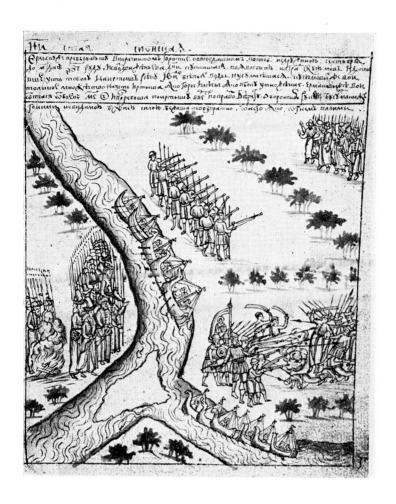

58. Yermak, who was living in Karacha's stronghold in constant
fasting with his company till the 14th day of September 7090 [1581],[1]
set out against Kuchyum's city on the day of the Raising of the Cross.
When they had sailed to the mouth of the Tobol on the Irtysh and saw
the white waters they were seized with doubt. Kuchyum's warriors were
as numerous at the mouth of the Irtysh as mountains and forests, as
countless as sands, while of Yermak's force there remained after the
battles 45 men.[2] So they rowed up the Irtysh along the right bank with
weapons in their hands while the infidels, pursued by God's invisible
might, fled from them without looking back as though burnt by flames.

[1] 1582 is likelier. The next few dates are all probably a year out.
[2] This really is pitching it a bit strong. The main battle is still to come.

155

59. Yermak went on with the cossacks to the tents[1] beyond the island and there captured the stronghold of Atik *murza*, taking refuge in it with all their possessions to withstand a siege. They spent the whole night without sleep and much exercised in their minds, some wishing and attempting to flee to Russia, others taking the decision: 'when we were robbers in Russia, we killed our own Christians on the Volga and wished to die; we were of one mind and died; where are we to go now that winter is near? Yermak and the elders are here, and it behoves us to die bravely like Christians for the Christian faith so that God may glorify our race now and in times to come'.

[1] Russ. *yurta*, the felt tent of the steppe nomad; though the picture shows no such thing.

60. And they all remained in Atik's stronghold in deep apprehension for they saw a multitude of infidels which could mean one man fighting against ten or twenty warriors, and this stronghold was surrounded as by a dark cloud. In the main square where the cathedral stands now Yermak and those with him saw the following vision: they saw a pillar of fire and a town with a ringing of bells mounting to the clouds, and a finger pointing to the square, so they understood that God wished to glorify this site with His holy and glorious name.

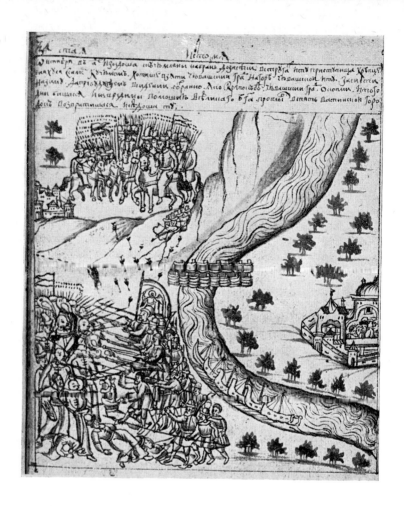

61. On the first day of October they sallied forth in their boats up to
the barrage to fight Kuchyum's men, and here they made a strong attack,
fighting Kuchyum himself, for they wished to seize the Chyuvash town
on the Chyuvash hill in order to entrench there for the winter 'so that we
could withstand a siege there in safety,' the Chyuvash town being well
defended by trenches. They fought on that day and sailed unharmed
with the help of the great God back to Atik's stronghold, and settled
down there.

62. They stayed in Atik's stronghold many days sallying forth up to the barrage and returning to the stronghold. Keeping in mind the winter and the need for food they collected a small quantity of barley, spelt and oats.

63. All the cossacks decided on a final blow, and this was the fourth battle with Kuchyum's men. Kuchyum was standing on the hill with his son Mametkul by the barrage when the cossacks by God's will issued forth from the town saying of one accord: 'God is with us! Understand this, ye peoples, and submit, for God is with us!' And all together they joined battle, and the fighting was terrible on the 23rd day of October, hand to hand, foe cutting down foe. Kuchyum was shooting from the hill while the cossacks raked them with their fire so that they died of wounds or were killed. The unbelievers, driven by Kuchyum, suffered great losses at the hands of the cossacks, they lamented, fought unwillingly, and died.

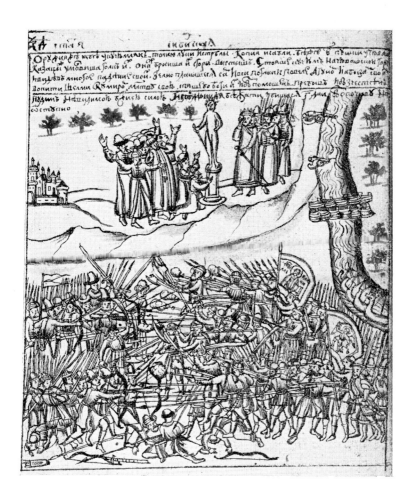

64. Kuchyum's men had no guns, only bows and arrows, spears and
swords. The Chyuvash[1] had two cannon which the cossacks silenced, so
they hurled these down the hill into the Yrtysh. Kuchyum as he stood on
the Chuvash hill saw the carnage wrought among his men and lamented
with all the unbelievers and ordered his chanters and mullahs to shout
their prayers to their idols because their gods were asleep. Helpless and
dishonoured, hard pressed by God's might he meditated flight. They
fought on ceaselessly for three days without respite.

[1] Either the term is used as a synonym for Tatar, or there were some genuine
Chuvash fighting with Kuchum. More likely the latter, for the place where the
battle was fought clearly had Chuvash connexions.

65. On the 24th day of October the Ostyak princelings of the lower reaches were the first to disobey Kuchyum's orders and fled on horseback to their homeland without return, to live there like animals in wild forests keeping out of sight of the Russian people. And to this day it is their custom to flee and disappear when our people come.[1]

[1] No doubt true; but not for the reasons the chronicler had in mind. It was the excesses associated with collection of fur tribute that later drove the Ostyaks and others into the woods.

66. On the 25th day of October Kuchyum, as he lay on his couch at night weary and sorrowful, had a vision sent by God: the skies suddenly opened at the four corners of the universe and there issued forth to destroy him shining warriors armed, winged, and terrible, who on reaching his residence surrounded the whole of his army saying: 'Unclean son of the dark demon Bakhmet,[1] leave this land, for the land and its fulness is the Lord's and all the Christians living in it are blessed; fly to your habitations near the abyss of the thrice accursed demon Bakhmet.' Kuchyum rose trembling in his whole body and said: 'Let us flee from here, from this terrible place, so as not to perish.' And God's angel drove them along, for the way for them was dark and slippery.

[1] Perhaps a corruption of Makhmet, Mohammed.

67. On the same date, in the evening, the Voguls also secretly abandoned Kuchyum's defences, fleeing to their homes beyond the impassable swamps and lakes of Yaskalba so as not to be tracked down by Yermak and die a cruel death. They took refuge with their families in inaccessible places to remain undiscovered, and to this day a man on skis can see in the overgrown swamps and lakes earth-walls in front and behind.

68. Kuchyum, after seeing in the night vision the final loss of his kingdom and wholesale devastation, fled from his city Kashlyk, which is called Sibir', on the 26th day of October. He secretly rose and said to all his people: 'Let us flee immediately so as not to die a cruel death at the hands of the cossacks.' And without looking back all fled from the city to the steppe, to the Kazakh Horde, to their former habitations, leaving empty the towns of Chuvash and Kashlyk, Suzgun, Bishik, Abalak and others, driven by God's invisible power.

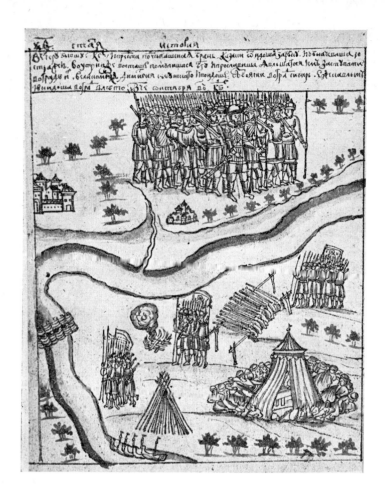

69. On the evening of the 25th the Chuvash battle ceased. The cossacks retired beyond the river and spent the night with guards on the watch. In the morning they rose, prayed to God, glorified the great martyr Demetrius of Salonika who had appeared to defend them in their town, and proceeded without fear to the city of Sibir', otherwise Kashlyk, and entered it in the year 7090 [1581], on the 26th day of October.

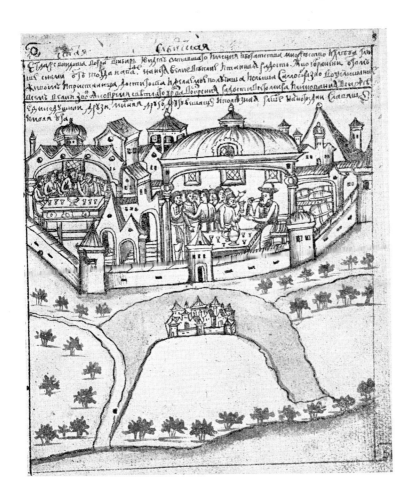

70. When they entered the city of Sibir' and saw the abondoned property and riches and corn, they said: 'God is with us!' Then great joy and inner happiness filled them that God had spared their lives, that they had reached a safe harbour and had their wishes fulfilled. And a wonderful great ringing of bells was heard by all, like on Easter Sunday, to the rejoicing and exultation of the whole world. All friends of one mind gave one another peaceful greetings and good words, throughout many days glorifying God and praying to Him.

71. The rumour about Yermak and the cossacks sped over the entire land of Sibir', and the fear of God seized all the infidels living in that country. And on the fourth day after the taking of Sibir' Boyar, prince of Dem'yan,[1] came to Yermak with many gifts, bringing all needful provisions and delivering tribute. Yermak received them with honour and dismissed them. There also began to come to him Tatars living in the neighbourhood with their wives and children and kinsfolk, bringing tribute. And Yermak ordered them to go on living in their homes as before, as they had done under Kuchyum.

[1] The Dem'yanka river is a tributary of the Irtysh, about 150 km below Sibir'.

72. The cossacks boldly rode to Tatar habitations and fishing and hunting grounds, fearing nothing. Twenty cossacks, who had gone to fish on the Abalak lake on the 5th day of November and were calmly sleeping in the night, were killed by the khan's heir Mametkul. Only one of them escaped to carry the news to Yermak about the killing.

73.[1] In 90 [1582], on the 5th day of March Yermak sent down the
Irtysh to the Dem'yan and Nazym strongholds and districts Bogdan
Bryazga, commander of fifty, with his fifty men to seize all the Nazym
districts and bring them to the true faith, and to collect a poll-tax. On
reaching the first Aremzyan district he attacked and captured the stronghold, and hanged many of the best stalwarts by one leg and shot them.
And he gathered tribute by his sword which he laid bloody on a table
with orders to give a loyal oath of allegiance to the lord tsar to serve him
and to pay tribute every year without fail. And they took from them to
Sibir' the tribute and provision of corn and fish which they sent to the
city. All the natives were seized with terror, and, awed by the threat,
not only dared not lift a hand but even to utter a word in the entire

[2] Chapters 73–80 are another insertion from the Short Kungur Siberian
chronicle.

Nadtsyn district. They reached the Turgay settlement, and those gathered there gave them battle and were immediately defeated, and tribute was soon collected from their princelings and headmen.

74. They rode as far as the mouth of the river Dem'yanka, to their chief, the princeling Demayan. Their town is large and strongly fortified, and 2000 Tatars and Voguls and Ostyaks were gathered there. They attacked for three days but could not penetrate into the stronghold on the hill, and wishing to return, deliberated how to take the place, for roads would soon be unusable and hunger was at hand. They enquired from those who had come with them on carts and with the tribute as to how they prayed. One of them, a Chuvash who had been among the Russian prisoners in Kuchyum's hands said: 'They pray to the Russian god, and this Russian god is cast in gold and sits in a bowl.[1] And they pour water into the bowl and drink it, and call him Christ. It is

[1] Bakhrushin points out (in Müller, 1937, p. 490) that this ritual is a mixture of Ostyak and Christian tradition. Drinking from a golden vessel was a ceremony found in these parts of Asia, and it normally accompanied oath-taking.

172

said that he has been brought from Vladimer's christening and therefore they live without fear. Let me go to them, I can bring him away and shall tell you all about what they are thinking.'

75. He left at night and returned to the camp early in the morning saying: 'They are soothsaying and saying: "it is better for us to surrender alive", and so they have decided. I was unable to take their god for they all sit and pray and stand in front of him, while he is set on a table and around him grease is burning, and they fumigate with sulphur as in a dipper.' When they began advancing up the hill many of the others, seeing their number, fled with their families to their homes belonging to other princes of Roman the Renowned.[1] Those in the town swore allegiance, and the cossacks took tribute and spent the spring there, but could not discover the place of worship.

[1] Russ. *Roman Slavnyy*. His renown, as far as we know, did not extend outside his own territories.

76. At the spring floods they built themselves light boats and sailed downstream collecting tribute from the conquered peoples. As for Roman, their chief prince, he fled from his residence up the Kovda[1] to Pelym with his family by ski and dog-sledge. When they reached the township of Rachevo here the valley devil-priests had gathered people from all the tents in great numbers for prayers to the devil Rach. They fled to the woods to the last man, into the thick fir forest, abandoning their sacrifices. The cossacks waited a day and a night but as the others did not return they went on, collecting tribute on the way.

[2] The Konda is meant.

77. The others had gathered between two rocky promontories on
the Irtysh above the river Tsyn'yala which rushes turbulently through
a narrow place. They thought that their god would not let the cossacks
go down the river in their boats and would stop them there, and they
would then kill them all. They provided themselves with hand-weapons,
boat-hooks, and ropes with hooks, and built a barrage and prepared
ropes to stop them. But Bogdan with his comrades hearing their wicked
gathering halted and prayed. At sunrise they took to the water and
reached the rapids. The Ostyaks tried to catch them with their boat-
hooks and hooked ropes but the cossacks fired their guns on both sides
so that the others fell crushing one another. The cossacks sailed up to the
Tsyn'yala and the Narim stronghold where the wives and children of the
others were half-dead with fright, weeping and shrieking and running
about. The plotters returned by night one by one and looking about and

seeing that their wives and children were not being killed but treated kindly, gathered in the morning, some of them dispersing while those who remained paid homage with tribute.

78. The tribute was received on the 9th day of May, and they sailed down to the Kolpukhov district, to their commander of a hundred and the devilish praying-place. They gave battle and fought for about three hours but seeing the killed they surrendered and paid sufficient tribute. On the same date they sailed to the Kolpukhov stronghold, collecting tribute both by force and without fighting. On the 20th day of May they reached the princeling Samar, and here there were eight princelings gathered expecting to gain victory by strength of numbers. Bogdan with his comrades, praying to God, sailed on a Sunday along a branch of the river up to the very town of Samar and surprised many Ostyaks on guard who were fast asleep without apprehension. They shot the sleeping sentries and slew the princeling Samar with his family, while all those who had been gathered there dispersed to their homes. There remained a few local inhabitants who brought tribute with humility

and swore the oath of allegiance. Bogdan stayed a week and set up as chief the prince Alachey, he being affluent, and let him go honourably with his people.

79. From there they went on to the Ob' and saw large wastes and few
habitations, and landed at Belogor'ye. Here the inhabitants have an
important place of worship[1] to an ancient goddess: she sits naked on a
chair with her son; she receives gifts from her people who bring her a
part of all they catch and hunt. Whoever does not give according to his
promise is tormented by her and caused to languish, and whoever brings
sparingly falls dead before her. They have a great gathering and public
worship. When the news of Bogdan's coming reached them she commanded them to conceal her and for all to flee. And much of the idola-
trous assemblage is hidden to this day.

[1] N. P. Nikol'skiy noted in the 1930's (in Müller, 1937, p. 491) that Belogor'ye
was until recently the most hallowed place of sacrifice among the Ostyaks.

80. Seeing the empty dwellings Bogdan deliberated with his comrades and decided that it was useless to go any further, and after waiting for three days returned to the town of Sibir'. What fighting there had been on the way as they sailed downstream is difficult to describe in detail: none were killed but all were many times wounded. They arrived rejoicing with the tribute on the 29th day of May. While passing through the destroyed strongholds they saw that many had settled down permanently in submission, meeting and seeing off the cossacks with honour; when the tribute was brought the receivers were all arrayed in bright garments in honour of the glory of the royal greatness. When they returned to Yermak with the collectors of the tribute, safe and sound, in their joy they all glorified God.[1]

[1] The third insertion ends here.

81. Yermak with his company followed Mametkul in close pursuit
and overtook him at the Shanshinsk landmark where he gave a great
battle. They killed many pagans while the others fled headlong from him
on their horses. As for Yermak, he went back and buried his dead on the
Sauskan headland in the royal cemetery, at the edge of the headland to
mark the place. This was the first killing of cossacks in Sibir'.[1]

[1] This is incomprehensible; we have been told of endless deaths.

82. On the 6th day of December there came from the Yaskalba districts beyond the marshes, from impenetrable places and from Suklem the princelings Ishberdey and Suklem with many gifts and tribute, and necessary provisions, paying their respects to Yermak and his company. On his part Yermak, having accepted the tribute and given them presents, dismissed them to their homes, commanding them to serve him well. Prince Ishberdey was so zealous in his service that he was the first among many to seek out princelings and bring them to tribute. He brought the tribute and described many roads, and was an excellent guide to the cossacks against the unpeaceful, and was extremely loyal.

84.[1] After consultation with his like-minded company Yermak wrote
a letter to the Pious Sovereign, Tsar and Great Prince Ivan Vasil'-
yevich of All Russia, acknowledging his guilt and pointing out his
services in having brought down the most proud Khan Kuchyum and
taken all his towns and brought many princes and *murzas*, Tatar,
Vogul and Ostyak and other peoples under his sovereign hand and
collected tribute, and sent it to you, Lord, with the *ataman* Ivan
Koltsov and fighting men on the 22nd day of December along the
wolf's trail,[2] by sledges and skis drawn by reindeer. Their guide was the
Yaskalba prince Ishberdey with his Voguls up to Perm' the Great, from
where they reached Moscow.

[1] Chapter 83 is omitted in the manuscript – a mistake in numbering chapters,
no doubt due to the insertions. See *Sibirskiye letopisi*, 1907, p. xxxvi.
[2] Evidently the name of the route taken. Müller thought (1750, p. 142) it was
the route up the Tavda to Cherdyn', but could not explain the name. Bakhrushin
comments (Müller, 1937, p. 490) that Müller and others derive the adjective
volch'ya, normally meaning wolf's, from *volok*, a portage, which Bakhrushin
thinks wrong. He thinks 'wolf's' may imply 'seldom used'.

85. When they reached the Moscow kingdom and the Pious Sovereign, Tsar and Great Prince Ivan Vasil'yevich of All Russia, they handed over the letter and the tribute. As the sovereign began to read and to hear that the kingdom of Sibir' had been conquered and the khan defeated, and that Tatars, Voguls and Ostyaks had been brought under his hand, and tribute collected and sent by the *ataman* and others, he greatly rejoiced and glorified God, and sent to Yermak great gifts: two coats of mail and a goblet and a fur coat of his own, bestowing on the *atamans* bounty and favours, and soon sent them back to Yermak with a laudatory charter along the same road by which they had come.

185

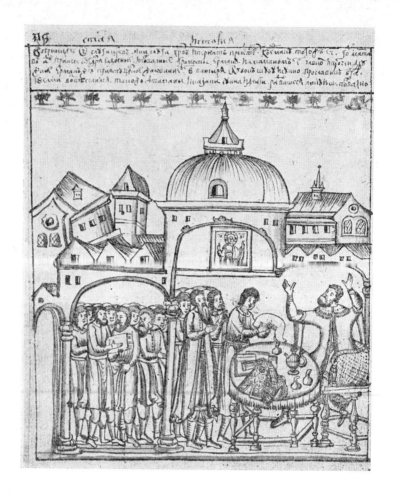

86. A man of trust, a servant of the tsar, like a winged servant of
Christ came flying to Yermak on the first day of March in the same year
90 [1582] bringing from the tsar gladdening and praiseful charters to
Yermak, the five *atamans* and the rest of the company. Yermak accepted
the tsar's gifts – two coats of mail, the goblet, the fur coat and the cloth,
praising God. He rejoiced greatly, as too the *atamans* and the cossacks,
glad of the cloth and the money, rejoiced and cheered.

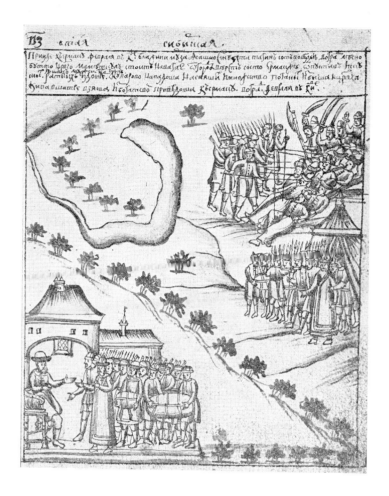

87. There came to Yermak on the 20th day of February the neighbouring *murza* Senbakhta Tagin, a tribute-payer, ingratiating himself
by bringing the information that, so he said, the khan's heir Mametkul
was standing on the Vagay, some one hundred versts from the city.
Yermak sent sixty able fighting men who, on reaching Kularovo, fell on
the sleeping men. They slew a great number of pagans and took the
khan's heir alive in his tent, returning to Yermak in the city, laden with
rich booty on the 28th day of February.

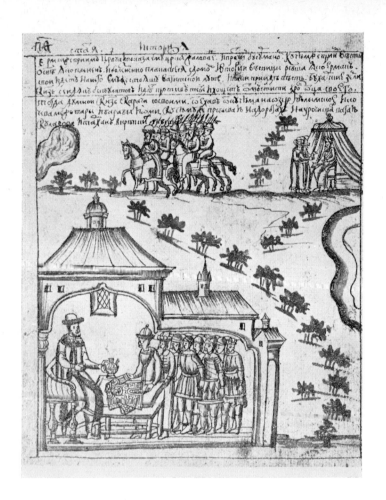

89.[1] Yermak received the khan's heir and showed royal favour to him and to the other infidels. When the news of his son's capture came to Kuchyum he lamented bitterly with his household. News that followed made him decide that Yermak was coming against him with his warriors. He was encamped on the Agitskiy river-bend and again came the news: 'The prince of the land of Bukhara Seydyak son of Bekbulat is coming against you and wants to avenge the blood of his father.' Then Prince Karacha of Kuchyum's council left him for the Chulym lake and nomadised between the Tara and the Baraba and the Om'[2] while Kuchyum stayed in fortified places on the roads at the natural boundaries of the Vagay, Kularovo and Tarkhany.

[1] Chapter 88 is missing, for the same reason as chapter 83.
[2] That is, to the south-east, on the steppes between modern Omsk and Novosibirsk.

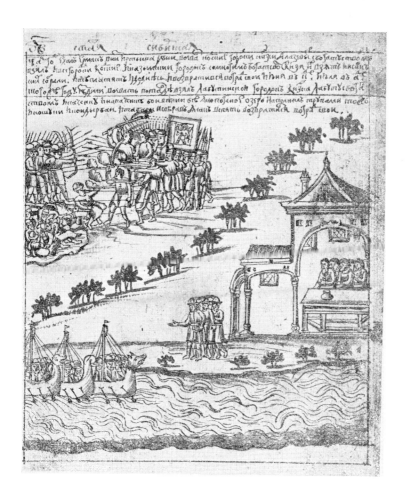

90. In the year 91 [1582] Yermak descended the river Irtysh and
made war on the Koda strongholds. He captured the Alazev princes
with their riches and all the Koda and Nazym strongholds with much
wealth, capturing their prince and collecting tribute from them, who pay
it to this day. He then returned to his town on the 20th day of June. On
the 1st day of July of the same year he waged war on the Tavda: he took
Prince Labuta's stronghold, captured Prince Labuta together with his
wealth and the Pachenka; at the Pachenka there was a great battle so that
the Poganoye lake was filled with dead bodies, and so it was also at
Koshuki and Kondyrbai and Tabary. And having collected tribute he
returned to his town.

91. In the year 91 [1582], on the 21st day of November, Yermak sent the khan's heir Mametkul and the collected tribute to Moscow. He was brought to the Tsar Fedor Ivanovich,[1] and by the tsar's order he was met and on arrival favourably received, and all the fighting men were much honoured and received favours and praise.

[1] One of the more glaring discrepancies of date: Fedor Ivanovich came to the throne only in 1584 – which is the likely year for this event.

92. In the same year 91 [1583], on the 10th day of May, *voyevodas* were sent to Yermak from Moscow at the command of the great lord Vasiliy Ivanovich Shuyskiy. They were Prince Semen Bolkhovskoy and Ivan Glukhoy with 500 men, and they went by the Volga across the portage. When they reached Sibir' on the 2nd day of November, winter had set in, and there was a great famine so that people were forced to eat human flesh, and many died of hunger, and so did the *voyevodas*.[1] When spring came the Tatars and Ostyaks brought first fruits of fish and vegetables and provisions, and the cossacks satisfied their hunger.

[1] In fact only Bolkhovskoy died. Glukhov (as he should be called) returned later to Moscow. The dating here is correct; but arrival in Sibir' is thought to have been in November 1584, not 1583, because the party wintered in the Perm' region.

93. In the year 92 [1584], on the 10th day of September, there came
from Karacha a false envoy who took the oath of allegiance according to
his faith, asking Yermak for defence against the Kazakh Horde. After
taking council, Yermak, deceived by their godlessness, let the *ataman*
Ivan Koltsov go with 40 men. When they came to Karacha they were
taken by surprise and killed. When the news of their killing reached
Yermak he greatly lamented. The ungodly ones seeing that Koltsov had
been killed began to slay the Russians in many places, districts and
encampments.

94. In the same year 92 [1584], on the 12th day of March, during Lent, Karacha came to Sibir' with many warriors and beleaguered the city with pack-trains and camps, himself taking up position on the Sauskan river bend, two versts from the city. He remained till the beginning of summer maliciously causing much fatal harm to the cossacks.

95. In the same year 92 [1584], on the 9th day of May, Yermak and
the cossacks sent up prayers to God and St Nicholas the Miracle
Worker appealing for help. They left the town secretly, and on coming
up to Karacha's camp fell on them in the night where they were sleeping without any apprehension; they killed two of Karacha's sons, while
others fled in all directions, Karacha escaping with three men beyond
the lake.

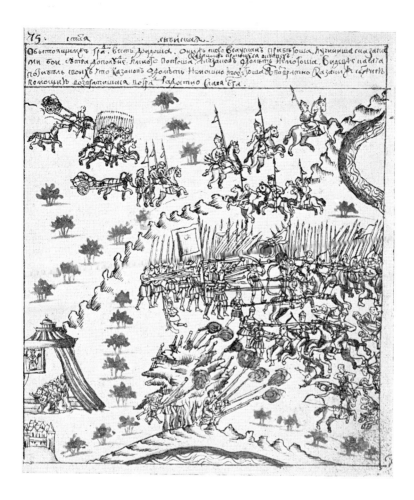

96. When news of this reached the besiegers of the town they came swiftly to Sauskan and gave battle to the cossacks from the morning till noon and many perished, but the cossacks took cover in the undergrowth and could not be overcome. When Karacha saw the destruction of his men and that the cossacks could not be overcome, he fled headlong while the cossacks, with God's help, joyfully returned to the town praising God.

97. In the night there appeared to Yermak as he was at prayer and to five other men St Nicholas of Mozhaysk who commanded them to live clean lives and observe fasts strictly and exercise all virtues with brotherly love. And he prophesied: 'Henceforth there will be on Krasnaya Gora a house and a dwelling for God and me. As for you, if you do not obey me I shall cease to help you and you will soon come to an end for your sins of not observing virtue and falling into evil ways.' Yermak told everyone about this vision.

98. By God's will in the year 7092 [1584], on the first day of August,
informants came from the steppe alleging that Kuchyum would not let
the Bukharans through to Sibir'. Yermak set out swiftly with fifty men
and went up the Irtysh to meet the Bukharans in boats. In the Agitskiy
river-bend he had a channel dug across the portage.[1] Having reached
the mouth of the Vagay without meeting the Bukharans he went in boats
up the Vagay to Adbash, and from there returned to the channel and the
mouth of the Vagay. They made camp on the channel and spent the
night there without setting guards, and slept soundly without fear. But
Kuchyum in his malice secretly observed them and sent Tatars in all
directions.

[1] This channel was seen by Müller (1750, p. 179), who had no doubt it was
made at Yermak's command, for it was still called Yermak's channel in his time.
It is the 'cross-channel' referred to in the other chronicles.

99.[1] On the taking of Sibir' in the year 92 [1584], on the 6th day of
August, following information from spies, Yermak set out with three
hundred cossacks to meet the travelling Bukharans carrying many goods.
Kuchyum was said to be encamped far away in the valley of the river
Vagay. When they went up the Irtysh, all the districts showing themselves obedient in everything, there was no news whatever of Kuchyum
and they did not find the Bukharans. They rowed up the Irtysh to
Sartezer' and to the chief prince Begish in his princely stronghold, and
here fought a mighty battle with assembled Tatars and Karacha's men.
Begish had two iron cannon brought from Kazan'. The cossacks silenced
them so they could not fire at the cossacks a second time and they pushed

[1] This and the next three chapters are an insertion from the Short Kungur
Siberian chronicle; hence the duplication.

them straight down hill into the Yrtysh.[1] And here in their fury they slew them all to the last man while very few escaped. And they took much property which they buried in cellars with their belongings. They rowed to Shamsha and to Kryanchiki, and in Saly there was some fighting. Then they rowed to Kaurdak where all the Tatars had concealed themselves in a dense fir wood and in marshes. And they rowed as far as Khan Sargachik of Ishim, established since ancient times, and took him in battle and subdued him.

[1] This seems to be another version of the earlier story about two cannons, told in chapter 64 above.

100. And from there to Tebendi, known as the down-river stronghold of the princeling Yelygay, where there was a captain with a few
inhabitants. Hearing and seeing that Yermak did not kill those who
submitted, they brought gifts and tribute as he had previously demanded what was good and honourable. He brought him his beautiful
daughter in honour as a gift. Yermak did not accept and refused the gift
and forbade it to the others. Kuchyum was endeavouring to get her for
his son as this girl was of noble descent from Khan Sargachik and was
beautiful. From there they rowed to the mouth of the Ishim, and at the
mouth of the Ishim there was a great battle, not with weapons but hand to
hand, each seizing whomsoever he could. In that battle five of Yermak's
cossacks were killed. They overcame the infidels and buried their own
dead. About these five cossacks the Tatars sing with tears at assemblies
in songs with the burden: 'Yanym, yanym, bish kazak, bish kazak,'

which means: warriors, warriors five, five men conquered and destroyed.[1] And this song of theirs is called the queen's lament.

[1] In Turkish the refrain means 'At my side, at my side, five cossacks, five cossacks'.

101. From there they travelled to the stronghold Kulary, the frontier defence stronghold of Kuchyum against the Kalmucks, and on the whole upper Irtysh there is none stronger.[1] After attacking it for five days Yermak could not take it and left it saying: 'We shall take it on our way back.' And they rowed on to the Tashatkan stronghold. In that stronghold a stone had fallen from the sky, like a cart with a sledge in size, red in colour, exuding from time to time cold, rain and snow; about it Yermak and his comrades wondered at the works of God.[2] The inhabitants here were submissive in everything and gave all that

[1] This seems to imply rather deep incursions by Kalmucks, for there were settlements owing allegiance to Kuchum well beyond Kulary (the rest of this chapter provides some evidence of this). But of course any concept of a frontier between groups of steppe nomads has to be very flexible.

[2] Bakhrushin notes (in Müller, 1937, pp. 493–4) other examples of stones fallen from heaven among Siberian peoples. Such legends are common in many parts of the world.

Yermak demanded, for they were frightened and had witnessed all the battles in Sibir' and at Chyuvashi, and had fled to their kinsfolk living here. And all wondered at not having heard anything about Kuchyum and the Bukharans and how they might get some news.

102. They reached the mouth of the Shishtamama and here they finally found the fugitives and Karacha's men, and those of the captives who had been captives of Yermak recognised him because they had lived in his camp. This district is known as that of the Turalian[1] people, and all saw how poor they were and did them no harm. From here they quickly returned to the lower reaches; and in Tashatkan they were told that the Bukharans had come to Sibir' rowing past all the strongholds and districts to the mouth of the Vagay river. They hastily rowed up the river Vagay with difficulty as far as the Agitskiy stronghold but found nothing, and heard and saw nothing. Tired of waiting they turned downstream to the river mouth and stopped there without noticing the observers of Kuchyum and Karacha, well-known robbers, lying hidden beyond the river at a distance of less than three versts, in a wild dark

[1] Russ. *Turalintsy*; presumably a local clan name.

wood by a steep and very boggy stream. Across it Kuchyum had a wide ford made, wide enough for three or four carts abreast; in one place it was solidly packed with stones and sand, and whoever missed it would drown.[1]

[1] The insertion ends here.

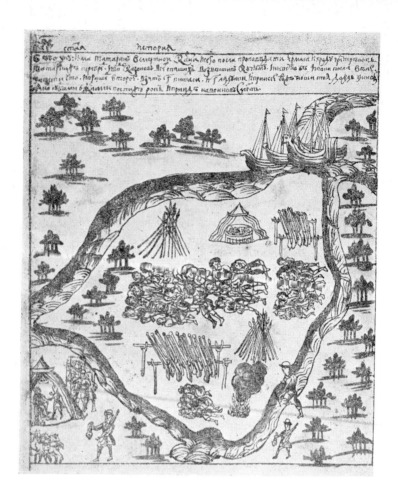

104.[1] Kuchyum had a Tatar condemned to death, and he sent this
man to find out about Yermak and the ford across the channel. The
Tatar crossed over and saw the cossacks all asleep and informed
Kuchyum. Kuchyum did not believe him and sent him again to bring
back something. So he went a second time and took three muskets and
three ammunition pouches which he brought back. That night the rain
increased because by divine destiny the time had come, and death
overtook the cossacks.

[1] Chapter 103 is missing, for the same reason as chapters 83 and 88.

105. In the year 92 [1584],[1] on the 6th day of August, at midnight, Kuchyum with a large number of warriors fell upon Yermak and his company as they were calmly sleeping, and their hour of death came and they were all slain, but for one cossack who escaped and came to the town and gave the news to those there.

[1] 1585 is likelier.

106. Yermak, seeing the killing of his men and no help from any-
where to save his life, ran to his boat but could not climb into it for he
was clad in two of the royal coats of mail and the boat had floated away
from the bank so that, unable to reach it, he was drowned on the 6th day
of August. When the other cossacks in the town heard the news they
wept bitterly about him for he was most courageous and shrewd, and
humane, and well-favoured and endowed with every kind of wisdom,
with a flat face, black of beard and with curly hair, of medium stature,
thickset and broad-shouldered.[1]

[1] This is the only description we have of Yermak's physical appearance – and
it was written more than a century after his death.

107. The remaining cossacks, seeing their leader with his company killed, mourned at the parting; there remained 150 men in all, not enough to stand up against the forces of the infidels, while if they were to continue living there they would starve to death. They got into their boats on the 15th day of August and with the *voyevoda* they rowed down the Ob', and along the Irtysh and the Soba, and across the mountains came to Russia to their homes, leaving the town deserted.[1]

[1] The rather clumsily described route seems to indicate the longest detour: right down the Irtysh and Ob', almost to the sea, and then taking the old northern route by the Sob' (as it is now called) and the Usa. Perhaps they really did go that far round; and the picture shows the ships heading downstream (compare chapter 9). But the Stroganov chronicle, chapter 32, speaks of the returning party meeting Mansurov's relief party on the Tura; in which case they must have withdrawn along the more direct route, which seems likelier.

108. When Kuchyum's son Aley, who was nomadising among the Abigun strongholds, saw that the cossacks had left the town deserted, he came there and settled in the town of Kashlyk with his warriors. When Prince Seydyak, son of Bekbulat, heard about all this, that Yermak had been killed on his waterway and the others had fled to Russia while Aley, Kuchyum's son, had installed himself in the town, he collected his household troops and, entering the town, defeated Aley and his warriors, avenging the blood of his father. He took up his inheritance and stayed in the town.

109. After drowning Yermak floated up on the 13th day of August and was carried by the waters of the Irtysh to the river bank by Yepancha's encampment. The Tatar grandson of Yanysh Begish was fishing and baiting his net when he noticed human legs floating near the bank. He caught them with a looped rope of the net and pulled them out on to the bank where, seeing the coats of mail, he understood that this was no ordinary man. Knowing that many cossacks had been drowned he hastened up the hill to the encampment giving the news to the inhabitants and calling all to hurry to see what had happened.

110. They all recognised by the coats of mail that this was Yermak, for they knew that the tsar had sent him two coats of mail which they had seen. When Kaydaul *murza* began to take them off the body, blood gushed from the body's mouth and nose as from a living man's. When Kaydaul, who was an old man, saw that the flowing of living blood had not ceased he understood that this was a man of God, so he laid his naked body on a trestle and sent messengers into the neighbouring towns calling the people to come and see imperishable Yermak exuding living blood. He gave out that this cried for the avenging of his blood and that this miracle should make them perceive the Christian God and one eternally glorifying God.

111. When people began to gather at the call, all who came thrust an
arrow into Yermak's dead body, and blood issued afresh from the thrusts,
while birds flew around not daring to touch him. And he lay on the
trestle six weeks till the first day of November until at last there came
Kuchyum with *murzas* and the Konda and Obdaria princes who thrust
their arrows, and his blood flowed as from a living man. And he appeared
in a vision to many infidels and to Khan Seydyak himself that they
should bury him. Because of him some lost their minds; and to this day
they swear and vow by his name, and he is so wonderful and awe-
inspiring that when they speak of him among themselves they do not
remain tearless.

112. They called him a god and buried him according to their law in the Baishevskoye cemetery under a spreading pine tree.[1] His coats of mail were divided: one was presented as an offering to the devil spirit of Belogor'ye,[2] and this one was taken by Prince Alach' who was famous in all the strongholds; the second one was given to Chaydaul *murza* Zakaydam.[3] His coat was taken by Khan Seydyak; his belt and

[1] This cemetery, also called Begishevo, was well known to Tatars in the 17th century. It contained a mausoleum to one Shaikh Hakim, and this was later thought by many to be Yermak's tomb (Bakhrushin in Müller, 1937, p. 494).

[2] See chapter 79 above.

[3] Bakhrushin (in Müller, 1937, pp. 494–5) reports that these coats of mail are mentioned later in the records of the Siberian office (Sibirskiy Prikaz) in Moscow. That given to Chaydaul (more correctly Kaydaul) was still in his family in 1658, and magical properties were attributed to it. What happened to the other coat of mail is not known certainly; but Bakhrushin suggests its possible identification with one which was in the possession of Prince P. I. Shuyskiy in 1646 and is now in the Kremlin Armoury (Oruzheynaya Palata) in Moscow.

sword were given to Karacha, and a mullah collected for a commemoration feast 30 oxen and 10 sheep, and held a ceremony according to their traditions, saying as they mentioned him: 'Had you been alive we would have made you our khan, but here we see you dead, an insensible Russian prince.'

113. Miracles were worked by Yermak's body and clothing, the sick
were healed, mothers and babes were preserved from disease, success
came in war and in fishing and hunting. Mullahs and *murzas*, seeing
that their law was profaned and their miracles were ceasing, forbade
everyone, old and young, to mention Yermak's name so that his honour
and fame should fade away and his grave become neglected. Yet to this
day the infidels see on the Saturdays of the commemoration of the dead a
pillar of fire rising to the sky, and on ordinary Saturdays a great candle
burning at his head. Thus God reveals his own.

216

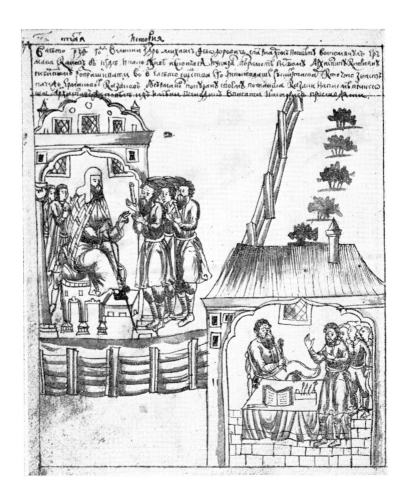

114. In the year 129 [1621] the Great Sovereign Mikhail Feodoro-
vich, taking counsel with the patriarch, called Yermak to memory,
desiring to know what he was like, and where and how he had lived and
died, and he commanded Kiprian, the first archbishop of Siberia, to
make enquiries. In the second year of his installation he questioned
Russians and Tatars on what they knew, and most of all Yermak's
cossacks. The infidels following their Koran revealed nothing, while the
cossacks brought their information in writing, and the archbishop
ordered their names to be entered in the book of names for the commemoration of the dead[1] and to be honoured in history.

[1] This is the *Sinodik*, preserved as chapter 37 of the Yesipov chronicle.

115. In the year of 7158 [1650] envoys from the Kalmat Ablay[1] came secretly to Tobol'sk asking for the above-mentioned royal coats of mail and naming Kaydaul *murza* and the Konda prince as having them in their possession. Following this embassy in the year 7159 [1651] the Great Sovereign Aleksey Mikhailovich ordered these coats of mail to be taken from the Alacha princes and Kaydaul's sons and sent to Obrey.[2] In that year the boyar Prince Ivan Ondreyevich Khilkov took the coats of mail away from the sons of Kaydaul with great threats, but it was not believed that the Alach' princes had the down-river one, and to this day it has not been heard of. On the 18th day of July the coat of mail was sent from Tobolsk with the Tobol'sk lieutenant of the *streltsy* Ul'yan Moseyevich Remezov[3] and his men.

[1] A Kalmuck chieftain of some importance, who had many dealings with the Russians. See Bakhrushin, 1955, pp. 36–8.

[2] Evidently Ablay.

[3] The father of the chronicler; and this is no doubt how the story got into the chronicle.

218

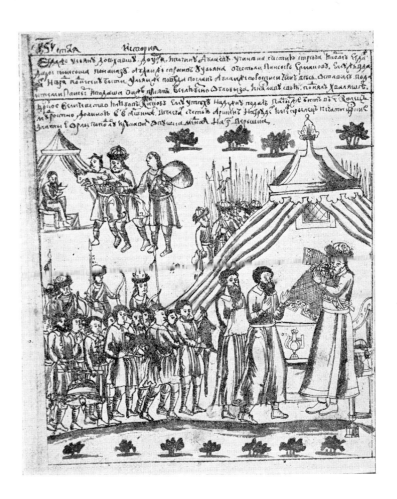

116. When Ul'yan reached the encampment he was awarded an
honourable reception and given food according to the custom of Ablay.
Ablay asked Ul'yan: 'Is it about the honour of Yermak's coat of mail
which was to be presented to me among the gifts?' And Ul'yan replied:
'It has been sent.' Ablay ignored the order of the inventory and said:
'Give me the coat of mail.' And when he was given it he took it, lovingly
kissed it and lifted it to his head, praising the tsar's greatness and love
for giving him a lasting pleasure. The coat of mail is most cunningly
forged in five links, two *arshins*[1] long, one *arshin* and a quarter in the
shoulders with gold seals of the tsar's eagles on the chest and between
the shoulder-blades, and with five inches of brass edging along the hem
and at the sleeves.

[1] One arshin: 28 inches or 71 cm.

117. After that Ablay asked: 'Do you know, Ul'yan, where your
Yermak is lying?' Ul'yan, who was smooth-spoken and cunning in
dealings, replied to this question: 'To this day we do not know where he
is buried and how he died.' So Ablay began to relate about him according to his history, how he had come to Sibir' and had fled from Kuchyum on the waterway and was drowned, and found, and shot with
arrows, and how blood flowed, and how the coats of mail were divided
and taken away, and how miracles were worked by the coats of mail and
the clothing, and how the Tatars had given a pledge not to tell the
Russians about him on pain of death. Ul'yan asked Ablay for a receipt
with his acknowledgment and seal, while Ablay promised to give
detailed information about Yermak.

118. Remaining seated, he accepted the other gifts and, the embassy being ended, he rejoiced with his people that the great monarch had acceded to his request and sent the coat of mail. In that year 7159 [1650], on the 4th day of September, he related in detail all about Yermak, how he had lived, according to their records, and how he had died according to our stories, exactly how he had been found and worked miracles, as has been described in chapter 81.[1] 'For many years I have lived here. When I was a child and ailing in my stomach I was given to drink of the earth from his grave, and have remained healthy to this day. When earth has been taken from the grave and I go with it to war, I am victorious, but when there is no earth I return empty-handed. I have asked the monarch for the coats of mail that I might go against the

[1] Another wrong reference, no doubt due to renumbering. The miracles are described in chapters 111 and 113.

Kazakh Horde. Your Yermak is lying in the Baishevskoye cemetery under a pine-tree, and on your days of commemoration of the dead there are pillars of flame over him, and on other days the Tatars see a candle, whereas the Russians do not see it.' And he set his seal to this.

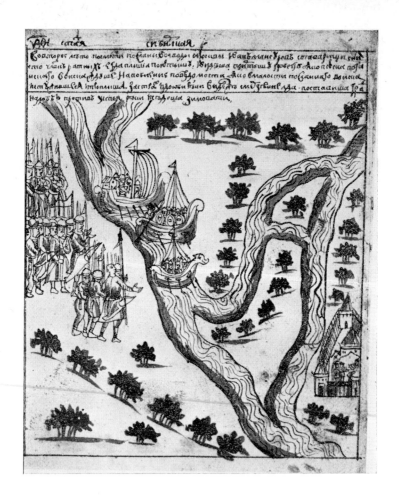

119. In the second year after the death *voyevodas* were sent from Moscow, Ivan Mansurov and comrades, and with him one hundred fighting men. When they were sailing on the Irtysh and saw along the bank of the Irtysh pagan troops like sand prepared for a massacre, knowing how small was the army sent, they were worried, and sailed in fear to the river Ob'. When they saw ice freezing over they built a stronghold above the Ob', opposite the river mouth,[1] and settled down for the winter.

[1] That is, at the confluence of the Ob' and the Irtysh.

120. A great number of Ostyaks gathered from the Yrtysh and the Ob' and besieged the stronghold, and fought all day, but at nightfall the pagans drew back. In the morning they brought the large idol of Belogor'ye and, setting it up under a birch tree, prayed and worshipped that they might take the stronghold. And during their worshipping a cannon was fired from the stronghold and their idol with the tree was shattered into many pieces. The pagans were very frightened, thinking in their ignorance that a man had done the smashing with his bow, and all dispersed to their homes, and later brought tribute. In the spring they crossed over the mountains.

121. In the year 7093 [1585][1] there were sent from Moscow the *voyevodas* Vasiley Borisovich Sukin and Ivan Myasnoy and the administrator[2] Danilo Chyulkov with three hundred men; and they founded the town of Tyumen' on the 29th day of July, known as Chingi, and built a church dedicated to the Most Merciful Saviour, the first of Sibir', and collected tribute from many Tatars along the Tura and the Tobol and the Iset' and the Pyshma.

[1] Tyumen' dates its founding from 1586; but for Tobol'sk (next chapter) 1587 is correct.
[2] Russ. *pis'mennyy golova*, an official working under a *voyevoda* on secretarial and administrative duties.

122. In the year 7095 [1587], under Tsar Fedor Ivanovich, a ukase was sent to the *voyevoda* Danilo Chyulkov: 500 men have been sent to build the town of Tobolesk. And by God's providence *voyevoda* Danilo Chulkov sailed to his destination and opposite the mouth of the Tobol built a town named Tobolesk on a hill, the first capital among all the other towns, and erected the first church dedicated to the Holy Trinity, and on the ascent another to the All-Merciful Saviour.

РИТ СПА ИСИЦА
Китъ иррами рудиансрь оте имаимонь Урате Казатан Ордее. Буделика Колкыдае иУслинф
Записнирелии Астрвоак Иосмдаа тоснаии поскоб тосицлиф тоб смити тиб амерб.
Имеилефаленбон иниаб поря ибеленоукенбеньь Ценайтоб посрсилан Засланы.

123. Prince Seydyak, who was the ruler, and Saltan, the heir of the
Kazakh Horde, and a counsellor of Kuchyum,[1] were sending hawks
after birds. The *voyevoda* sent envoys to Seydyak offering to live in
peace and inviting them to come to the town for friendly counsel about
living in brotherly union.

[1] The counsellor of Kuchum was Karacha, as the next chapter makes clear.
The phrase could not be taken to refer to Saltan, for he, as an associate of
Seydyak's, was no ally of Kuchum's.

124. When the envoys came to Seydyak he took counsel with Saltan and Karacha, and after taking counsel took with him 100 men; and they came to the *voyevodas* in the town and sat at the table, and out of fear spoke words of deceit. But Seydyak was lost in thought, neither eating nor drinking. The *voyevoda* said to him: 'What evil are you plotting against us?' And taking a cup presented it to him, saying to all three: 'If you harbour no evil thoughts against us, drink this cup to our health.' When Seydyak took it and began to drink, he choked. The same happened to Saltan and Karacha: God revealed their evil thoughts.

125. The *voyevoda* and his men saw that they intended evil, so he stealthily waved his hand to the cossacks, who fell upon the pagans. Seeing the killing of his men, Seydyak rushed to a window, Saltan followed and so did Karacha, but they were caught and tied up while those who stood outside the town, on hearing that Seydyak and all with him had been overcome, out of great fear took to flight and did not enter their town of Sibir' but fled past it. When the rest in the town heard about this they hastened away to the Vagay to Kuchyum.

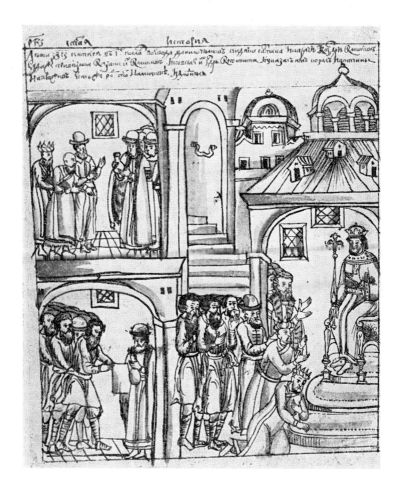

126. In the year 7097 [1588], on the 10th day of September, the *voyevoda* Danilo Chyulkov sent Seydyak, Saltan and Karacha to the sovereign in Moscow. When the cossacks brought them to Moscow the sovereign commanded that they should be christened and assigned to them revenue and estates for their living. Their descendants exist in Moscow to this day.

127. Kuchyum in his flight wandered about and found no place to settle, always making plans against Tobol'sk but holding back out of fear. Once in the year 7098 [1590], on the 23rd day of July he gathered all his men intending to march on Tobolesk, and coming by stealth upon some troops of his own infidels he killed his own people and hastily fled on to the steppe, intending to attack again. Fear and trembling and terror overcame him so he did not march upon the town but devastated the infidel villages Kaurdatskaya and Salinsk.

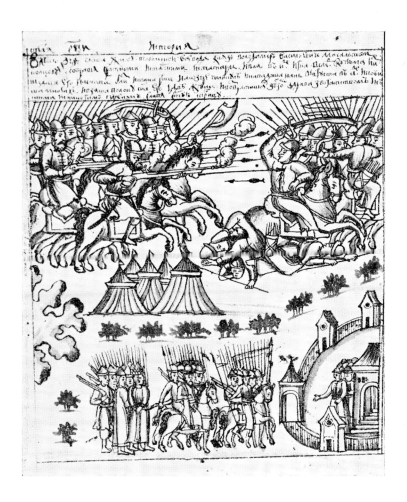

128. In the year 7099 [1591], complaints having reached him, the
voyevoda of Tobol'sk, Volodimer Vasil'yevich Masal'skoy-Koltsov, set
out with his troops and men of Tara and Tatars on the 8th day of July
on the track of Kuchyum and found him on the steppe near the river
Ishim at lake Chilikul. They fell upon him on the first day of August and
slew many and captured his son and two of his wives, returning in good
health and with rich booty and horses and a number of prisoners,
giving praise to the Holy Trinity.

129. Kuchyum however escaped with a few remaining Tatars, and with his wives and children in order to avoid death from a surprise attack by the Russians fled to the Kalmuck border, to the headwaters of the rivers Ishim and Nor-Ishim, Osha and Kamyshlov, between the lakes, to fortified places.[1] He dwelt there in hiding sorely harassing the Russians and the tributary tribes in the neighbourhood of Tara. He often planned vengeance against Tobol'sk but was filled with a great fear from his very first excessive terror of the Russian troops, because owing to his self-will his friends abandoned him and became enemies. Here Kuchyum lived with his people nomadizing till the year 105 [1597]. The *voyevoda* of Tara learnt through tributaries about Kuchyum's encampments and nomad camps and wrote to the sovereign in Moscow about taking the field against him.

[1] That is, eastwards, towards modern Omsk.

234

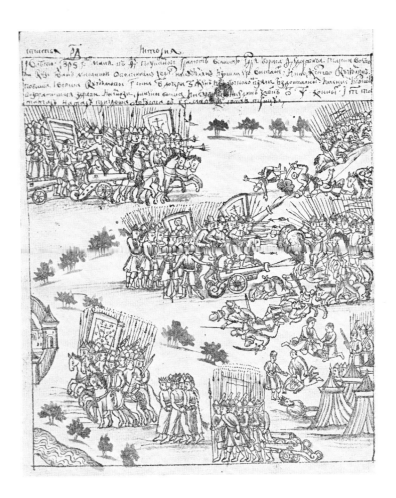

130. In the year 7106 [1598], on the 9th day of May, following a written order of the Great Sovereign Boris Fedorovich, the *voyevoda* of Tara, Prince Ivan Masalskoy, set out against Kuchyum's people. They overtook him in the camps killing many of Kuchyum's men and capturing three of his sons, two daughters, six wives and many prisoners, and with much booty and cattle returned safely. Not many had been wounded and not a single man killed out of 700 horsemen and 300 Tatars. They returned to Tara on the 23rd day of August, praising the Holy Trinity.

131. From Tara and Tobol'sk the captured kin of Kuchyum, his
three sons, two daughters and six wives were sent to Moscow with an
escort by the *voyevoda* Yefim Varfolomeyevich Buturlin. When the
captives were brought to Moscow in the same year 106 [1598] to Tsar
Boris Fedorovich, the sovereign received them and glorified the Holy
Trinity and the Most Pure Mother of God and the Moscow Miracle
Workers for the conquest, while he highly praised the Siberians. He
rewarded each for their service with gold coin and special payment and
living allowance, and sent the same reward in gold to the others in
Sibir'.

132. As for Kuchyum, he kept in hiding and could not find a dwelling place as he was bereft by the settled Siberians of his whole family, his property and cattle, and people. With a few men he fled to the Kain land, to the headwaters of the Irtysh at lake Zaysan-Nor, robbed the Kalmucks of a great number of horses and fled to another place with his men. The Kalmucks pursued him and overtook him on the Nor-Ishim by lake Kurgal'chin,[1] and here killed many of Kuchyum's men and took back their horses and herds, and plundered the remainder of his possessions. Kuchyum however escaped from them with a few men to the Nagay land to live and subsist in beggary.

[1] If we can believe these reported travels of Kuchum and his followers, great distances must have been covered, and through hostile territory. Lake Zaysan is 1100 km in a direct line south-east of Omsk, and Lake Kurgalchin (now Kurgaldzhin) the same distance west of Zaysan.

133. When Kuchyum with his men came to the Nagays, the Nagays lost no time in gathering their clans, slew Kuchyum and pillaged all his possessions. They enslaved his men saying to him: 'You are a renowned and famous robber, son of Murtaza, and your father inflicted much harm on us. You, though you are beggared, would do the the same to us as to your other people who have been needlessly killed by you and embittered.'

134. When Kuchyum's remaining infidels, who lived on the steppe, saw that Kuchyum had been cruelly slain, they came to the town of Tobol'sk and agreed to pay tribute, as is still done to this day. And some became Christians and were enlisted on the roll of new converts. Some 300 *murzas* and lesser nobles were taken into service at salaries of fifteen and seven roubles, and a Russian official was put at their head, and so they serve to this day. After the baptism of many infidels Sibir' expanded, and towns and monasteries were built with everything necessary to their subsistence.

135. In the year 7144 [1636] on the 16th day of February, the council of the blessed assembly, the Most Holy Patriarch Filaret and the Sovereign Mikhail Fedorovich of All Russia issued a decree to the first Nektariy, archbishop of Siberia,[1] that he should proclaim eternal memory[2] to Yermak, son of Timofey Povol'skoy, and to all who had been killed: in the year 88 [1579], on the 23rd day of October, to 107 men slain by Kuchyum at Chyuvashi – the great commemoration; in the next year 89 [1580], on the 5th day of November, to 20 men fishing

[1] Nektariy (Nikolay Telyashin) was the third archbishop of Tobol'sk and Siberia (1636–40). He is called the first Nektariy to distinguish him from a later Nektariy who was Patriarch of Jerusalem, 1661–69.

[2] This chapter gives in abbreviated form the *Sinodik* which forms chapter 37 of the Yesipov chronicle. The years are wrong (as we have come to expect in this chronicle), being one or two years too early; some are also inconsistent within the chronicle, for instance Yermak's death is given as 1583 here, and 1584 in chapter 105 – while the likeliest date is 1585.

on lake Abalak slain while sleeping without apprehension – the lesser commemoration; in the year 89 [1581], in July and June, to those who fought down the Irtysh on the Ob' and the Tavda, and who captured the strongholds of Nazym, Koda and Labuta – the intermediate commemoration; in the third year 90 [1582], on the 17th day of April, to the *ataman* Ivan Koltsov with 40 men, treacherously killed by the crafty Karacha – the great commemoration; in the fourth year 91 [1583], on the 6th day of August, to Yermak son of Timofey with 300 men – a commemoration, the great extolment. And from then until now there has been established a universal memorial service in Moscow and here in Tobolsk to Yermak and those like him now faithfully serving, with a great extolment to the eternal memory of those killed for the Orthodox faith

On an ancient prophecy[1]

136. With regard to this Kuchyum, the prophecy of Isaiah was fulfilled, and the word was carried out by the Christian warrior Yermak
with his faithful company in Siberia: rejoice not, all strangers, because
the yoke of him who made ye rejoice is broken; for out of the serpent's

[1] The narrative is again interrupted at this point, and the tone becomes more
ecclesiastical. Of the remaining chapters in the chronicle, numbers 140–7 are an
interpolation from an unknown source, somewhat similar to the earlier interpolations from the Short Kungur chronicle. The other fourteen (136–9, 148–57)
each have a separate heading of a sort which calls to mind some kind of devotional
book. But this source too has not been identified. Western influence is apparent
in the picture, for, while the coat-of-arms on the left of the house is the Russian
State seal in its late 17th-century form, the one in the sky on the right is that of
the City of London (I am indebted to Dr W. F. Ryan for this fascinating indenti-
fication).

242

root shall come forth grandchildren as an asp, and their grandchildren will come forth as a fiery serpent, and the poor shall be saved by God, and the needy shall lie down in peace; God will kill thy root with famine, O asp, and the remnant; the gates of cities will weep, and the strong towns of all the strangers will be taken, for smoke from the north is coming, and there is no sojourning in his appointed times.[1] And thus the prophecy is perfectly fulfilled with regard to the Turks.[2]

[1] A much garbled version of *Isaiah* xiv. 29–31, which reads in the English Authorised Version: 'Rejoice not thou, whole Palestina, because the rod of him that smote thee is broken; for out of the serpent's root shall come forth a cockatrice, and his fruit shall be a fiery flying serpent. And the firstborn of the poor shall feed, and the needy shall lie down in safety: and I will kill thy root with famine, and he shall slay thy remnant. Howl, O gate; cry, O city; thou, whole Palestina, art dissolved: for there shall come forth from the north a smoke, and none shall be alone in his appointed times.' One might suppose that the chronicler was using a text which predated Patriarch Nikon's reforms of the 1650's, thus showing how necessary they were. But his version, whatever it was, differs almost as much from that of the main pre-reform text – the *Ostrog* bible of 1581 – as it does from the modern Orthodox bible. Either the chronicler's memory failed him, or he was using a text that has not been identified.

[2] Andreyev (1960, p. 255) points out that this comment by Remezov could scarcely have been made before the Russian capture of Azov from the Turks in 1696; and so this must be the *terminus post quem* for the dating of the chronicle.

Thanksgiving service of the Siberians

137. On the return from captivity to Tobolesk in the year 106 [1598], on the 23rd day of August, all those in authority and the clergy, truly conscious of their joy, spoke in one voice: 'We praise the Lord for gloriously has our Father been exalted, God in the Trinity, blessed art thou, Lord, who hast destroyed the heads of the snakes in the waters, as also the wicked men of Kuchyum.' And before all the people a thanksgiving service from the whole heart was offered to the Holy Trinity, the Mother of God and all the saints, with bellringing, thus terrifying the infidels even more, while the hearts of the faithful rejoiced and everyone with all his soul confidently placed his hope in God and his Most Pure Mother, the intercessor for the entire world, asking them to give quiet and peace to their servants and grant them mercy and allay

discords and rebellions among us, dispel the fear and trembling that oppress us, so that we may add to our many blessings the taking of Sibir', proclaiming to all the truth of the visions, the protection and the great mercy and miracles from long past on the 28th day of November of the year 88 [1579] for ever and to this day.

The heavenly blessing of life for the Siberians

138. The Siberian exploits were accomplished, and God blessed
Noah and his sons and said to them: Be fruitful and multiply, replenish
the earth and possess it. And the fear of you and the dread of you shall be
upon every beast of the earth, and upon every fowl in the air, upon all
that moveth upon the earth, and upon all the fishes of the sea; and every
reptile I have delivered into your hand, for I have created all the days,
the seed time and harvest, winter and heat, summer and autumn, day
and night shall not cease.[1]

---

[1] *Genesis* ix, 1–2, and viii, 22. Here again, there is some garbling in the last
verse, which is also misplaced, In the picture the Hebrew letters in the sky are a
garbled version of the tetragrammaton, the ineffable name of God. The named
kneeling figures are (left to right) Japheth, Ham, Noah and Shem. The words
above their heads read: 'And Noah said, Blessed be the Lord God of Shem; and

Canaan shall be his servant. God shall enlarge Japheth, and he shall dwell in the tents of Shem. Genesis IX. And unto them were born sons after the flood. The sons of Japheth, Remes, Elisa, Meshech and others. Genesis x'. These are correctly quoted (ix, 26–27, and x, 1–2), except for the names of two of Japheth's sons. The whole of this picture, according to Gol'denberg (1965, p. 116) is taken from one in the *Sinopsis* of Innokentiy Gizel', Kiev, 1680.

I

*Siberia is illumined by divine
manifestations and glorified*

139. Since ancient times Siberia was darkened by idolatry but today
the Siberian land and country, and above all the principal city Tobolesk,
under God's protection, have become filled with the holy glory of divine
manifestations: in the year 96 [1588] a vision of the Almighty Himself to
the glory of His name, also in the year 144 [1636], on the 20th day of
July, that of the most pure Mother of God, Intercessor for the whole
world, also those of St. John the Baptist, of the Archangel Michael on the
Shamtalyk, of St Nicholas the Miracle Worker to Yermak and his
company in the year 7110 [1602],[1] and on Yermak's arrival a vision of the

[1] Yermak was long dead by this date. The incident may relate to that described in chapter 95, which is said to have happened in 7092 [1584].

great martyr Demetrius, in the year 7089 [1580], on the 23rd day of
November, and the land was illuminated by such a light of inexpressible
joy and enlightened by the all-holy and life-giving Spirit in the form of
an eagle, that it was as though an eagle had covered his nest Sibir' with
his fledglings and had given to each city a feather of his glory; blessing
shone forth, all-present and all-pervading, and was glorified to all the
ends of Sibir'. Lesser manifestations came from the mystery and power
of saints pleasing to God, supplicants for the providing of Sibir'. Also
through its priests and warriors, in the love of Christ and brotherly love
it remains luminously golden and filled with light, exuding spiritual
grace, finally manifesting divine guidance and serenely gathering the
community of the Orthodox in a spiritual union.

140. In the year 6672 [1164], on the first day of August, the Great
Prince Andrey Bogolyubskiy,[1] who lived and died in the year 6683
[1175], had a custom; when setting out against a foe he took into his
army the glorious and holy icon of our most pure sovereign the Mother
of God with the eternal child, holding Christ our Saviour on her arm,
and with it the sublime cross of our Lord which two priests in vestments
carried in the regiments and took among the troops going to war with
many tearful prayers to Christ the Lord and the most pure Mother of
God. These gave the communion of the divine most pure mysteries of
the body and the blood of Christ, arming the troops with such unconquerable weapons, better than sword or spear, and relying more on the
Supreme aid than on the courage and strength of his soldiers, according

[1] Son of Yuriy Dolgorukiy and ruler of Vladimir-Suzdal'. He was born about
1111 and died in 1174, not 1175.

to the words of David, psalm 146.[1] 'He hath no pleasure in the strength of an horse: neither delighteth he in any man's legs. But the Lord's delight is in them that fear him: and put their trust in his mercy.' And again: 'It is not that my sword shall help me; but it is thou that savest us from our enemies.'

[1] Actually, *Psalms* cxlvii, 10–11, and xliv, 6–7. But the text is nearly correct.

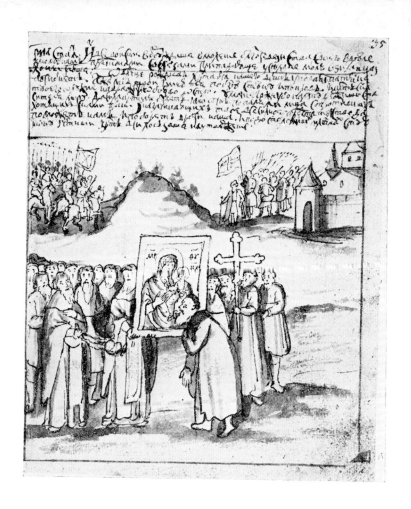

141. And the entire army inspired to prayers in its reverence for the divine service fell on its knees before the icons with tears, fervently praying looking at the icons and saying: 'O holy Virgin who bore Christ our God, whoever places his hope in thee will not perish; I, thy servant, have in thee through God a rampart and a protection, and in the cross of thy Son, a double edged weapon against the foe; entreat him whom thou holdest on thine arm, the Saviour of the world, that the power of the cross may be as fire, burning the faces of the adversaries who seek war with us, and against the instigators may thine all-powerful protection help us and overcome our foes.' And after suitable prayers all kissed the holy icon and the sublime cross in confirmation.

142. They boldly set out against their foe, God helping them with the power of the cross, and the most pure Mother of God giving aid in everything, through the intercession before God, just as in ancient times the great king Constantine had done on venturing forth; he fought shield to shield with the Bulgar forces and overcame them and pursued them and captured four of their towns, the fifth being Bryakhinov on the river Kama,[1] and when he returned to his camp after fighting the infidels he saw icons of Christ and of his most pure Mother illumined by rays like flames issuing forth, blessing the entire army on the first day of August. And he acquired courage and daring, turning his strength against the pagans, burning down their towns and devastating their

[1] Bryakhimov was a town of the Volga Bulgars, and flourished in the 12th century. But Constantine (whichever it was) had to do with the Bulgars of the Danube, a distantly related people. There seems to be some confusion between the two.

land; and on the remaining towns he laid a heavy tribute. Thus, too, did the Greek king Manuil[1] who led his troops against the Saracens see the same miracle and vision, rays issuing from the icons of the holy Virgin, and conquered with his soldiers and with the sublime cross. According to the Scriptures they each instituted this August thanksgiving festival, rendering thanks to the powers of the cross, kissing it and glorifying God in the Trinity forever.

[1] Presumably the Byzantine Emperor Manuel I Comnenus, 1143–80.

143. In the year 6888 [1380], on the 9th day of May, at the time when the Great Prince of Moscow Dimitriy[1] was at war with the Tatar Mamay,[2] a night sentry Foma Khaltsybeyev had the following revelation, a vision from God: high above a great cloud appeared, and it was as if some great armies were advancing from the east, while from the south there came two shining youths holding tapers and naked swords. These were the holy martyrs Boris and Gleb who said to the Tatar commanders: 'Who ordered you to destroy our fatherland given to us by God?' And they began to cut down the foe so that not one of them remained whole.

[1] Dmitriy Ivanovich (1350–89), a great hero of Russian history who, as ruler of Moscow, defeated the Mongols at the battle of Kulikovo in 1380 and earned the name Donskoy (of the Don).

[2] The Mongol leader of the Golden Horde. Most of his men were Tatars, so their designation as such in this chapter and the next is reasonable.

144. In the morning the sentry told the great prince about his vision. And the prince, raising his eyes to heaven and stretching up his arms prayed with tears, saying: 'Lord who lovest men, through the prayers of the holy martyrs Boris and Gleb, help me in the same way as Moses against Ammalik, David against Goliath, Yaroslav against Svetopolk, and my grand-sire the Great Prince Aleksandr against the German king,[1] thus too give me aid against Mamay!' And on that day Dimitriy with the aid of the holy martyrs Boris and Gleb defeated Mamay, king of the Tatars, about which there is a vast history; and he killed Mamay, and spread human bodies over 40 versts. There were 200,000 Russians in the engagement, and of Tatars twice as many – 400,000.

[1] These Russian princes are the great heroes of Russian Orthodoxy: Yaroslav, prince of Novgorod, defeated his brother Svyatopolk, who had Roman Catholic allies, to become ruler of Kiev in 1019; and Alexander Nevsky (actually Dimitriy's great-great-grandfather) defeated the Teutonic Knights at lake Peipus in 1242.

145. In the year [year omitted], on the 13th day of January, in the days of yore, Savoriy, king of Persia, came with a great host and besieged the town of Nisivia which had formerly defeated Savoriy, the town being rendered unconquerable and strong over many years by virtue of the prayers of the bishop St Jacob.[1] Now Savoriy dammed the river flowing through the town with stones and earth, holding back the current, and when much water had collected released it against the town so that the walls fell from the pressure of the waters which with great force flooded a large part of the town. The citizens were terrified while the Persians rejoiced thinking that the town was going to fall into

---

[1] Sapor II (309–79), the Shah of Persia, attacked Nisibis, a chief town of upper Mesopotamia, in about 337 and was repulsed by the defenders, who were led by 'St Jacques' (J. Labourt, Le christianisme dans l'Empire perse sous la dynastie sassanide, Paris, 1904, p. 45).

their hands. They did not attack the town on that day because of the wetness of the water and put off till the morning the assault with all their forces.

146. When night came all the people of the town, inspired by the
bishop to action and labour by his encouraging prayers, repaired the
town walls so that not only horsemen but even men on foot could not get
in without ladders, nor could the town be easily taken by surprise. The
citizens put their trust in the aid of the Almighty and prayers of Bishop
Jacob, and all came out on to the walls to curse the enemy host. The
bishop ascended the wall and seeing the innumerable regiments of the
Persian host prayed God to send against them mosquitoes and gad-flies
to make them feel the power of God and retire from before the town.

147. God hearkened to the prayer of his servant and sent on to the Persian host a great cloud of mosquitoes and flies whose stinging was so cruel that the horses and elephants were unable to bear it and broke their reins and bits and rushed wildly hither and thither; and not only to the dumb beasts but to the Persians themselves those mosquitoes and flies were terrible and unbearable, worse than armed warriors. The infidel king saw that his endeavours were wasted and the power of his host was broken by the mosquitoes and flies. Perceiving the holy man Jacob the Bishop striding along the town wall he took him for the king for he seemed to him to be clad in royal purple with a brightly shining crown on his head; he was angry with his men who had informed him that there was no king in the town, and had them put to death. He retreated from the town and fled to his own land pursued by the flies and mosquitoes.

*Christians since ancient times awe-inspiring to
other peoples, and Yermak*

148. In olden times everywhere and in all places when Orthodox
Christians went their way and to war, they inspired with awe infidels
and others who know not God, because our holy Christian faith was
embraced by the pious Tsar and Great Prince Vladimer of All Russia,
when the holy Gospel of the Redeemer of our stronghold did not burn in
the fire, and God gave us Christians power, strength, courage and
success over all to crush underfoot the serpent and the scorpion and the
entire enemy host, and move mountains, and because of the divine
command one Christian defeats a thousand infidels and two overpower a
hundred thousand, and this was a fitting example to the Siberians.

On the Roksolan foul vagabonds

149. The foul vagabond Roksolans, rebelling against God, accepted
the Latin abomination from Satan and not God's help, relying on the
bows of their armament.[1] They fell like sheaves during harvest with
unreasonable and not spiritual understanding. As a barren fig-tree
buffeted by a high wind scatters its buds, so they fled in flaming lawlessness to the north, and condemned by God for tolerating foul sins
were destroyed: one infidel drove one thousand, and two moved one
hundred thousand, and this is clearly written in their histories: if a
righteous man is barely saved, where will the wicked and sinner go?

[1] The Roksolans were a group of Iranian tribes who lived on the north shore of
the Black Sea between the 2nd century B.C. and the 4th century A.D. At first they
fought the Romans, later, in the Danube region, they sided with them. Just what
the 'Latin abomination' was, and why the chronicler is so angry with them, is not
clear. They had ceased to be a distinct people long before his time.

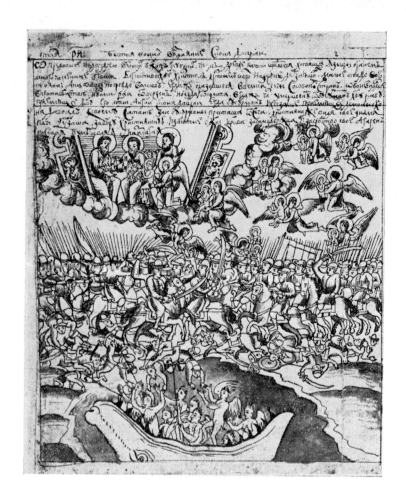

The reward of a warrior's life – from horse to paradise

150. O wonderful miracle, the work of God's great profound miracles! In olden times peoples assembled in the field for war in numerous hosts, while pious Christians, courageously placing their trust in Christ's word, were as a small flock of sheep surrounded by wolves. When a great battle was joined both sides saw opposite them the heavenly paradise wide open and an abyss disclosed. When the hour comes for a servant of Christ to be slain by an infidel, holy angels carry his soul from his mount to paradise. When an infidel perishes, demons carry him from his mount to hell to Satan himself. Wherefore the infidels ceased to fight while the Christians, beholding their sign, began to act boldly for the Christian faith and for the holy churches of God, for the sovereign and for their kinsfolk, cutting down the infidels and killing them and laying them low.

Example of the conquest of peoples by Christians

151. The tree of life grows from the fruit of truth for the Siberians:
natives doing good seek the grace for the good; intruders seeking evil are
overtaken by evil. If they were to abandon former evil, then like all
creatures submitted to Adam in Paradise, they would evidently submit
to any Christian. All who follow blameless ways are pleasing to God, the
roots of the pious are firm and will not be taken from them; those who
sow truth will receive justice, a just reward; the righteous son is born to
live, the desires of the righteous are all good; nothing wicked is pleasing
to the righteous, and it is better to acquire the Lord's grace and to serve
loyally, for whoever acts in good faith is pleasing to him.

On peaceful organisation

152. In striving for peace, for instance in directing words to people of the realm for useful intercourse, a well informed man must know a host of customs and rules and laws in order the better to acquire the art of taking over cities and strongholds, and establish a laudable ruling of ranks, the cross of peace, devotion and joy for the angels. Philosophy requires us to preserve justice in all things, through which great love lives among all races, to introduce no innovations, and to send intruders beyond the frontier because we must have care that our Siberian population should live forever, because our fatherland demands now as before good counsel and wisdom, and just, not rash, decisions to create good examples that can pacify personal strife and quell intrigues and wickedness in towns so that they be not destroyed. In narratives it is not art

that should be sought but firm peaceful order in a pure world, for those who do not agree and do not stand firm criminally introduce temptation into the heart and thus create evil. Those who keep the peace will rejoice; the steed is known for what it is on the day of battle, help comes from God.[1]

[1] While such relevance as this chapter has seems to lie in its exhortation to colonial rulers to exercise wisdom and justice, no explanation comes to mind for the fact that the angel's banner carries the inscription 'peace' in old Dutch. This, together with the western numerals (see p. 86, note 1), is more evidence of western influence. The whole picture may well be a copy of some Dutch original. It is not known what caused the excision in the bottom left corner – also apparent, of course, on the back of the sheet, in chapter 155.

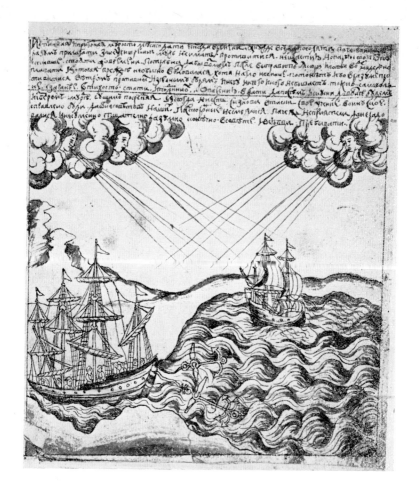

On military reverses

153. True and useful wisdom is sometimes to give place to time and always aid necessity, to apply wisdom increasingly to writing, for a man of experience does not oppose misfortune, but hauling down his sails waits for a suitable time in order to be able later to weigh anchor and safely navigate those waters which had previously been unusually turbulent. Although by accident one can innocently drown, because it is within reason to oppose unfavourable winds and great storms and the skies, there is nothing else to be done than voluntarily to take shelter and give in to true apprehension. Thus we shall become sufficiently experienced and will choose the wisest means, in order that, at any time when in straits our military experience is called upon, other people should not mock our wrong decisions nor the foe rejoice, and we remain in the end without doubt, careful and wise in good counsel and love.

Prescription of the holy fathers on loyal service

154. When the holy fathers saw Greek honour hard pressed and ready to fall they gave this advice to autocrats about the faithful servant: better one righteous man than a thousand beggars, and better the support of one wise man than that of a multitude of fools, for it is not with cruel weapons that peoples are brought low but it is by the word coming from God that foes are swiftly overcome and cities and many thousands of one's own people are saved, because a wise man had more wisdom than the strong and is better than a man of action. Great power with reason is called valour, spiritual strength is wisdom, defeating visible foes will in every way defeat the invisible. When a man's own house stands firm then all he builds is firm. Strive to share God's spirit. Wisdom gives to the wise man power greater than that of the strong and better than that

of the brave displaying senseless courage. The thought of a wise man is greater than many rivers and it shines in his countenance. For this reason autocrats should exercise wisdom or follow the example of the wise, extolling the holy fathers on whom truly God rests as on a throne. Wisdom reigns over all virtues and has more power in a city than the strong, and dominates everything.

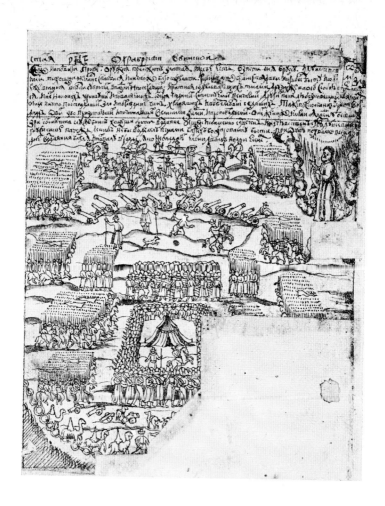

On military valour

155. Another argument about deeds of valour. Weapons must be of
gold: you must take them in your hands and act, by their means you do
not intend vaingloriously to save yourself and accomplish no good. Tell
me, if a battle was being fought in the presence of the king who saw
some persons driving into the thick of the enemy host, killing and per-
forming many deeds of valour, and others in single combat, and some
riding about and praised by the king, admired, applauded and crowned
with laurels, and some others approving, but having come to no harm,
and the rest keeping to their ranks and sitting in silence whom after the
battle we also see summoned and honoured with great awards though
even their names were not known – see, which kind you would wish to
see rewarded: the hardhearted, the unfeeling, the abominably devoid of

spiritual qualities, and the lazy, or would you not wish the good to be loaded with gifts, publicly highly commended to their faces and praised for generations to come, for it is not the deer that dominates the lion but the lion that dominates the deer.

Drift not hither and thither, let us follow the royal road

156. Vanity of vanities and all is vanity, says the sage, beholding what is happening under the sun, and that is vanity. In war iron is more precious than gold, and in our life it is more than riches. Therefore it is good not to deviate either to the right or to the left, and for us to proceed in our lives along the royal road, because in life nothing remains stable and nothing is firm,[1] but all is uncertain: the day changes between

---

[1] Here again, as in chapters 136 and 152, the western influence is marked. The centre piece of the picture is the wheel of fortune – a common symbol in mediaeval European culture (see for instance H. R. Patch, *The Goddess Fortuna in mediaeval literature*, London, 1967). The concept was known in Russian literature of the time, having been apparently introduced by Maksim the Greek, but no occurrence is known in pictorial art (see L. S. Kovtun, 'Planida – furtuna – schastnoye koleso', *Trudy Otdela drevnerusskoy literatury*, Tom xxiv (1969), pp. 327–30).

morning and night, the mountain is not the affair of the valley, nor the valley that of the mountain. For this reason it is necessary not to rejoice at good fortune, nor to be dejected by adversity, but in both cases to strive only towards the sun, for a virtuous life brings closer to God. If you wish to be great before God and men, humble yourself for you will gain renown in all things through heavenly goodness. Avoid worldly blindness, for a temple is created with wisdom and is served with reason, treasures are accumulated by actions, and one who has attained wealth earns fair renown. Youth and bodily excellence of the foolish are altered by old age, fame is altered by sorrow, and wealth is destroyed by death and corruption, and all joy in this life ends in tears, whereas virtue endures forever. The thief hates the sun, and the proud man hates the humble one. The wise man is a friend of the judicious and an enemy of the foolish. From where there are quarrels and discord God withdraws. Brother, be an eye to the blind, a foot to the lame, food to the hungry, clothing to the naked, a visitor of the sick, a deliverer from misfortune, do not seek esteem from everyone, and on this we end here.

The last chapter

157. Having sailed up to here and hauled down the sail of words, we shall gladly rest in the safe haven of history. No one is more lenient towards himself than God is to us all. You, reader, seeing what has been written above, remember God, revere Him by deeds to the last breath, glorify Him by word and thought, fear Him, hold your soul for a leader, your body for a warrior, so that the warrior should in all things be obedient to his leader, and not the leader to the warrior, thus healthy food out of an earthen dish tastes good. I have briefly spoken about the staunch cossacks in their Siberian life, I have clearly shown them in the city of Tobol'sk for all to see, and if I have not attained eloquence and have opened with an iron key, I have prepared for the future a golden one so that the whole nation may be sustained. And by this token I call for

my name to be known among the usefully renowned in the Siberian land and in the capital city.

[There follow five groups of letters which do not spell words. These are in the same code as Yesipov used (see p. 86, note 1). The solution, given in *Sibirskiye letopisi*, 1907, p. xxxv, reads as follows: 'Written by Semen Remezov. Leontey Semenov. Ivan Semenov. Semen Semenov. Petr Semenov.' The last four names, which are those of the writer's sons, are in the genitive case, and so are not part of the first phrase. The shields contain monograms of the five names, but there is still argument about the interpretation of some of the letters (see Sergeyev, 1970, p. 55, and Alekseyev, 1974, pp. 193–4).]

THE BOOK CALLED THE NEW CHRONICLE[1] . . . AT THE BEGINNING OF THE BOOK, ON THE TAKING OF THE KINGDOM OF SIBIR'; COMMENCED TO BE WRITTEN IN 92 [1584] AND CONTINUES UP TO THE PRESENT

1. From the ruling city of Moscow to the east of the country lies a kingdom called Sibir', and Khan Kuchyum lives in it; their faith is infidel according to the law of Mohammed, and some peoples serve and worship idols, and other lost Chud'[2] know neither faith nor law; so it must be told from the beginning, how God brought it under the hand of the Moscow kingdom. There is in the south of the country a river called the Don, and on it live cossacks; not far from the Don is the river called Volga, and on it cossacks lived and plundered much on the Volga and on other rivers: sometimes they would raid the tsar's ships, sometimes they would raid and kill Kizilbash[3] and Bukharan ambassadors and many others. Tsar Ivan, seeing their plundering and wicked unruliness, sent his *voyevodas* against them and ordered them to take them and hang them there; many were caught and executed, but others, like wolves, scattered. Six hundred men fled from them up the Volga at the summons of Maksim Strogonov, among them their leader, an *ataman* called Yermak, and many other *atamans*. And they went to the river Kama and up the Kama to the Chesovaya, where they reached the patrimony of the Strogonovs. There they asked the people living there, to what kingdom that land belonged; they told them: 'there is not far from here a kingdom called Sibir', in it lives Khan Kuchyum.' Yermak prepared stores for himself, and took with him about 50 people from there, and went up the river Serebryanaya, and took his boats over the portage to the river Tagil, and went to the river Tura, and by the river Tura went to the river Tobol, and by the Tobol went to the river Irtish, and by the river Irtish went to the stronghold where Khan Kuchyum was nomadising, and came up to that kingdom of Sibir'. And he fought with them for many days, and by God's will took the kingdom of Sibir', Khan Kuchyum fled, and his queen and sons were taken captive. Yermak

<hr>

[1] The text translated is in *Polnoye sobraniye russkikh letopisey*, Tom 14, 1910, pp. 33–4. Probably compiled in 1630 (see p. 28). Only the first two chapters out of 422 are relevant.
[2] See Introduction, p. 22.
[3] The ordinary word for Persian. See p. 95, note 2.

stayed in the kingdom of Sibir', and sent fifty cossacks to the tsar in Moscow with a report of good news[1] – Tsar Ivan Vasil'yevich was already dead – and he himself began to bring under the tsar's hand all the land of Sibir' and many other kingdoms: some he subdued for the tsar, and from these he obtained an oath of allegiance; and those who did not submit he took captive and destroyed. The lord Tsar Feodor favoured the bringers of the report, and sent with them his *voyevodas* Prince Semen Bolkhovskoy and Ivan Glukhov, and to Yermak and to the *atamans* and cossacks he sent his great and royal favour; and the sovereign ordered that Yermak should be addressed not as *ataman* but as prince of Sibir'.[2] And Prince Semen Bolkhovskoy did not become a *voyevoda* in Sibir'.

2. On the fight, how they killed Yermak and the cossacks, and on the record of Sibir'. News came to the *voyevoda* and to Yermak, that Bukharans were coming to Sibir' with trade goods. Yermak took with him *ataman* Ivan Koltso and about a hundred and fifty cossacks and marched against the Bukharans to the river Vokhay;[3] and just short of the river they stopped for the night at the crossing-place[4] and went to sleep, and not one of them remained on guard. Kuchyum approached and saw them on the island. Kuchyum had a Tatar who had committed a crime, and Kuchyum sent him to the river: 'Find out for me where there is a ford in the river; if you find out, I will pardon you.' The Tatar crossed the river and saw them asleep, and the Tatar came and told Kuchyum. Kuchyum did not believe him and sent him again and ordered him to take something from them. So the Tatar went again and came up to them and took from the cossacks three muskets and three slings and brought them to Kuchyum. Khan Kuchyum then killed Yermak and all the cossacks on the island; only one of them fled to the *voyevoda* in the town with the news. The *voyevoda* Ivan Glukhov and the *atamans* and cossacks, taking fright at this, rowed from the stronghold by the river Irtish downstream to the river Ob', and by the river Ob' they rowed to Berezov, and from Berezov they went over the mountains to Moscow. Tsar Feodor Ivanovich did not show disfavour towards them and immediately sent his *voyevoda* Vasiley Borisovich Sukin with soldiers; and they reached the stronghold of Tyumen' and founded the first town in Sibir', Tyumen'; and from Tyumen' *voyevoda* Vasiley sent the leader Danilo Chyulkov, and Danilo came and established at the mouth of the river Tobol and the Irtish a fort, and gave to

---

[1] Russ *seunch*.

[2] Much is made of this apparent elevation to the nobility by the émigré cossack writer Mel'nikov (1961, p. 25). But no other evidence survives, and from this one sentence it is not altogether clear whether the tsar meant it formally, or was paying a graceful compliment. The point arouses little interest among Soviet scholars.

[3] Modern Vagay.

[4] Russ. *pralir*, which means nothing. The editor of the printed edition of 1910 suggests it might be intended for *proliv*, a strait.

that fort the name Tobol'sk; and now in the kingdom of Sibir' that town is the capital. And they founded many other towns in the kingdom of Sibir'.

[continues to §422]

ROYAL CHARTERS AND LETTERS RELATING TO THE ADVANCE ACROSS THE URALS[1]

A.D. 1558, 4th April. *Charter granted by Tsar Ivan Vasil'yevich to Grigorey Stroganov on financial, juridical and trade privileges in the empty lands along the river Kama.*

This I, Tsar and Great Prince Ivan Vasil'yevich of All Russia, have granted to Grigorey, son of Anika, Stroganov, who has humbly beseeched me and has related that in our possessions 88 versts below Perm' the Great[2] along the river Kama, along its right bank from the mouth of the stream Lysva, and along the left bank of the Kama opposite the Pyznovskaya backwaters, along both banks of the river Kama up to the river Chyusovaya,[3] lie empty lands, dense forests, wild streams and lakes, empty islands and pools, in all 146 versts of this wilderness. Until now no ploughing has been done and no dwellings built there, and no kind of dues have come from there to my royal treasury, and this land has not been given to anyone and has not been entered in anyone's name in registers, deeds of sale or legal documents. And Grigorey Stroganov has humbly beseeched us wishing to build on that land a stronghold, and to mount in it cannon and muskets, and to station gunners, musketeers and artillery men there for defence against the Nagay people and other hordes, and to fell the forest along the streams up to their headwaters and around the lakes, and to plough the cleared land, and to build dwellings, and to recruit unregistered and untaxed men, and to seek salt-pans and to build salt works and extract salt. And would I make a grant to Grigorey Stroganov and commend him to build a stronghold in that place, and to set up in it cannon and muskets, and station gunners,

[1] The text translated is printed in Müller, 1937, pp. 332–44. The texts printed in the first edition of Müller's book (1750) came presumably from the Stroganov archives, but for the modern edition they were re-checked against surviving originals.

[2] In the 16th century there was no town of Perm' (that was a settlement founded in 1723 and named Perm' only in 1781). Perm' the Great was a tract of land on the Kama – earlier it had connoted a much bigger area – of which the chief town was Cherdyn', the most important outpost of Muscovite power in the approaches to the Urals. Modern Perm' (renamed Molotov, 1940–57) is 300 km downstream.

[3] The modern reader finds it hard to locate these lands on a map: there are three rivers Lysva in the region, and the 'Pyznovskaya backwaters' are not identifiable now. But the general region is clear: the Kama and Chusovaya basins between about lat. 58° and 61°N. The Russian *Atlas* of 1745 marks this as Stroganov land.

281

musketeers and artillery men in that stronghold for defence against the
Nagay people and other hordes and order him to fell forests along the
streams up to their headwaters, and around the lakes, and having
cleared the land to plough it and build dwellings, and recruit men, and
search for salt-pans, and where they are found to extract salt. And here in
Moscow, our treasurers questioned about those parts Kodaul, a man
from Perm', who had come bringing tribute from all the Perm' people.
And this man of Perm' told our treasurers: that place about which
Grigorey makes his humble request to us has always since the beginning
of time lain waste, and there is no income from it to our treasury, and the
people of Perm' have no settlers there. And should it be so as Grigorey
petitions and as Kodaul of Perm' has said that from those empty lands
we have had no tribute until now, and no tribute comes today, and the
people of Perm' pay no taxes on them, nor has any tribute been paid to
Kazan' or is being paid now, and that there would be no hindrance for
the people of Perm' or travellers, I, Tsar and Great Prince Ivan
Vasil'yevich of All Russia, have granted this to Grigorey, son of Anika,
Stroganov, and commanded him: that in that empty land, 88 versts
below Great Perm' along the river Kama, on the right bank of the river
Kama from the mouth of the river Lysva, and on the left bank of the
river Kama opposite the Pyznovskaya backwaters, downstream along
both banks of the Kama as far as the river Chyusovaya, he should build
a stronghold in the dense forest, in a safe and easily defended place, and
mount in this stronghold cannon and muskets, and I have ordered him
to bring gunners, musketeers and artillery-men there for defence against
the Nagay people and other hordes; and let him fell the forest near this
stronghold along the streams and lakes up to their headwaters, and
plough the land around this stronghold, and build dwellings, and recruit
unregistered and untaxed men. But he is not to recruit or to accept
registered and tax-paying men from Perm' or other towns of our realm,
nor is he to admit robbers and fugitives from among boyars' men with
their families, or thieves and outlaws. And if there come to Grigorey
from other towns or districts of our realm tax-paying men with their
wives and children, and if governors or heads of districts or elected
headmen send enquiries about them, Grigorey is to send these tax-
paying men with their wives and children back to those towns from
which there were precise enquiries about them, and not keep them and
give them shelter. But if any men from our realm or other lands, men
with money or with merchandise come to buy salt or fish or some other
goods, these men are to sell their wares freely, and purchases are to be
made from them tax-free. And whatever people come from Perm' to live
there, those Grigorey is to admit but exclusively the unregistered and
the untaxed. And in what place a salt-pan is found, there he is to set up
salt-works and extract salt. Fishing in the lakes and rivers in those parts
is to be untaxed. And wherever silver ore is discovered, or copper or tin
ore, Grigorey shall immediately write about those ores to our treasurers

and not work those ores himself without our knowledge. And he is not to enter the hunting and fishing grounds belonging to Perm'. I have granted him this exemption from taxes for 20 years from Annunciation Day of the year 7066 [1558] till Annunciation Day of the year 7086 [1578]. Whoever of unregistered and untaxed men come to him into the town, its suburbs and the ploughland around the town, and to the villages, and on to newly cleared land, for these during those privileged twenty years Grigorey is exempt from tribute to my royal and great princely treasury, as well as from relay levies, saltpetre money, ploughing and defence service, and some other taxes, and from levies on salt and fisheries in those parts. And whatever people travel past this stronghold from our realm or from some other country, with goods or without them, they shall not be made to pay any dues whether they trade or not. But if he takes or sends this salt and fish to other towns he is to pay all taxes on that salt and fish the same way as our taxes exacted from other merchants. And whatever men, whether ploughmen[1] or not, settle in that stronghold of his, our governors of Perm' and their bailiffs shall have no jurisdiction whatsoever over Grigorey Stroganov and men of his stronghold and villages, and their sheriffs and constables and their men are not to come to Grigorey Stroganov, to his stronghold and his villages on any account, nor to hold them to bail[2] or to send anyone out to them. Grigorey will be in charge of his local inhabitants and is to judge them in all cases. And whoever from other towns will have any litigation with Grigorey shall take out the legal documents here, and according to these legal documents both plaintiff and defendant are to appear in person before our treasurers in Moscow during that same period of time till Annunciation Day. When these determined years have come to an end, Grigorey Stroganov is to bring to Moscow all our taxes to our treasury on the same date of Annunciation Day, to the amount which our scribes will have set. This too I have granted Grigorey son of Anika Stroganov: when our envoys travel from Moscow to Siberia or from Siberia to Moscow, or when our envoys travel from Kazan' to Perm' or from Perm' to Kazan' past his stronghold, Grigorey and his local people during those privileged twenty years will not have to give carts, and guides, and fodder to our Siberian envoys and to any of our other messengers; but the merchants of the town are to keep bread and salt, and all other stores and sell them to envoys, and messengers, and travellers, and wayfarers at the same price as they trade among themselves: and every traveller may hire at an agreed price carts, and boats, and oarsmen, and helmsmen, whomever will wish to hire out cheapest. This too I have granted Grigorey, son of Anika, Stroganov: not to exact any

---

[1] Russ. *pashennyye*, which is derived from the verb *pakhat'*, to plough. But in a more technical sense the word implied those peasants who paid their feudal obligation to the government by work (for example, ploughing), in contrast to those who paid by produce or by money.

[2] Russ. *davat' na poruki*. The system was to make the whole community answerable for the man. No money was generally deposited.

taxes from the men of Perm' and not to have any accounts with them during those determined years. And the men of Perm' are not to enter Grigorey's property either of land or forest from the river Lysva along the Kama, along the streams and lakes up to their headwaters as far as the river Chyusovaya, nor any new gainful appendages to his property. Let the men of Perm' hold the old hunting grounds which they have held of old, and let Grigorey hold his new hunting grounds for which and for other gainful holdings no dues have been coming to our treasury, and no fur tribute had gone to our boyars and *voyevodas* in Kazan' for our treasury and have not been until now delivered to Kazan'. But if it appears that Grigorey has been false in his humble request to us, or if he begins to act out of keeping with this charter, or takes to thieving, then this my charter will be null and void. This charter was granted in Moscow in the year 7066 [1558], on the 4th day of April.

The original has been lost. The document is published from a copy included in the text of the charter of 1564, 2nd January, preserved in the Leningrad Department of the Central Historical Archives (LOTSs IA), in the library of auxiliary historical studies; in the copy the verso of the 1558 charter is described as follows: 'at the back is a lengthy addendum by the secretary Petr Danilov; at another place: ordered by the courtiers Fedor Ivanovich Umnoy and Oleksey Fedorovich Adashev, as well as by the treasurers Fedor Ivanovich Sukin and Khozyain Yur'yevich Tyutin; addendum by the secretary Tret'yak Karacharov'.

A.D. 1568, 25th March. *Charter granted by Tsar Ivan Vasil'yevich to Yakov Stroganov on financial, juridical and trade privileges with regard to the salt-works on the river Chusovaya.*

I, Tsar and Great Prince Ivan Vasil'yevich of All Russia have granted to Yakov, son of Anika, Stroganov what he has humbly requested saying that in our possessions in those parts for which we have granted them exemption from taxes and a charter to his brother Grigorey, from the stream Lysva to the river Chyusovaya, on both banks of the river Kama, lie empty lands, dense forests, wild streams and lakes, and the extent of this empty land along the Kama is 100 by 40 by 6 versts.[1] Up the river Chyusovaya in the wilderness they have found salt-pans but dare not set up forts at those salt-pans without our knowledge. And on the other side of the river Chyusovaya, from its mouth to its headwaters, and from the river Chyusovaya down the river Kama till the Lasvinskiy pine

---

[1] The meaning is not clear. Possibly the wording implies that the land stretches 100 versts along the river, and reaches back 40 versts on one side and six on the other.

wood, on both banks of the river Kama lie empty islands and water-meadows, dense forests and wild streams and lakes extending over 20 versts, which have not been given to them, and in our charter these empty spaces have not been entered. No fields have been ploughed there, no dwellings built, and no taxes whatsoever have been paid to our royal and great princely treasury; nor has this land been given to anyone, or entered in anyone's name in registers, deeds of purchase or legal documents, and the people of Perm' have no settlers there entered in registers and rolls. Yakov wishes to fortify that place by the salt-pans, build a stronghold and set up salt works, and recruit unregistered and untaxed men, and mount quick-firing defence cannon and hand and heavy muskets, and establish gunners, musketeers, smiths, carpenters and artillery-men, and keep guards against the coming of Nagay men and other hordes. And could we grant to Yakov, son of Anika, Stroganov the following: that on that empty land at the salt works by the river Chyusovaya which has been given to them free from taxes, from the river Lysva down the river Kama to the river Chyusovaya, and up the river Chyusovaya from its mouth and on the other side of the river Chyusovaya from its mouth to its headwaters, and from the Chyusovaya river down the Kama river to the Lasvinskiy pine wood, on both banks of the Kama river, he should build forts, and a stronghold, and set up salt works, and recruit unregistered and untaxed men, mount quick-firing defence, cannon and hand and heavy muskets, and establish gunners and musketeers, and smiths, and carpenters, and artillery-men, and keep watchmen against the coming of Nagay men and other hordes. And near that place he is to clear the forest along the streams up to their headwaters and around the lakes, and plough fields, and cut hay in the cleared spaces, and hold hunting, fishing and other profitable grounds. So let it be as Yakov, son of Anika, Stroganov has humbly requested, and I, Tsar and Great Prince Ivan Vasil'yevich of All Russia, have granted to Yakov, son of Anika, Stroganov his humble request and ordered him, in that wilderness along the Chyusovaya river and the same places which have been registered in his name in our former charter, at the salt works where they have found salt pans, to build forts and a stronghold, and mount quick-firing defence, cannon and hand and heavy muskets, and establish gunners, musketeers, smiths, carpenters and artillery-men, and keep watchmen for defence against the Nagay men and other hordes, and near the stronghold, by the salt-pans to set up salt-works and build houses on either side of the Chyusovaya river along the streams and lakes up to their headwaters, and from the Chyusovaya river along both banks of the Kama river 20 versts downstream to the Lasvinskiy pine wood, and fell the forest along the streams and lakes, and plough fields, and clear land for hayfields, and hold hunting and fishing and other profitable grounds, and recruit unregistered and untaxed men, so that our treasury suffers no loss. And Yakov is not to recruit registered and tax-paying men from Perm' and various towns of our realm and not to admit them, nor to accept runaway boyars' men with their families, or thieves and robbers. And if there come to Yakov from other towns or districts of our realm tax-paying men with their wives and children, and if our governors or district bailiffs and elected headmen enquire about them Yakov is to send back those tax-payers with their wives and children to the towns from which enquiries have been made about them, and he is not to keep or admit these people. But whatever men come to that town from our realm or from other lands, with money or merchandise to buy salt or fish or other wares, these men are to sell their goods freely, and purchases are to be made from them without any payment of dues. And if any people come from Perm' to live there, Yakov is to admit them but exclusively the unregistered and untaxed. And where in those parts salt-pans are found, there he is to set up salt-works and extract salt. And on fishing in the streams and lakes at those places there will be no levy. And where silver or copper or tin ore is found Yakov is to inform us immediately about those ores and not work those ores himself without our knowledge. And Yakov is not to enter Perm' fishing and hunting grounds which have been recorded by the Permians in registers and legal documents. I have granted him exemption from taxes for those new lands about which Yakov has humbly beseeched me, on the other side of the Chyusovaya river, and from the Chyusovaya river 20 versts downstream the river Kama on both its banks up to the Lasvinskiy pine wood, for 10 years, the same privilege as I have previously granted on the humble request of Grigorey from Annunciation Day of the year 7066 [1558] till Annunciation Day of the year 7086 [1578]. And for those men, unregistered and untaxed, who come to him into the stronghold, its suburbs, and the ploughlands around the town, and to the villages and on the newly cleared land, for these during those privileged ten years Yakov need not pay my royal and great princely tribute, and relay levies, saltpetre money, ploughing and defence service, and levies on salt and on the fisheries in those parts. And whatever people travel past that township from our realm or other countries with goods or without them, they shall not be made to pay any dues whatsoever, whether they trade or not. But if he takes or sends this salt and fish to other towns he is to pay all the taxes on this salt and fish, the same as those exacted from other merchants. And whatever men, whether ploughmen or not, who come to settle in that stronghold of his, our governors of Perm' and their bailiffs shall have no jurisdiction whatever over Yakov Stroganov and men of his stronghold and villages, and their sheriffs and constables and their men are not to come to Yakov Stroganov, to his stronghold and villages on any account, nor to hold them to bail or send anyone out to them, but Yakov will be in charge of his local inhabitants and is to judge them in all cases himself or through whomever he will order to do so. And whoever from other towns will have any litigation with Yakov shall take out the legal documents here, and according to these legal documents both plaintiff and defendant will appear in person before us in Moscow during that same period of time till Annunciation Day. When these determined years have come to an end Yakov Stroganov is to bring to Moscow all the taxes to our treasury on the same date of Annunciation Day to the amount which our scribes will have set. This too I have granted Yakov, son of Anika, Stroganov: when he or his men or peasants from his settlement travel from their settlement from the Vychegda salts[1] past Perm' on to the Kama to their settlement, or from their settlement to the Vychegda salts, our governors and their bailiffs and constables and all officials of Perm' shall not put Yakov or his men and peasants on bail, nor bring them to court on any matter. This too I have granted to Yakov, son of Anika, Stroganov: when our envoys travel from Moscow to Sibir' or from Sibir' to Moscow, or when our envoys travel from Kazan' to Perm', or from Perm' to Kazan' past his stronghold, Yakov and his local people during his privileged ten years will not have to give carts or guides or fodder to our Siberian envoys and any of our other messengers; but the merchants of the town are to keep bread and salt and all other stores and sell them to envoys, and messengers, and wayfarers, and travellers at the same price as they trade among themselves; and every traveller may hire carts, and boats, and oarsmen, and helmsmen for their need from whomever will wish to hire himself out cheapest. This too I have granted Yakov, son of Anika, Stroganov: not to exact any taxes from the men of Perm', and not to have any accounts with them during those determined years. And the men of Perm' are not to enter Yakov's property of land or forest from the river Chyusovaya along both banks of the Kama to the Lasvinskiy pine wood, along the streams and lakes up to their headwaters, into none of the new gainful appendages to his property which have not been entered in the registers and legal deeds of the men of Perm', but let the men of Perm' hold the old hunting grounds which they have held of old according to the registers, and let Yakov hold his new hunting grounds for which hunting grounds and other gainful property no dues have been coming to our treasury and no fur tribute has been paid to Kazan' to our boyars and governors for our treasury. But if it appears that Yakov has been false in his humble request to us, or if he begins to act out of keeping with this charter or takes to thieving, then this my charter will be null and void. This charter was granted in Moscow in the year 7076 [1568], on the 25th day of March.

A red seal is appended to the original.
On the verso of the original document is written: Tsar and Great Prince Ivan Vasil'yevich of All Russia. Secretary Druzhina Volodimerov.
The original has been lost. Reprinted from Dopolneniya k Aktam Istoricheskim, Tom I, 1846, pp. 172–75.

[1] Russ. Vychegodskaya sol'. Later written as one word, Sol'vychegodsk.

A.D. 1572, 6th August. *Ivan Vasil'yevich's letter to the settlement on the Kama to Yakov and Grigorey Stroganov on the sending of fighting men for the subduing of the Cheremis and other peoples marauding on the river Kama.*

From Tsar and Great Prince Ivan Vasil'yevich of All Russia to the settlement on the Kama to Yakov and Grigorey, sons of Anika, Stroganov. In the year 80 [1572] our *voyevoda*, Prince Ivan Yur'yevich Bulgakov with his man Ivan Borisov wrote to us from Perm' about news of Cheremis attacks on merchants' boats on the Kama. Prince Ivan has also written to us that your man Tret'yachko[1] had written to him on 15th July from the mouth of the river that 40 Cheremis, traitors to us, had come in war on to the Kama with Ostyaks, and Bashkirs, and Buintsy and had killed on the Kama 87 Perm' merchants and fishermen. When this our letter reaches you, you should live very much on your guard. Choose a good leader and with him as many volunteer cossacks as can be had, with all kinds of weapons, with muskets and quivers, and also Ostyaks and Voguls who are true to us, with volunteer cossacks who have not broken away from us, and order them to assemble, and for their wives and children to stay inside the stockade. And when you have chosen a leader and have had the volunteer bowmen and cossacks entered on a roll, and however many Ostyak and Vogul volunteers have been assembled, have them listed by name; and having sorted them out according to what weapons they carry, and noted how many of these volunteers, and Voguls, and Ostyaks have gathered against our traitors, and having had a copy made of this list of names, keep it and send the list under your seal with whomever is suitable to us in Moscow, to the office in the Kazan' palace, to our secretaries Ondrey Shchelkalov[2] and Kirey Gorin, so that we should know about their numbers. And send out these leaders with the volunteers, and musketeers, and cossacks, and Ostyaks, and Voguls to fight our traitors, the Cheremis, the Ostyaks, the Votyaks, and the Nogays who have turned traitor and have seceded from us. Whoever of these traitors come to attack the settlements, let the volunteers fight those Cheremis, but protect themselves and retreat from them carefully and guardedly. And let them without fail fight our traitor Cheremis, and Ostyaks, and Votyaks, and Nogays who have betrayed us and have seceded from us. But if some good Cheremis or Ostyaks wish to persuade their comrades to leave the rebels and be true to us, whoever of them agrees is not to be killed but kept safe and we

---

[1] The ambassador Tret'yak Chubukov, who was killed the following year. See below, p. 289.

[2] Andrey Yakovlevich Schelkalov (d. 1597) was a very powerful official, who held the post of head of the Posol'skiy Prikaz (the Ambassadors' Office, and therefore Foreign Office) from 1571 to 1594, and so was known to many foreign ambassadors (see references in modern index of Hakluyt 1589). He signed the important letter of 16 November 1582 (see below, p. 294). It is significant that Siberian affairs were at this time engaging the attention of the senior official.

ROYAL CHARTERS AND LETTERS

shall show them favour. As for those who have been guilty of some
wrongdoing, but now wish to be true to us and show their loyalty, let
them be spoken to and told about our merciful words, that we shall
pardon them and remit punishment, and will make all things easy for
them, while they should prove their loyalty by gathering with their
leaders and joining the volunteers to fight our traitors, and make war on
them, and defeat them, and whoever is overcome his life will be theirs,
and their wives and children will be their slaves. As for those Cheremis
who become loyal to us and honestly turn to us and fight our traitors,
and have seized their wives, and horses, and cows, and clothing, and any
kind of livestock, you must give orders that no one should take the
living booty from them. Written in Moscow in the year 7080 [1572], on
the 6th day of August.

On the verso: Tsar and Great Prince of All Russia – Secretary Kirey
Gorin.
A black wax seal is affixed to the verso.
In State Archive of the Feudal and Serf Epoch (GAFKE),[1] *Stroganovs
file, No. 6.*

A.D. 1574, 30th May. *Charter of Tsar Ivan Vasil'yevich to Yakov and
Grigorey Stroganov on exemption for 20 years from various taxes and
levies of their lands and people in the Takhchei and on the Tobol.*

This I, Tsar and Great Prince Ivan Vasil'yevich of All Russia have
granted to Yakov and Grigorey, sons of Anika, Stroganov: they have
humbly informed us that in our possessions beyond the Yugrian range,[2]
on the borders of Sibir', between Sibir' and Nagai, the Takhchei and
the river Tobol with rivers and lakes up to their headwaters, is where
assemble warriors of the Siberian sultan and make war. In the year 81
[1573], on St Elias's Day, there came from the Tobol the brother of the
Siberian sultan, Mametkul,[3] together with an army, to spy out roads on
which to lead his men against Perm'. They killed many of our Ostyak
subjects and took their wives and children into captivity, and this
Siberian also killed our envoy Tret'yak Chebukov and serving Tatars
who were on their way to the Kazakh Horde. He came within 5 versts of
their fort where their works and establishments are situated by our grant.
And Yakov and Grigorey say that they do not dare send their hired
cossacks after the Siberian forces from our granted land and their fort

[1] This archive, in which this and some of the later charters translated here
were located in the 1930's, has now been incorporated in the Central State
Archive of Ancient Documents (TsGADA) in Moscow.
[2] Russ. *Yugorskiy kamen'*, the ordinary phrase for the Urals at that time.
[3] The chronicles generally call Mametkul Kuchum's son. Here he is the
brother. In fact he was probably the nephew.

289

without our order. Even before this the Siberian sultan with his army had killed our subject Ostyaks, Chagir' with his comrades, in those same parts where Yakov and Grigorey have their hunting and fishing grounds, and works, and settlements. The Siberian seizes other subjects of ours, and kills some of them, and orders our Ostyaks, Voguls, and Yugrians not to pay any tribute to our treasury. He also forces these same Ostyaks and Voguls to fight with him on boats against the Yugrians. And to those Cheremis who have betrayed us the Siberian sent word through Takhchei and took over Takhchei. He says that until now Takhchei did not send tribute to us or to Kazan' but sent tribute to the Nagays. And those Ostyaks who live around Takhchei order them to pay our tribute as do other of our Ostyaks, and not to pay tribute and levies to the Siberian, and to join them in the struggle against the Siberian. And would we grant to Yakov and Grigorey the following: in Takhchei and on the river Tobol, and on those lakes that empty into the Tobol up to the headwaters, to clear a defensible place and build forts, and hire guards and keep various firearms, and produce iron, and plough fields, and hold hunting grounds. And whichever Ostyaks desert the Siberian and begin to pay tribute to us, those Ostyaks to be defended against him. So let it be as Yakov and Grigorey have humbly requested, and I, Tsar and Great Prince Ivan Vasil'yevich of All Russia, have granted to Yakov and Grigorey, sons of Anika, Stroganov, according to their humble request the following: in Takhchei and on the river Tobol they are to build forts, and keep firearms, and gunners and musketeers, and guards against the Siberian and the Nagay people, and around the forts by the iron works, the fishing places and ploughlands on both sides of the Tobol river and along the rivers and lakes up to the headwaters they are to build houses, fell trees, plough fields, and hold hunting and fishing grounds. They are to recruit unregistered and untaxed men but they are not to recruit outlaws and fugitive boyars' men with their families or thieves and robbers, and should guard against all evil. And where in those parts they find iron ore they are to work that ore; and wherever they discover copper ore, or tin ore, or lead ore, or inflammable sulphur, they are to work this ore. If other people wish to engage in this work let them do so freely, and make them pay a levy so that our treasury benefits. And whichever people wish to ply their trade let them have the material and write to us when each work is begun, and what payment for the ore used is set, and about the levies from those who are to pay them, and we shall issue a decree on the matter. The exemption from taxes in Takhchei and on the river Tobol with rivers and lakes up to their headwaters for the ploughed fields we have granted from Trinity of the year 7082 [1574] till Trinity of the year 7102 [1594] for twenty years. Whoever of unregistered and untaxed men come to live in those strongholds of Yakov and Grigorey, and begin to clear and plough fields, from those places during the privileged years my tsar's and great princely tribute is not needed, nor are relay levies or saltpetre money, or ploughing and defence service, nor some other taxes, nor levies from their works and hunting, fishing and other profitable grounds in those places till the end of these years. But where there are in those parts old villages and hamlets, and newly cleared land with inhabitants, Yakov and Grigorey are not to interfere in those places which are to remain as of old paying taxes and all our other dues. On those goods which Yakov and Grigorey, and those men who will come to the new places, take or send to other towns they are to pay custom duty the same as do other merchants according to our decree. Whichever Ostyaks, and Voguls, and Yugrians desert the Siberian and begin to pay tribute to us, those men are to be sent with the tribute to our treasury; if they do not go themselves with the tribute, then Yakov and Grigorey are to choose reliable men from among the inhabitants who wish to settle in the new places and send them with our tribute to our treasury to pay it in. Those tribute-paying Ostyaks, and Voguls, and Yugrians, and their wives and children are to be defended by Yakov and Grigorey in their strongholds against the incursions of hostile Siberians. And Yakov and Grigorey are to gather volunteers, and Ostyaks, and Voguls, and Yugrians, and Samoyeds and send them together with their hired cossacks and artillery to fight the Siberian, and capture Siberians, and have them pay tribute to us. This I have also granted to Yakov and Grigorey: if there start coming to their new places merchants from Bukhara, and from the Kazakh Horde, and from other lands with horses and all kinds of merchandise, such as do not come to Moscow, they are to trade in every kind of wares freely without duty. Whatever men, whether ploughmen or not, come to live near their strongholds, our governors of Perm' and their bailiffs shall have no jurisdiction whatsoever over Yakov and Grigorey and the inhabitants of their settlements, and sheriffs and constables and their men are not to come to Yakov and Grigorey and their settlers on any account, nor to hold them to bail, nor to send anyone out to them; Yakov and Grigorey will be in charge of their local inhabitants, and are to judge them in all cases themselves, or through whomever they will order to do so. And whoever from other towns have any litigation with Yakov and Grigorey, they are to obtain legal documents from our boyars and officials, and according to these legal documents both plaintiff and defendant are to appear in person before us in Moscow during that same period of time till Trinity Day. When these determined years have come to an end, Yakov and Grigorey are to bring to Moscow all our taxes to our treasury on Trinity Day according to the books, to the amount which our scribes will have set. This too I have granted Yakov and Grigorey, sons of Anika Stroganov: when they or their men or peasants from their settlement travel from the Vychegda salts past Perm' to the Takhchei settlements, or from the settlement to the Vychegda salts, our governors of Perm', their bailiffs and constables and all officials of Perm' shall not put Yakov and Grigorey, and their men and peasants on bail, nor bring them to court on any matter. This too I have granted Yakov and Grigorey: when our envoys or messengers travel from Moscow to Sibir', or to the Kazakh Horde, or from Sibir' and from the Kazakh Horde to Moscow past their stronghold, Yakov and Grigorey and their local people during those privileged 20 years will not have to give carts or guides or fodder to our Siberian envoys and any of our other messengers. And the envoys, and messengers, and travellers, and wayfarers are to buy bread and salt and all other stores at the same price as the people trade among themselves. And the travellers shall hire boats, and oarsmen, and helmsmen according to local custom, as suitable. This too I have granted to Yakov and Grigorey: on the Irtysh and the Ob', and on other rivers in places suitable for mooring, and for those who would wish to spend the night there, they are to build a stronghold and keep guards armed with firearms. And from the stronghold fishing and hunting shall be free during the same privileged years. This charter was given in the Sloboda in the year 7082 [1574], on the 30th day of May.

A lesser state seal of red wax is appended on a red silk cord to the recto of the document, and is somewhat damaged.
On the verso: Tsar and Great Prince of All Russia.[1]
Leningrad Department of the Central Historical Archives (LOTs IA), Library of auxiliary historical studies, Ustryalov list No. 8. One sheet.

A.D. 1581, 6th November. *Letter from Tsar Ivan Vasil'yevich to Nikita Stroganov about his sending his men to the aid of Semen and Maksim Stroganov against the Pelym prince and the Voguls.*

From Tsar and Great Prince Ivan Vasil'yevich of All Russia to Nikita, son of Grigorey, Stroganov. Semen and Maksim Stroganov have humbly petitioned us and have said: the Pelym prince together with the Voguls have attacked their settlement, burnt down many villages, and are carrying peasants into captivity. And now the Pelym prince is encamped with the Voguls near the Chyusovaya fort. They beg our favour to order fighting men to be sent to them from Perm' the Great. They say that you are not joining them against the Voguls and are not helping them with men. When you receive this our letter you are to send as many men as needed with those of Semen and Maksim to fight the Voguls, and your men are to stand as one with those of Semen and Maksim, and defend themselves together with them. Orders have been given to district headmen to gather men from Perm' for help, and to send them, taking the men into account according to what number of Vogul warriors come, and to order them to stand together as one with

[1] The signature of the secretary Petr Grigor'yev, as noted in the previous editions of the charter, is absent from the verso.

the men of Semen and Maksim against the prince of Pelym. And you are to order your men to stand together with those of Perm' and of Semen and Maksim against the Pelym prince, and prevent them from fighting so that you all should avoid war. Written in Moscow in the year 7090 [1581], on the 6th day of November.

On the verso: Tsar and Great Prince of All Russia.
A black wax seal is affixed to the verso of the letter.
In State Archive for the Feudal and Serf Epoch (GAFKE), Stroganovs file, No. 10.

A.D. 1582, 16th November. *Letter from Tsar Ivan Vasil'yevich to Maksim and Nikita Stroganov on the Chusovaya about sending to Cherdyn' the Volga cossacks Yermak Timofeyevich and his comrades.*

From Tsar and Great Prince Ivan Vasil'yevich of All Russia to the Chyusovaya, to Maksim, son of Yakov, and Nikita, son of Grigorey, Stroganov. Vasiley Pelepelitsyn has written to us from Perm' that you sent out from your forts Volga *atamans* and cossacks, Yermak with his comrades, to make war on the Votyaks and the Voguls, and the lands of Pelyn and Sibir', on the first day of September, and that on the same day the prince of Pelyn assembled with his Siberian troops and Voguls and went to war against our lands of Perm', attacked the town of Cherdyn' and the fort, and killed our men and caused grievous harm to our people. And this was done through your treachery: you have estranged the Voguls and Votyaks and the Pelyn people from our favour, and provoked them and gone to war against them. By this provocation you have made mischief between the Siberian sultan and us, and by calling in the Volga *atamans* you have hired robbers to serve in your forts without our permission. These *atamans* and cossacks before this brought us into conflict with the Nagay horde, they killed Nagay envoys on the Volga crossings, and robbed and killed Ordobazartsy, and have robbed many of our people and caused them losses. They could have redeemed their guilt by guarding our land of Perm' but they acted in concert with you since they have committed acts and robberies such as they did on the Volga: on the day when the Voguls marched on Cherdyn' in Perm', on the first day of September, on that same day Yermak and his comrades set out from your forts and went to make war on the Voguls, and gave no aid whatsoever to Perm'. And all this happened owing to your dishonesty and treason. You should have rendered service to us by not sending those cossacks to make war at that time, but by sending them with your own men from the forts to defend our Perm' lands. We have sent to Perm' Voin Onichkov and have commanded that those cossacks, Yermak with his comrades, should be taken and brought to Perm' and to Usol'ye Kamskoye, and we have commanded that they should stay there, separately; and from those parts we have ordered all those cossacks together with the men from Perm' and Vyatka, and their envoys, and Voin Onichkov and Yvan Glukhov to march in winter with sledges against the prince of Pelyn in order that the fighting men of Pelyn, and the Ostyaks, and the Voguls should not invade and conquer our land. And we have ordered those cossacks to remain in Perm' till the spring, and go with Voin to fight the Otyaks and the Voguls and bring them to subjection on our command. You should agree by an exchange of letters with Vasiley Pelepelitsyn and Voin Onichkov in Cherdyn' and send your men to fight the Voguls and the Otyaks. You personally, in conformity with this letter, must immediately send those cossacks who will just have returned from the wars to Cherdyn', and not keep them by you. If until their return you cannot remain in the fort, retain a few men, up to a hundred with an *ataman*, and send away all the rest to Cherdyn' without fail immediately. But if you do not send out of your forts to Perm' the Volga cossacks, the *ataman* Yermak son of Timofey and his comrades, and keep them with you, and do not defend the lands of Perm', and if by that treachery of yours any harm comes henceforth to the lands of Perm' at the hands of the Voguls, and the men of Pelyn, and the troops of the Siberian sultan, then you will fall into our great disfavour, and the *atamans* and cossacks who obeyed you and served you and betrayed our land we shall order to be hanged. And you should without fail send those cossacks away from you to Perm', and deal with our matters concerning the men of Pelyn, and the Voguls, and the Otyaks in accordance with our order, exchanging letters with Vasiley Pelepelitsyn and Voin Onichkov, so that God may help us to defeat them and bring them under our rule, and guard the Perm' land and your forts. Written in Moscow in the year 7091 [1582], on the 16th day of November.

On the verso: Tsar and Great Prince of All Russia – Secretary Andrey Shchelkalov.

A black wax seal is affixed to the verso.

In State Archive for the Feudal and Serf Epoch (GAFKE), Stroganovs file, No. 12.

A.D. 1584, 7th January. *Letter from Tsar Ivan Vasil'yevich to Semen, Maksim and Nikita Stroganov on the fitting out for the spring of 15 boats for men and stores being sent to Siberia.*

From Tsar and Great Prince Ivan Vasil'yevich of All Russia to Semen, son of Onika, and Maksim, son of Yakov, and Nikita, son of Grigorey, Stroganov. By our decree Prince Semen Dmitriyevich

Bolkhovskoy had been ordered to take 50 mounted men from you from your forts for our service on a winter campaign in Sibir'. Now the rumour has reached us that it is impossible to go on horseback to Sibir' in winter. We have ordered Prince Semen not to march now to Sibir' from Perm' till spring and its floodwaters, and not to take the fifty mounted men from you into our army as had been ordered, and we have ordered Prince Semen when starting for Sibir' in spring to take from you for our forces and stores 15 boats fully fitted out, such as can carry 20 men with their stores each, and have ordered him not to take from you fighting men, carts, guides and fodder. And we have given orders not to cause any harm to you, your men and peasants on their way to Sibir'. When this letter reaches you, immediately give orders to prepare for our army for the spring and the arrival of Prince Semen Bolkhovskoy 15 good boats fully fitted out which will each carry 20 men and their stores. And when in spring Prince Semen Bolkhovskoy, or the commanders Ivan Kireyev[1] and Ivan Glukhov come to Sibir' with our army and supplies, you are to hand over immediately these fully fitted out boats for our army and supplies to Prince Semen Bolkhovskoy or the commanders Ivan Kireyev and Ivan Glukhov so that they should not be delayed in your forts because of the boats. But if you do not speedily provide boats for our fighting men with all ships' supplies, but bring harm to our cause, then you will incur our great displeasure. Written in Moscow in the year 7092 [1584], on the 7th day of January.

A black wax seal is affixed to the verso.
In State Archive for the Feudal and Serf Epoch (GAFKE), Stroganovs file, No. 13.

[1] Ivan Kireyev's appointment as *voyevoda* is made quite clear here, but as Müller points out (1750, p. 172), he evidently never carried out the assignment.

REFERENCES

Adrianov, S. A. (1893) 'K voprosu o pokorenii Sibiri' [On the subjugation of Siberia]. *Zhurnal Ministerstva narodnago prosveshcheniya*, Tom CCLXXXVI, Otdel 4, pp. 522–50.

Aleksandrova, Ye. A. (1959) 'K voprosu o metodike analiza istoricheskikh pesen' [On the method of analysing historical songs]. *Uchenyye zapiski Gosudarstvennogo pedagogicheskogo instituta, Daugavpils, Seriya gumanitarnykh nauk*, Vypusk 2, pp. 79–112.

Alekseyev, V. N. (1974) 'Risunki "Istorii Sibirskoy" S. U. Remezova (problemy attributsii) [The drawings in S. U. Remezov's 'Siberian history' (problems of attribution)]. *Drevnerusskoye iskusstvo. Rukopisnaya kniga. Sbornik vtoroy*, Moscow, pp. 175–96.

Allen, W. E. D., ed. (1970) *Russian embassies to the Georgian kings (1589–1605)*. Cambridge, 2 vols. Hakluyt Society Second Series, Vols. CXXXVIII–CXXXIX.

Andreyev, A. I. (1942) 'Cherepanovskaya letopis'' [The Cherepanov chronicle]. *Istoricheskiye zapiski*, Tom XIII, pp. 308–23.

Andreyev, A. I. (1960) *Ocherki po istochnikovedeniyu Sibiri. Vypusk pervyy. XVII vek. 2-oye izdaniye* [Outlines in source studies of Siberia. No. 1. 17th century. 2nd edition]. Moscow, Leningrad.

Atlas (1745) *Atlas rossiyskoy . . . [Russian atlas . . .]*. St Petersburg.

Baddeley, John F. (1919) *Russia, Mongolia, China*. London, 2 vols.

Bagrow, L., ed. (1958) *The atlas of Siberia by Semyon U. Remezov*. Facsimile edition with an introduction by Leo Bagrow. Supplement I to *Imago Mundi*. 'S-Gravenhage.

Bakhrushin, S. V. (1955) *S. V. Bakhrushin. Nauchnyye trudy, III. Izbrannyye raboty po istorii Sibiri XVI–XVII vv. Chast' pervaya. Voprosy russkoy kolonizatsii Sibiri v XVI–XVII vv. [S. V. Bakhrushin. Scientific works. III. Selected works in the history of Siberia of the 16th and 17th centuries. Part 1. Questions of the Russian colonisation of Siberia in the 16th and 17th centuries]*. Moscow.

The papers reprinted here which are of greatest interest to us are in a series called 'Outlines in the history of the colonisation of Siberia in the 16th and 17th centuries' and were originally published between 1916 and 1927.

Bakhrushin, S. V. (1955a) *S. V. Bakhrushin. Nauchnyye trudy. III. Izbrannyye raboty po istorii Sibiri XVI–XVII vv. Chast' vtoraya. Istoriya narodov Sibiri v XVI–XVII vv. [S. V. Bakhrushin. Scientific works. III. Selected works in the history of Siberia in the*

REFERENCES

16th and 17th centuries. Part 2. History of the peoples of Siberia in the 16th and 17th centuries]. Moscow. The paper on fur tribute (pp. 49–85) was first published in 1927, and that on Ostyak and Vogul principalities (pp. 86–152) in 1935.

Belov, M. I. (1956) *Istoriya otkrytiya i osvoyeniya severnogo morskogo puti. Tom pervyy. Arkticheskoye moreplavaniye s drevneyshikh vremen do serediny XIX veka* [*History of the discovery and utilisation of the northern sea route. Vol. 1. Arctic seafaring from ancient times to the middle of the 19th century*]. Moscow.

Cherepnin, L. V. (1956) *Russkaya paleografiya* [*Russian palaeography*]. Moscow.

Dal', V. I. (1956) *Tolkovyy slovar' zhivogo velikhorusskogo yazyka* [*Explanatory dictionary of the living Great Russian language*], Reprint of 2nd edition. Moscow, 4 vols.

Dergacheva-Skop, Ye. (1965) *Iz istorii literatury Urala i Sibiri XVII veka* [*Literary history of the Urals and Siberia in the 17th century*]. Sverdlovsk.

Dmitriyev, A. A. (1892) *Permskaya starina. Sbornik istoricheskikh statey i materialov preimushchestvenno o permskom kraye. Vypusk 4. Stroganovy i Yermak* [*Permian antiquity. Collected historical articles and sources chiefly on the Perm' region. No. 4. The Stroganovs and Yermak*]. Perm'.

Dmitriyev, A. A. (1894) 'Rol' Stroganovykh v pokorenii Sibiri' [The role of the Stroganovs in the subjugation of Siberia]. *Zhurnal Ministerstva narodnago prosvesheniya,* Tom CCXCI, Otdel 2, pp. 1–45.

Dolgikh, B. O. (1960) 'Rodovoy i plemennoy sostav narodov Sibiri v XVII v.' [Clan and tribal composition of the peoples of Siberia in the 17th century]. *Trudy Instituta etnografii imeni N. N. Miklukho-Maklaya.* Tom LV.

Dvoretskaya, N. A. (1957) 'Arkheograficheskiy obzor spiskov povestey o pokhode Yermaka' [Archaeographic summary of versions of the accounts of Yermak's campaign]. *Trudy Otdela drevnerusskoy literatury,* Tom XIII, pp. 467–82.

Dvoretskaya, N. A. (1958) 'Ofitsial'naya i fol'klornaya otsenka pokhoda Yermaka v XVII v.' [Official and folklore evaluations of Yermak's campaign in the 17th century]. *Trudy Otdela drevnerusskoy literatury,* Tom XIV, pp. 330–4.

Fennell, J. L. I., ed. (1965) *Prince A. M. Kurbsky's history of Ivan IV.* Cambridge.

Fischer, J. E. (1774) *Sibirskaya istoriya s samogo otkrytiya Sibiri do zavoyevaniya sey zemli rossiyskim oruzhiyem . . .* [*Siberian history from the discovery of Siberia to its conquest by Russian arms . . .*]. St Petersburg.

Fisher, R. H. (1943) *The Russian fur trade, 1550–1700.* Unviersity of California Publications in History, Vol. XXXI.

297

YERMAK'S CAMPAIGN

Fletcher, Giles (1591) *Of the Russe Common Wealth* ... London. Facsimile edition, with notes, edited by R. Pipes and J. V. A. Fine, Cambridge, Mass., 1966.

Fomenko, Yu. V. (1960) 'K voprosu ob imennom sklonenii v russkoy pis'mennosti XVII veka (na materiale sibirskikh letopisey)' [Noun declension in 17th-century Russian writing (on the basis of the Siberian chronicles)]. *Uchenyye zapiski Moskovskogo gosudarstvennogo pedagogischeskogo instituta*, Tom CXLVIII, pp. 392–412.

Fomenko, Yu. V. (1961) 'Nablyudeniya nad glagol'nymi formami v yazyke sibirskikh letopisey XVII v.' [Observations on verb forms in the language of the Siberian chronicles of the 17th century]. *Voprosy istorii i dialektologii russkogo yazyka*, Magnitogorsk, pp. 35–51.

Gessler, E. A. (1941) *Die schweizer Bilderchroniken des 15./16. Jahrhunderts*. Zürich.

Gol'denberg, L. A. (1965) *Semen Ul'yanovich Remezov sibirskiy kartograf i geograf, 1642–posle 1720 gg.* [*Semen Ul'yanovich Remezov, Siberian cartographer and geographer, 1642–after 1720*]. Moscow.

Gordeyev, A. A. (1968–71) *Istoriya Kazakov* [*History of the cossacks*]. Paris, 4 vols.

Gorelov, A. A. (1961) 'Trilogiya o Yermake iz Sbornika Kirshi Danilova: polemicheskiye zametki' [The Yermak trilogy from Kirsha Danilov's Book: polemical notes]. *Russkiy fol'klor. Materialy i issledovaniya*, No. 6, pp. 344–76.

Hakluyt, Richard (1589) *The principall navigations, voiages and discoveries of the English nation*. London, 2 vols. Facsimile reprint, with introduction by D. B. Quinn and R. A. Skelton and index by Alison Quinn, published by the Hakluyt Society as Extra Series No. 39, 1965.

Hakluyt, Richard (1598–1600) *The principal navigations, voiages, traffiques and discoveries of the English nation*. London, 3 vols. Reprinted London, 1809–12, and Glasgow, 1903–5.

Horsey, Sir Jerome (1968) Travels. In L. E. Berry and R. O. Crummey, eds. *Rude and barbarous kingdom*, Madison, Wisconsin, pp. 262–369. Probably written about 1589–90.

Howorth, H. H. (1876–88) *History of the Mongols from the 9th to the 19th century*. London, 5 vols.

Ides, E. Ysbrantszoon (1710) *Driejaarige reize naar China* ..., Amsterdam. English translation *Three years travels from Moscow overland to China* ..., London, 1706.

Ilovayskiy, D. (1889) 'Yermak i pokoreniye Sibiri' [Yermak and the subjugation of Sibir']. *Russkiy vestnik*, No. 9, pp. 3–39.

Itogi (1973) *Itogi vsesoyuznoy perepisi naseleniya 1970 goda. Tom 4. Natsional'nyy sostav naseleniya SSSR* [*Results of the All-Union census of 1970. Vol. IV. National composition of the population of the USSR*]. Moscow.

298

REFERENCES

Karamzin, N. M. (1818–29) *Istoriya gosudarstva Rossiyskogo* [*History of the Russian state*]. St Petersburg, 12 vols.

Katanayev, G. Ye. (1893) 'Yeshche ob Yermake i yego sibirskom pokhode' [More on Yermak and his Siberian campaign]. *Zapiski Zapadno-Sibirskago Otdela Imperatorskago Russkago geograficheskago obshchestva*, Kniga 15, Vypusk 2, pp. 1–36.

Khramova, V. V. (1964) 'The West-Siberian Tatars'. In M. G. Levin and L. P. Potapov, eds. *The peoples of Siberia*, Chicago, pp. 423–439.

Kovtun, L. S. (1969) 'Planida – furtuna – schastnoye koleso (k istorii russkoy idiomatiki)' [Planet – fortuna – wheel of fate (history of Russian idiom)]. *Trudy Otdela drevnerusskoy literatury*, Tom XXIV, pp. 327–30.

Kruglyashova, V. P. (1961) 'Predaniya reki Chusovoy' [Legends of the river Chusovaya]. *Uchonyye zapiski Ural'skogo gosudarstvennogo universiteta imeni A. M. Gor'kogo*, Vypusk 18, pp. 34–53.

Labourt, J. (1904) *Le christianisme dans l'Empire perse sous la dynastie sassanide (224–632)*. Paris.

Lantzeff, George V. and Pierce, Richard A. (1973) *Eastward to empire. Exploration and conquest on the Russian open frontier, to 1750*. Montreal and London.

Levin, M. G. and Potapov, L. P. eds. (1964) *The peoples of Siberia*. Chicago.
    Translation of *Narody Sibiri*, Moscow, 1956.

Likhachev, D. S. (1947) *Russkiye letopisi i ikh kul'turno-istoricheskoye znacheniye* [*Russian chronicles and their significance in cultural history*] Moscow, Leningrad.

Listopadov, A. M. (1946) *Donskiye istoricheskiye pesni* [*Historical songs of the Don*]. Rostov-na-Donu.

Longworth, Philip (1969) *The Cossacks*. London.

Lunt, Horace G. (1970) *Concise dictionary of old Russian (11th–17th centuries)*. Munich.

Matthews, W. K. (1951) *Languages of the USSR*. Cambridge.

Matthews, W. K. (1960) *Russian historical grammar*. London.

Matuz, J. (1968) *L'ouvrage de Seyfī Çelebī, historien ottoman du XVIe siècle*. Paris.

Maykov, L. N. (1881) 'Khronologicheskiye spravki po povodu 300-letney godovshchiny prisoyedineniya Sibiri k russkoy derzhave' [Chronological information on the 300th anniversary of the annexing of Siberia to Russia]. *Zhurnal Ministerstva narodnago prosveshcheniya*, Tom CCXVII, Otdel 4, pp. 21–36.

Mel'nikov, N. M. (1961) *Yermak Timofeyevich, knyaz' sibirskiy, yego spodvizhniki i prodolzhateli* [*Yermak Timofeyevich, prince of Siberia, his companions and successors*]. Paris.

Miller, V. F. (1915) 'Istoricheskiya pesni russkago naroda XVI–XVII vv.' [Historical songs of the Russian people in the 16th and 17th centuries]. *Sbornik Otdeleniya russkago yazyka i slovesnosti Imperatorskoy Akademii nauk*, Tom XCIII.

Mirzoyev, V. G. (1960) *Prisoyedineniye i osvoyeniye Sibiri v istoricheskoy literatury XVII veka* [Annexation and utilisation of Siberia in the historical literature of the 17th century]. Moscow.

Müller, G. F. (1750) *Opisaniye Sibirskago tsarstva* ... [Description of the kingdom of Siberia ...]. St Petersburg.
See also Müller, G. F. (1937).

Müller, G. F. (1937) *Istoriya Sibiri*, Tom *1* [History of Siberia, Vol. *1*]. Moscow, Leningrad.
First published as *Opisaniye Sibirskago tsarstva*, St Petersburg, 1750. The 1937 edition, however, is the first complete one. It differs in many respects from the 1750 edition, and also has annotation by by A. I. Andreyev, S. V. Bakhrushin and others.

Nebol'sin, P. I. (1849) *Pokoreniye Sibiri* [The subjugation of Siberia]. St Petersburg.

Nolde, B. (1952) *La information de l'empire russe. Etudes, notes et documents.* Paris.

Novyy letopisets (1910) Novyy letopisets [The new chronicle]. *Polnoye sobraniye russkikh letopisey*, Tom XIV, pervaya polovina, pp. 33–154.

Ogorodnikov, V. I. (1924) *Ocherki istorii Sibiri do nachala XIX st. Chast' 2, vypusk 1. Zavoyevaniye russkimi Sibiri* [Outlines in the history of Siberia before the beginning of the 19th century. Part 2, No. 1. Conquest of Siberia by the Russians]. Vladivostok.

Okladnikov, A. P. ed. (1968) *Istoriya Sibiri. Tom vtoroy. Sibir' v sostave feodal'noy Rossii* [History of Siberia. Vol. 2. Siberia as part of feudal Russia]. Moscow.

Olearius, Adam (1656) *Vermehrte Newe Beschreibung der Muscowitischen und Persischen Reyse* ... Schleswig.
Facsimile reprint, with notes, Tübingen, 1971. The 1656 edition was the 2nd, revised by the author and much fuller than the first (1647).

Patch, Howard R. (1967) *The Goddess Fortuna in mediaeval literature.* London.

Platonov, S. F. (1924) *Proshloye russkogo severa* [The past of the Russian north]. Berlin.

Porokhova, O. G. (1962) 'Vzaimodeystviye russkoy i staroslavyanskoy (po proiskhozhdeniyu) leksiki v russkom pis'mennom yazyke XVII v. (na materiale sibirskikh letopisey)' [Interaction of Russian and (originally) Old Slavonic vocabulary in written Russian of the 17th century (on the basis of the Siberian chronicles)]. In *Istoricheskaya grammatika i leksikologiya russkogo yazyka*, Moscow, pp. 115–37.

Porokhova, O. G. (1969) *Leksika sibirskikh letopisey XVII veka* [Vocabulary of the Siberian chronicles of the 17th century]. Leningrad.

Preobrazhenskiy, A. A. (1972) *Ural i Zapadnaya Sibir' v kontse XVI–*

nachale XVIII veka [*The Urals and western Siberia in the late 16th to early 18th century*]. Moscow.

Putilov, B. N. (1953) 'Istoricheskiye pesni o Yermake' [Historical songs about Yermak]. *Russkoye narodnoye poeticheskoye tvorchestvo*, Tom I, Moscow, Leningrad, pp. 325–35.

Putilov, B. N. (1958) 'K voprosu o syuzhetnom sostave i istorii slozheniya pesennogo tsikla o Yermake' [On the content and history of a song cycle about Yermak]. *Voprosy izucheniya russkoy literatury XI–XX vekov*, Moscow, Leningrad, pp. 38–48.

Radlov, W. (1872) *Die Sprachen der Türkischen Stämme Süd-Sibiriens und der Dsungarischen Steppe. 1 Abtheilung. Proben der Volkslitteratur. Übersetzung. 4 Theil.* St Petersburg.

[Remezov, S. U.] (1882) *Chertezhnaya kniga Sibiri, sostavlennaya Tobol'skim synom boyarskim Semenom Remezovym v 1701 godu* [*Atlas of Sibeiia compiled by the Tobol'sk boyai son Semen Remezov in 1701*]. St Petersburg.

Romodanovskaya, Ye. K. (1970) 'Sinodik yermakovym kazakam' [The book of names for the commemoration of Yermak's cossacks]. *Izvestiya Sibirskogo otdeleniya Akademii Nauk SSR, No.* 11, pp. 14–21.

Romodanovskaya, Ye. K. (1973) *Russkaya literatura v Sibiri pervoy poloviny XVII v* [*Russian literature in Siberia of the first half of the 17th century*]. Novosibirsk.

Seredonin, S. M. (1914) 'Istoricheskiy ocherk zavoyevaniya Aziatskoy Rossii' [Historical outline of the conquest of Asiatic Russia]. In Glinka, G. V., ed. *Aziatskaya Rossiya*, St Petersburg, Tom I, pp. 1–38.

Sergeyev, V. I. (1959) 'K voprosu o pokhode v Sibir' druzhiny Yermaka' [On the Siberian campaign of Yermak's band]. *Voprosy istorii*, No. 1, pp. 117–29.

Sergeyev, V. I. (1970) 'U istokov sibirskogo letopisaniya' [At the sources of Siberian chronicle writing]. *Voprosy istorii*, No. 12, pp. 45–60.

Shlyakov, N. (1901) 'Yermak Timofeyevich letom 1581' [Yermak Timofeyevich in the summer of 1581]. *Zhurnal Ministerstva narodnago prosveshcheniya*, Tom CCCXXXVI, Otdel 2, pp. 33–45.

Sibirskiye letopisi (1907) *Sibirskiye letopisi* [*The Siberian chronicles*]. St Petersburg, Imperatorskaya Arkheograficheskaya komissiya. Edited by L. N. and V. V. Maykov.

Sidorov, A. A. (1956) *Risunok starykh russkikh masterov* [*Drawings of old Russian masters*]. Moscow.

Sinyayev, V. S. (1951) 'Okonchatel'nyy razgrom Kuchuma na Obi v 1598 godu' [The decisive defeat of Kuchum on the Ob' in 1598]. *Voprosy geografii Sibiri*, Sbornik II, pp. 141–56.

Slovtsov, P. A. (1826) *Pis'ma o Sibiri* [*Letters on Siberia*]. St Petersburg.

Sobraniye (1819) *Sobraniye gosudarstvennykh gramot i dogovorov* [*Collection of State charters and treaties*]. St Petersburg.

Sokolova, V. K. (1951) 'Russkiye istoricheskiye pesni XVI veka, epokhi Ivana Groznogo' [Russian historical songs of the 16th century, Ivan the Terrible's time]. *Trudy Instituta etnografii imeni N. N. Miklukho-Maklaya*, Tom XIII, pp. 7–91.

Sokolova, V. K. (1960) 'Russkiye istoricheskiye pesni XVI–XVIII vv' [Russian historical songs of the 16th to 18th centuries]. *Trudy Instituta etnografii imeni N. N. Miklukho-Maklaya*, Tom LXI.

Solov'yev, S. M. (1897) *Istoriya Rossii s drevneyshikh vremen*. [*History of Russia from earliest times*]. 2nd edition. St Petersburg, 25 vols. in 5.

Stavrovich, A. M. (1922) 'Sergey Kubasov i Stroganovskaya letopis'' [Sergey Kubasov and the Stroganov chronicle]. In *Sbornik statey po russkoy istorii, posvyashchennykh S. F. Platonovu*, Petrograd, pp. 279–93.

Stökl, G. (1953) *Die Entstehung des Kosakentums*. Munich.

Störmer, Carl (1955) *The polar aurora*. Oxford.

Strahlenberg, P. J. von (1738) *An historico-geographical description of the north and eastern parts of Europe and Asia*. London.

2nd edition of English translation of *Das Nord- und Ostliche Theil von Europa und Asia*, Stockholm, 1730.

Ustryalov, N. G. (1842) *Imenityye lyudi Stroganovy* [*The distinguished Stroganovs*]. St Petersburg.

Vasmer, Max (1953–58) *Russisches Etymologisches Wörterbuch*. Heidelberg, 3 vols.

Vernadsky, G. (1959) *Russia at the dawn of the modern age*. New Haven.

Vernadsky, G. (1969) *The tsardom of Moscow, 1547–1682. Part I*. New Haven.

Voronikhin, A. (1946) 'K biografii Yermaka' [On Yermak's biography]. *Voprosy istorii*, No. 10, pp. 89–100.

Vsevolodskiy-Gerngross, V. N. (1959) *Russkaya ustnaya narodnaya drama* [*Russian oral folk drama*]. Moscow.

Vvedenskiy, A. A. (1962) *Dom Stroganovykh v XVI–XVII vekakh* [*The house of Stroganov in the 16th–17th centuries*]. Moscow.

Witsen, N. (1698) *Noord en Oost Tartarye*. Amsterdam.

2nd edition 1703, 3rd 1785.

Yevgen'yeva, A. P. and Putilov, B. N., eds. (1958) *Drevniye rossiyskiye stikhotvoreniya, sobrannyye Kirsheyu Danilovym* [*Ancient Russian poems collected by Kirsha Danilov*]. Moscow, Leningrad.

Zagoskin, N. P. (1909) *Russkiye vodnyye puti i sudovoye delo v dopetrovskoy Rossii* [*Russian waterways and shipping in pre-Petrine Russia*]. Kazan'.

Zamyslovkiy, Ye. Ye. (1882) 'Zanyatiye russkimi Sibiri' [The seizure of Siberia by the Russians]. *Zhurnal Ministerstva narodnago prosveshcheniya*, Tom CCXXIII, Otdel 2, pp. 223–50.

REFERENCES

Ziyayev, H. (1962) *Ortä Asiya vä Sibir'* (*xvi–xix äsirlär*) [*Central Asia and Siberia* (*16th to 19th centuries*)]. Tashkent.

Zost, A. I., ed. (1880) *Kratkaya sibirskaya letopis'* (*Kungurskaya*) *so 154 risunkami* [*The Short* (*Kungur*) *Siberian chronicle, with 154 drawings*]. St Petersburg. Inaccurately titled. This is a facsimile and transcription of the Mirovich version of the Remezov chronicle, which contains interpolations from the Short Kungur Siberian chronicle. Zost financed publication.

INDEX

Abalak (Yabolak), opp. 18 (map), 32;
fight at, 51, 73–4, 169; commemoration of, 84, 241; abandoned by Kuchum, 165
Abalak (Agalak, Yabalak, Yabolak), Tatar prince, 47, 66, 112
Abigun strongholds, 210
Ablay, Kalmuck chief, 218–23
Abugay river, 166
Adashev, Aleksey Fedorovich, courtier, 36, 284
Adbash (Atbash), opp. 18 (map), 57, 78, 197
Ader, khan of Sibir′, 47, 66
Adrianov, S. A., 5, 26, 296
Agalak (Abalak, Yabalak, Yabolak), Tatar prince, 47, 66, 112
Agash (Agish, Aguish), khan of Sibir′, 47, 67, 112
Agitskiy river-bend, 188, 197, 204
Agtakov, Begbeliy, Vogul prince, 6, 41–2
Aguish (Agash, Agish), khan of Sibir′, 47, 67, 112
Alach′ (Alacha, Alachey), native prince, 179, 214, 218
Alazev district, 189
Aleksandrov, Cherkas, cossack, 74, 85n
Aleksandrova, Ye. A., 13, 296
Aleksey, cossack, 85n
Aleksey Mikhaylovich, tsar, 218
Alekseyev, V. N., 30–2, 277, 296
Alenin family, 11
Alexander Nevsky, 257
Aley, Ali see Alliy
Alim, khan of Kazan′, 111
Allen, W. E. D., 95n, 296
Alliy (Aley, Ali), son of Kuchum, 39, 47; reoccupies Sibir′, 58, 79, 210
Altanai Kuchumovich, Tatar prince, 32
Altaul, Tatar prince, 39
Altyn Yarginak, 113
Alyshay, Tatar captain, 132
Anana, cossack, 85n
Andrey, cossacks named, 85n
Andreyev, A. I., 10, 296, 300; on Siber-

ian chronicles, 28; on Stroganov chronicle, 5, 24–6; on Remezov chronicle, 27–8, 30, 243n
Anichkov (Onichkov), Voin, voyevoda, 45, 293, 294
animal life in Sibir′, 64; symbolic animals, 121–2, 153–4
Antokol′skiy, M. M., 12
Antsyfor, cossack, 85n
architecture, some pictures showing, 150, 167, 186, 196, 226, 231, 236, 239, 244
Arctic Ocean, 6
Ardobazartsy (Ordobazartsy), 40, 45, 293
Aremzyan district, 170
Artemiy, cossack, 85n
Astrakhan, 10, 95, 104; khanate of, 1
ataman, defined, 10
Atbash (Adbash), opp. 18 (map), 57, 78, 197
Atik murza, fights Russians, 48, 71, 156; his stronghold, 156–9
aurora borealis, 114, 152
Azov, captured by Turks, 27

Babasan murza, 135
Babasan (Babasany, Bobasan) river, fight at, 7, 48, 70, 137
Baddeley, J., 32n, 65n, 296
Bagrow, L., 27, 296
Baishevskoye cemetery, 214, 223
Bakhmet, devil, 163
Bakhrushin, S. V., 3n, 7n, 37n, 296–7, 300; on aurora, 114n; on Karacha, 48n; on Ostyaks and Voguls, 23, 172n; on river routes, 19, 184n; on Sinodik, 84n; on Siberian chronicles, 28; on Stroganov chronicle, 5, 25; on Yesipov chronicle, 26; on Yermak's army, 13; on Yermak's coat of mail, 214n
Bannoye Poganoye (Poganoye), 143, 189
Barancha river, 16, 106n
Basan river, 73

305

66; abandoned by Kuchum, 165; commemoration of fight at, 84, 240
Chyulkov *see* Chulkov
Chyusovaya *see* Chusovaya
Chyuvashevo, Chyuvashiye *see* Chuvashiye
ciphers, use of in chronicles, 86, 277
coats of arms, 242
Constantine, emperor, 254
cossacks, origins, 9–10; of the Don, 10; size of Yermak's army, 13, 69, 95, 106, 107, 130, 155; names of its members, 84n, 85n; its morale, 49, 71, 101, 107, 133, 156
Crimea, khan of, 2
Crummey, R. O., 32n, 298

Danilov, Kirsha, 16, 17
Danilov, Petr, secretary, 36, 284
dates – Old Style and New Style, 36
deer, 64; pictures of, 102
Dem'yan (Demayan), Ostyak prince, 172
Dem'yan strongholds, 168, 170
Dem'yanka river, opp. 18 (map), 168, 170, 172
Dergacheva-Skop, Ye., 17n, 297
Devlet-Girey (-Gerey, -Giray), khan of Crimea, 2
Devletim Bay, *murza*, 115, 119
Dmitriy Ivanovich Donskoy, Great Prince, 256–7
Dmitriyev, A. A., 5, 10, 17, 297
Dmitriyev, I. I., 12–13
Dolgikh, B. O., 20–3, 297
Dolgiy Yar, 138
Don river, homeland of cossacks, 10, 12, 15, 104, 278; law, 101
doshchanik, 19
Ducket, Jeffrey, 10
Dvoretskaya, N. A., 6, 28, 297
Dzungars, 23–4

Fedor Ivanovich, Tsar Fedor I, 7, 61, 77, 190, 227, 279
Fennell, J. L. I., 59n, 297
Feodor, cossack, 85n
Filaret Nikitich, Patriarch, 83, 240
firearms used by Russians, 37; impression on Tatars, 46, 125; use of cannon, 161, 198, 225
Fischer, J. E., 5, 28, 297
Fisher, R. H., 3, 297
Fletcher, Giles, ambassador, 32, 55, 298

folk tales associated with Yermak, 13–18
Fomenko, Yu. V., 29n, 298
frontier, Muscovy's eastern, 1–3
Funikov, Nikita Afonas'yevich, treasurer, 37
fur, industry, 3, 18; as booty, 50–1; presented to tsar, 53; tribute (*yasak*), 60–1, 111n, 124, 170–81, 183

Gengis (Chingis) Khan, 1, 20, 46, 47, 66
German *see* Yermak
Gessler, E. A., 31n, 298
giant warrior, 146
Gizel', Innokentiy, 247n
Gleb, Saint, 256
Glukhov (Glukhoy), Ivan, *voyevoda*, 8; ordered against Voguls, 294; ordered to Sibir', 53–4, 76, 191, 279, 295; sends Mametkul to Moscow, 55
Golden Horde, 1, 20
Gol'denberg, L. A., 27, 32, 247n, 298
Gordeyev, A. A., 9, 298
Gorelov, A. A., 16, 17, 298
Gorin, Kirey, secretary, 38, 288, 289
Grigoriy, cossack, 85n
Great Perm' *see* Perm', lands of
Grigor'yev, Petr, 40, 292
Groza, Ivan, *ataman*, 85n, 101
Gwagnin (Guagninus), Alexander, 30

Hagarenes, 41
Hakim, Shaikh, 214n
Hakluyt, R., 10, 22n, 145n, 298
Harrison, W., 13n
hawking, 81, 228
historical songs associated with Yermak, 13–18
Hoca *see* Khodzha
Horsey, Sir Jerome, ambassador, 32, 298
hostages taken by Russians, 38
Howorth, H. H., 22n, 66n, 298

Ichimek, native captain, 144
Ides, Evert Ysbrantszoon, ambassador, 32, 298
Idiger *see* Yediger
illustrations in the Remezov chronicle, 29–31
Ilovayskiy, D. I., 5, 12, 298
Imperial Archaeographical Commission, 24

307

INDEX

73–4, 136–7, 160, 169, 182, 289;
wounded, 50, 72; captured, 51–2,
75, 187–8; sent to Moscow, 55,
76–7, 190
Mamut (Mamet, Makhmet), khan of
Sibir', 47, 66, 67, 111, 112
Mangazeya, 65, 89n
Mansi see Voguls
Mansurov, Ivan, voyevoda, 8; arrives
on Ob', 7, 58, 79, 224
Manuel I Comnenus, emperor, 255
Mar, khan of Sibir', 47, 66
Mari see Cheremis
Martazey (Murtaza, Murtazey), ruler
of Uzbeks, 2, 39, 62, 67
Masal'skoy-Koltsov, V. V., voyevoda,
233, 235
Matthews, W. K., 20n, 23n, 86n, 299
Matuz, J., 8n, 299
Maykov, L. N., 5, 10, 24, 299, 301
Maykov, V. V., 24, 301
Mel'nikov, N. M., 11, 12, 13, 279, 299
Mel'nikov-Pecherskiy, 17
Meshcheryak, Matvey, ataman, 8, 40,
85n; attacks Karacha, 56; leaves
Sibir', 57; meets Mansurov, 58;
returns to Irtysh, 59; killed, 60
Mezen' river, 18, opp. 18 (map)
Mikhail, cossacks named, 85n
Mikhail, Fedorovich Romanov, tsar,
83, 217, 240
Mikhaylov, Yakov, ataman, 40, 55
Miller, V. F., 14n, 15, 299
mineral exploitation, Stroganovs en-
couraged to engage in, 290
miraculous events favouring Russians,
131, 139–40, 142, 212–13, 216–23
Mirovich, P. F., 26, 87
mirza (murza), defined, 3n
Mirzoyev, V. G., 5, 300
Mohammed, 66, 68, 163
Mongols, 24, 65, 103; dominate
Russia, 1; western, 23–24; Khalkha, 23; levy fur tribute, 61n
Moses, 68
Müller, G. F., 7n, 106n, 300; and
Remezov chronicle, 26, 28, 32;
travels in Siberia, 17, 33, 105n,
108n; on size of Yermak's army,
95n; on Stroganov involvement,
5; on Yermak's doings, 132n,
197n; on routes across Urals,
184n; uses Stroganov archives,
29, 281n
Murat, khan of Kazan', 118
Murashkin, Ivan, army officer, 10, 95

Murtaza (Murtazey, Martazey), ruler
of Uzbeks, 2, 39, 62, 67
murza (mirza), defined, 3n
Muscovy, eastern frontier of, 1–3
Muscovy Company, 10
Myasnoy, Ivan, voyevoda, 8, 80, 226

Nadtsyn district, 171
Nagais, Nagays, see Nogais
napisaniye, 24, 26, 83
Narym (Narim), opp. 18 (map), 89n,
176
Nazym (Nazim), opp. 18 (map);
cossacks reach, 52, 76, 170;
Yermak reaches, 189; fight at
commemorated, 85, 241
Nazym river, opp. 18 (map), 52
Nebol'sin, P. I., 8, 10, 300; view of
Stroganov chronicle, 5, 24
Nekotoraya sibirskaya istoriya, 10
Nektariy, Archbishop of Tobol'sk, 240
Nemirovich-Danchenko, V. I., 15
Nentsy see Samoyeds
Nepein, Senya, secretary, 37
New chronicle, 6, 28; text, 278–80
Neyva river, opp. 18 (map), 19
Nikol'skiy, N. P., 180n
Nikon, cossack, 85n
Nisibio (Nisivia), 258–61
Nitsa river, opp. 18 (map), 19, 65, 102
Nizhne-Chusovskiy Gorodok, 37
Noah, 246
Nogai, Prince, 22
Nogais (Nogaytsy, Nogai horde,
Nagais, Nagays), 21 (map), 22;
Stroganovs encounter, 36, 37, 45,
281, 285; hostile to Russians, 288;
kill Kuchum, 82, 237–8
Nolde, B., 5, 300
Nor-Ishim river, 234, 237
Nosovoy Gorodok, opp. 18 (map)
Novgorod, 1, 61
Novocherkassk, 12
Novosibirsk, 188n

Ob' river, opp. 18 (map), 65, 102;
early Russian penetration to, 1;
routes to, 18–19; Stroganovs
allowed to build forts on, 4, 292;
cossacks descend, 52, 180; cossacks leave, 209, 279; Mansurov
reaches, 58, 224
Obdaria, 213
Obskiy Gorodok, 9
Obva river, opp. 18 (map), 61
Ogorodnikov, V. I., 5, 300

310